Susan Magarey

Susan Magarey has degrees from the University of Adelaide and the Australian National University. At ANU she was Lecturer-in-charge of the Women's Studies Program 1978-1983. At Adelaide University, where she is now Professor Emerita, she founded the Research Centre for Women's Studies 1983-2000 and the journal, *Australian Feminist Studies* 1985— . In 2006, she was made a member of the Order of Australia for her work in establishing Women's Studies as a field of intellectual endeavour.

Susan Magarey, 2013
Photograph courtesy of Susan Magarey

Other books by this author:

*Unbridling the tongues of women: a biography of
Catherine Helen Spence, 1985, revised 2010*

*Roma the First: A Biography of Dame Roma Mitchell,
2007, revised imprint 2009, with Kerrie Round*

*Looking Back: looking forward. A century of the Queen
Adelaide Club 1909-2009, 2009*

Passions of the first wave feminists, 2001

Dangerous Ideas

Women's Liberation – Women's Studies – Around the World

by

Susan Magarey

History Department, Faculty of Arts
The University of Adelaide

THE UNIVERSITY
of ADELAIDE

UNIVERSITY OF
ADELAIDE PRESS

Published in Adelaide by

University of Adelaide Press
The University of Adelaide
Level 14, 115 Grenfell Street
South Australia 5005
press@adelaide.edu.au
www.adelaide.edu.au/press

The University of Adelaide Press publishes externally refereed scholarly books by staff of the University of Adelaide. It aims to maximise access to the University's best research by publishing works through the internet as free downloads and for sale as high quality printed volumes.

For the full Cataloguing-in-Publication data please contact the National Library of Australia: cip@nla.gov.au

ISBN (paperback) 978-1-922064-94-3
ISBN (ebook: pdf) 978-1-922064-95-0
ISBN (ebook: epub) 978-1-922064-96-7
ISBN (ebook: kindle) 978-1-922064-97-4

Editor: Rebecca Burton
Editorial support: Julia Keller
Book design: Zoë Stokes
Cover design: Emma Spoehr
Cover image: © Mary Leunig, used with permission

Contents

Acknowledgements

To everyone involved in Women's Liberation and Women's Studies — in Australia, and around the world — a thousand thanks for all that you taught me. Especially I offer my profound gratitude to all the people who contributed to the tales told here: friends, colleagues, sisters, comrades, intellectual and political inspirations. I learned much from you all. My debt to some will shout from these pages: to Daphne Gollan, Julia Ryan, Kay Daniels, Margaret Power, Anna Davin, Marian Quartly, Drusilla Modjeska; to Genevieve Lloyd, Carole Pateman, Marilyn Strathern, Terry Threadgold; to Sara Dowse, Elizabeth Reid; to Raewyn Connell, to Marion Halligan — I owe most of my intellectual and political formation and all that followed from it. I must thank, too, people who have worked with me as students for insights, argument and opposition enough to prove an important goad.

Some of the pieces reproduced here are preliminary efforts towards the history of the Women's Liberation Movement in Australia. A few quote from interviews recorded during the early days of research for that project, the interviews carried out by splendid Research Assistants Kate Borrett, Liz Dimmock, Ruth Ford, Ann Genovese, Judith Ion, Tristan Slade, Lizzie Summerfield, Inara Waldron, Deborah Worsley-Pine, and Sarah Zetlein who — to our enduring sorrow — took her own life at the end of 1996. That history has not yet been written. I had designed it as a collaboration with Ann Curthoys and Marilyn Lake, whose influence also shapes these pages. We did take a trio of papers to the Berkshire Conference on Women's History in North Carolina in 1996; Ann used them in her highly praised article for the *Oxford Companion to Australian Feminism*, 'Cosmopolitan Radicals'. And Marilyn says that without the research for that project she could not have written the relevant chapters in her wonderfully encompassing and incisive work, *Getting Equal: The History of Australian Feminism* (published by Allen & Unwin in 1999). I want to thank those splendid historians — colleagues all, these days — and the many people who agreed to be interviewed, to check the transcripts of their interviews and to correct them. Mary Lyons deserves an avalanche of thanks; she transcribed all of the interviews. I promise, now that I have put this present collection together, I will return to that project. It has been waiting for attention since the late 1990s; it is time it became a book which could perhaps be called *A History of the Women's Liberation Movement in Australia's World*.

For their contributions to this book I must thank the brilliant Mary Leunig for allowing the University of Adelaide Press to reproduce the cartoon on the cover, and John Emerson for an array of assistances that he has provided as Director of the University of Adelaide Press.

To my partner, Susan Sheridan, who helped me invent the title of this collection, I am also grateful for quality control — among many other things.

Figure 1: Ann Curthoys and Marilyn Lake, Sydney University, c. 1996
Photograph by Susan Magarey

Preface

I used to describe my life as 'ambivalent, ambidextrous, ambiguous, androgynous, ironic'. This book is similarly unorthodox: plural, haphazard and conjectural. It is a memoir, a — highly selective — *curriculum vitae*, and a history. However, there is *some* order in it. Each element is focused on the history and politics of the Women's Liberation Movement in Australia, on some of what we learned and thought in Women's Studies, and on some of what I learned about women and the conditions of their lives around the world during the last thirty years or so, partly in the course of editing a feminist journal. These are serious matters; they are about how people's lives and ideas changed, too little remembered or understood any longer, worth recalling for that reason alone. These ideas might well not seem dangerous any longer, but they certainly did when we first formulated them. They can be great fun, too — as I hope you will agree.

Looking into the rear-vision mirror at the roads that my life has travelled, I think I can spot the crossroads where I first encountered the possibility of such changes. I was walking along a corridor at the Australian National University past the offices that housed the people who taught history. I met Daphne Gollan, coming towards me. I had been so inspired by her teaching of Russian history, to say nothing of her wit and charm, that I had undertaken a research paper on the collapse of the western front during the First World War, a subject that allowed me to read about the Russian revolutions of 1917 in English-language sources. Subsequently, though, I had embarked on research on an Australian subject, the nineteenth-century Scottish South Australian, Catherine Helen Spence. I wasn't liking Miss Spence very much, at that time, and doing Australian historical research did not bring me into contact with Mrs Gollan much, either. So, that day in the passage in the middle of 1970, I greeted her enthusiastically. (Daphne was to say that I was like a big waggy dog who would bound up to you saying pat me, pat me.) She said, 'There's a meeting that I think you should come to'.

It was a gathering in a student house in Canning Street in the northern suburbs of Canberra: the first meeting of what became the Canberra Women's Liberation group and its dream of an entirely reordered world. To appropriate the words of North American political philosopher Wendy Brown, it was a dream of transformation that would bring into being 'a radical reconfiguration of kinship, sexuality, desire, psyche and the relation of private to public'.[1] It was a dream of an entirely new and different politics. It was a dream of friendships. It was a dream that also taught me to understand Catherine Spence better, to admire her, even to like her. I dubbed her 'Australia's first feminist'.

---

[1] Wendy Brown, 'Feminism unbound, revolution, mourning, politics', in Wendy Brown, *Edgework: critical essays on knowledge and politics*, Princeton University Press, Princeton, 2005, p. 106.

Part I

Women's Liberation

The first section of this book is concerned with the history of the Women's Liberation Movement in Australia. These chapters are about sex, politics, joy and anguish. They are not in the order in which I wrote them, but, instead, in an order approximating a chronology of the Women's Liberation Movement. Chapter One is concerned with the pre-history of the upsurge of activist feminism at the beginning of the 1970s, and argues against the widespread contention that its single cause was the appearance of the contraceptive pill on the mass market. Causes are, I would argue, usually plural. What about Ann Curthoys's conviction that the new movement originated in 'radical New Left politics'? 'The early Women's Liberation Movement', she contended,

> while in part a revolt against New Left men, was nevertheless imbued with New Left politics. It was concerned with imperialism, socialism, and the oppression of Third World and minority groups, with ideologies sustaining an evil capitalist system, with revolutionary strategy and tactics.[2]

Others' experiences brought other explanations to the fore. One focused on the women of the post-World War II baby boom gaining access to tertiary education in far greater numbers than ever before, learning about societies absolutely different in time, place or kinds of relationships from our own, and thence being able to

---

[2] Ann Curthoys, 'The Women's Movement and social justice', in Dorothy H. Broom (ed.), *Unfinished business: social justice for women in Australia*, George Allen & Unwin, Sydney, 1984, pp. 161-2, reprinted in Ann Curthoys, *For and against feminism: a personal journey into feminist theory and history*, Allen & Unwin, Sydney, 1988, pp. 79-80.

1

contemplate changes to our own. Sara Dowse begins the memoir of her marriage titled 'Bride Price — 1958' with brief accounts of the marriage of a young Gogo woman of central Tanzania, and of Princess Sophie Augusta Frederika Anhalt-Zerbst of Stettin, married to the unlovely and incapable Grand Duke Peter Feodorovich, who would eventually sit at her side as she occupied the throne of All the Russias as Catherine the Great. Sara learned about these two, she tells us, in tiered lecture theatres at the University of Sydney, 'enrolling in the last stages of pregnancy and taking night classes for the first year while my mother-in-law looked after my baby boy in her pub'. That mother-in-law, Sara decided, was her father-in-law's slave: 'She still did most of the cleaning, much of the cooking, and most of the accounts; my father-in-law went out every morning to one of his buildings, came back for his lunch, and spent the rest of the afternoon either at bowls or with his cronies at the bar'. Her own situation was 'on a minor scale' much the same, and she was bothered by not having any money of her own.

> How could you put a value on my services anyway? On dusting, or shopping, or motherhood? I would think about the Gogo woman's bride price, about Sophie-Catherine's jewels. It was as though I had entered a cage, but how could I call it that?[3]

Of course the story that ends with Sara Dowse leaving that marriage is more complicated than the version that I am offering here. But it shows how learning about women in other societies offered her a mirror that refracted, rather than simply reflecting, the conditions of her own life.

Others suggested explanations that emphasised what we were, suddenly, reading. Susan Ryan, in New York with her diplomat husband and two children, was already restless with her marriage. She

> seized upon *The Female Eunuch*, written in a brilliant explosion of frustration by Germaine Greer, our old acquaintance from St Joseph's Camperdown. Betty Friedan, Kate Millett and Gloria Steinem provided more grist to my new mill. All the intelligent women I met — my new neighbour, other Australians in town, university women, even some other wives of diplomats — were on fire with enthusiasm.[4]

---

[3] Sara Dowse, 'Bride Price — 1958', Chapter One of an unpublished autobiography, personal communication, email March 2014.

[4] Susan Ryan, *Catching the waves: life in and out of politics*, HarperCollins Publishers, Sydney, 1999, p. 115.

Figure 2: Daphne Gollan, late 1970s
Photograph by Susan Magarey

(Some of the works she was finding so exhilarating appear briefly, here, in Chapter Nine.) Yet other women explained the eruption of Women's Liberation by speaking of the exhilaration of discovering friendships with women, and even, sometimes, love: the bonding which brought solidarity to such a diverse array of women — at least now and again.

That is the subject of Chapter Two, on 'sisterhood'. There are three notes to add to the discussion presented there. The concept of sisterhood can also expand from a focus on individual growth and pleasure to an attempt to describe what bound the whole diverse Women's Liberation Movement together. At the first Women & Labour Conference, held in Sydney in 1978, Daphne Gollan — here she is again — suggested that it was 'women's universal role as life-givers' that provided the basis for 'the simple concept of sisterhood', though the context of that comment suggests that she didn't consider this a particularly strong source for the solidarity that was needed to bind such a variety of individual women into an 'imagined community'. I have appropriated the term 'imagined community' from Benedict Anderson's important and influential book, *Imagined Communities*, for two elements in his gloss on 'an imagined political community': 'imagined' because we would never actually *know* everyone involved, and 'community' implying that however different we might be, we would share 'a deep, horizontal comradeship'.[5]

However — the second note — that comradeship suffered an erosion fuelled by recognition of precisely those differences among us all. Initially, questions about difference arose in relation to differences between women and men. One strand of

5   Benedict Anderson, *Imagined communities: reflections on the origin and spread of nationalism*, Verso, London, 1983, pp. 15-16.

Women's Liberation insisted that those differences were not based in biology; there is more about this in Chapter Nine. Those differences were, rather, socially and historically constituted. Another strand held that women are, in essence, entirely different from men, not merely biologically but also ethically, politically, culturally and spiritually. Such questions were, for a time, subject to intense and often theoretically sophisticated analysis. Discussions ranged from the North American feminist Carol Gilligan's essentialist account of difference in moral reasoning between women and men to post-modernist French feminist Luce Irigaray's poetic exploration of bodily and psychic sexual difference in the formation of subjectivity.

By the late 1970s, questions raised within the Women's Movement about its capacity to speak for, or about, or to relate to, the conditions of life of women who were anything but white, heterosexual in preference, and middle-class, were prompting increasing attention to differences between women. In the language of personal experience, which is always political, but never as unproblematically so as many seem to assume, this meant that the Women's Movement's horizontal comradeship was overwhelmed by a variety of voices, speaking of experiences of class-based, homophobic, racist or ethnocentric discrimination that had no place in Women's Liberation's political and theoretical analyses. The fourth Women & Labour Conference in Brisbane in 1984 was witness to encounters over precisely those kinds of difference. No claim for universal sisterhood could be sustained after that, it seemed.

The third note is to give emphasis to the point made towards the end of this second chapter, about the changing economic and cultural context of the Women's Movement in the 1990s and 2000s, a point that offers a different angle on discussions of sisterhood and difference. This context has made us all familiar with a neo-liberal social ideology emphasising the individual; with profound economic conservatism emphasising the primacy of market freedom; and with a moral vacuity in which advertisements tell each of us to 'put yourself first'. They foster the concept of 'retail therapy', even 'retail fun', blamed for a greed-is-good culture and its consequential tectonic global shocks. As one academic observed in 2009, 'The personal pronoun has taken dominion in our period: there is the iPod and the iPhone; one spends time on MySpace or YouTube; universities simulate small group interactions using i-peer; you can even buy MyDog food'.[6] In a context like this, the feminisms of the Women's

---

[6] Mark Furlong, 'i-dolatry', *Arena: The Australian Magazine of Left Political, Social and Cultural Commentary*, no. 101, 8 September 2009, pp. 12-13.

Liberation Movement could be dismissed as having failed to provide to young women all that they wanted to *have*, while the market, if allowed free rein, would do just that. Memories of Women's Liberation talking about what women could or wanted to *do*, not *have*, are few and drowned out by advertising jingles. In this context, this chapter argues, the concept of sisterhood could readily become, instead of an assertion of solidarity, a claim that all women are the same — a claim only too vulnerable to contradiction. And with that contradiction, then, a splintering of solidarity.

Chapters Three and Five are about the exuberance, the joy for women in breaking the rules, behaving badly, in public — a feature of the Women's Liberation Movement that seems to have been entirely obliterated from memory and history. Chapter Five, in particular, asks if it is possible to adapt the brilliant argument of North American feminist historian, Natalie Zemon Davis, in 'Women on Top', from her empirical source-base in early modern Europe to all advanced capitalist cultures in the mid-twentieth century.

Chapter Four is the earliest of these essays. I wrote it in the later months of 1976 as a protest against what I saw as a diminishing allegiance in Women's Liberation groups to the socialism that those groups had taught me. In 1976, to my distress, some women in those same groups were describing socialism as 'male pie-in-the-sky'. I was just gaining confidence in my knowledge about and commitment to socialism; within just a few more years, I would be able to accept invitations to present, for instance, a paper on 'Women and Socialism' to a conference of the Australian Labor Party on the party's socialist objective.[7] How could my sisters sail off in a different direction, leaving me and my socialist-feminism marooned high and dry? And what about *their* commitment to eliminating differences of power between all people? I was distraught and angry. But I was not, as that fine scholar Margaret Henderson alleges, mourning the disappearance of the feminism that, by then, formed the central commitment of my life.[8] Rather, I was merely trying to persuade my sisters to remember the ideals that we had forged together. Looking back at the moment I was protesting against, I'm now inclined to think that I was making too much fuss about

---

[7] Susan Magarey, 'Women and socialism', in Bruce O'Meagher (ed.), *The socialist objective: Labor & socialism*, Hale & Iremonger, Sydney, 1983, pp. 110-18.

[8] Margaret Henderson, *Marking feminist times: remembering the longest revolution in Australia*, Peter Lang, Bern 2006, pp. 138-40. Henderson refers to me by my married name, Susan Eade, the name under which I published that article.

it; my sisters in Women's Liberation are still, today, as critical of the imperatives of unbridled capitalism as they were in the early 1970s.

Rereading this chapter so many years later also causes me wry amusement. Its emphasis on 'social' revolution should have been on a revolution that was 'socio-political and cultural'. But I was, at the time when I wrote it, in the throes of a messianic enthusiasm for 'the new social history' that I had absorbed while doing research for a PhD in England. There I met the socialist and feminist History Workshop pioneers — Raphael Samuel, Anna Davin, Sally Alexander and Catherine Hall — and read not only Edward Thompson, but also, and crucially, Eric Hobsbawm's account of a new — and highly political — social history.[9] Deemed a 'maturing' in the United States, and a new and exciting growth in Britain where it prompted the establishment of a new journal, called *Social History*, in 1976, the 'new social history' shared with the currently ascendant structuralist history a concern with theory and with, as the editorial to the inaugural issue of *Social History* put it, 'the essential task of explaining total social process and analysing the whole range of forces promoting change and transformation, stability and continuity in past societies'. The 'new social history' was also profiting from a general historicisation of the social sciences in the 1950s and 1960s, impelling historians to attend to the methodologies devised by anthropologists, demographers, economists and sociologists for discovering information about the non-literate, those whose descendants did not donate their papers to the archives. I was to write enthusiastically about 'the new social history', providing a survey of developments in Britain in an article published in the Australian journal, *Labour History*, and then, perhaps over-optimistically, I wrote another article about developments in Australia for the British journal, *Social History*. As the second observed, in Australia, *Labour History* was so impressed by the 'new social history' it changed its sub-title to include 'social history' in its brief.[10] Afire with this enthusiasm, I failed to see anything as not encompassed in a 'social' revolution.

Questions of the extent, the size, of the Women's Liberation Movement surface in this chapter, too. I exclaim at the 'overwhelming' numbers of one Women's

---

9   See, for example, Raphael Samuel (ed.), *History workshop: a collectanea 1967-1991*, History Workshop 25, Oxford, 1991; E.J. Hobsbawm, 'From social history to the history of society', first published in *Daedalus*, vol. 100, no. 1, Winter 1971, republished in M.W. Flinn and T.C. Smout (eds), *Essays in social history*, Clarendon Press, Oxford, pp. 1-22.

10   Susan Eade [Magarey], 'Social history in Britain in 1976 — a survey', *Labour History*, no. 31, November 1976, pp. 38-52; Susan Magarey, '*Labour History*'s new sub-title: social history in Australia in 1981', *Social History*, vol. 8, no. 2, May 1983, pp. 211-28.

Liberation conference which had brought together some 600 women — a reminder of how touchingly modest were our early expectations.

By the late 1970s and early 1980s, I was employed in teaching and developing Women's Studies in universities, and on occasion I was invited to give a public lecture. Chapters Six and Seven were public lectures, one to a conference on the future, the other in a series offered to the general public. They are, accordingly, cautious in their arguments while still focusing on subjects central to Women's Liberation at the time. My concern with the future revolved around our identification of the family as the principal agent of women's oppression; later, we defined it more precisely as 'the bourgeois nuclear family'. 'Smash the family', we had chorused, marching down the leafy avenues of Canberra. This was an idea that many thought very dangerous. From this distance in time, though, it is not difficult to see 'the family' in Australia, at least in white Australia, as already in the process of profound change. No doubt the objections fuelling our protests assisted, as did the Family Law Act of the government of Labor Prime Minister Gough Whitlam, but they were not the only drivers of those changes. We would learn, too, how limited, both historically and culturally, was our definition of 'the family', excluding most particularly our Indigenous neighbours for whom families could be a refuge from the state. By the time it reaches a conclusion, my sixth chapter hints at a different, if more abstract, agent of women's oppression — patriarchy.

The concept of patriarchy was not new to feminist debate in the mid-to-late 1970s. Kate Millett had used it in *Sexual Politics*, as early as 1971. But, as Hester Eisenstein was to observe, 'the word, although widely adopted, was something of a "Sleeper"'.[11] It was not until the second half of the 1970s that it was used so frequently that feminists were prompted to debate its meaning.[12] These debates may well have signalled a continuing effort to recapture some kind of unity in the Women's Movement. I think they indicated a strenuous engagement among feminists whose work was primarily theoretical and feminists who were primarily activists to

---

[11] Hester Eisenstein, 'Comment on the Women's Movement and social justice', in Broom (ed.), op. cit., p. 177.

[12] Women's Publishing Collective, *Papers on patriarchy: conference, London 76*, Women's Publishing Collective, London, 1976; Sheila Rowbotham, 'The trouble with "patriarchy"', *New Statesman*, December 1979, Sally Alexander and Barbara Taylor, 'In defence of "patriarchy"', *New Statesman*, February 1980, both reprinted in Raphael Samuel (ed.), *People's history and socialist theory*, Routledge & Kegan Paul, London, 1981; Susan Magarey, 'Questions about "Patriarchy"', in Broom (ed.), op. cit.

find common ground. They certainly signalled a continuing desire to find a single, all-encompassing explanation for the persisting oppression of women. But, as they developed, they demonstrated an increasing diversity in feminism.

For feminists reading such works by North American feminists as Susan Brownmiller's *Against Our Will*, or, later, Susan Griffin's book on rape or Andrea Dworkin's on pornography, or Mary Daly's *Gyn/Ecology*[13], or working in a women's refuge or shelter, or a rape crisis centre, or, perhaps, a women's health centre, the term 'patriarchy' was relatively straightforward. It stood for all the ways in which men oppressed women, degraded them symbolically, damaged them physically and psychologically. 'Patriarchy' was what the North American Redstockings Manifesto had called 'male supremacy': 'the oldest, most basic form of domination. All other forms of exploitation and oppression (racism, capitalism, imperialism, etc.) are extensions of male supremacy'.[14] For feminists endeavouring to integrate analyses of women's disadvantages in the labour market with their Marxist understanding of the workings of capitalism, however, the concept 'patriarchy' was more complex. Was it a function of capitalist relations? Was it an independent system of relations? Was it, as English feminist Juliet Mitchell suggests at the end of her monumental book, *Psychoanalysis and Feminism*, primarily ideological? Was it, as another English feminist, Sheila Rowbotham, objected, a trans-historical and therefore static notion which ignored differences in the relations between women and men, femininity and masculinity, at different periods of time?[15] How could the sexual politics of contemporary Sicily and contemporary Sweden be described by the same term? And for those women who had taken up jobs in the federal and state government

---

[13] Susan Brownmiller, *Against our will: men, women and rape*, Simon & Schuster, New York, 1975; Susan Griffin, *Rape: the power of consciousness*, Harper & Row, San Francisco, 1981; Andrea Dworkin, *Pornography: men possessing women*, The Women's Press, London, 1981; Mary Daly, *Gyn/Ecology: the Meta-ethics of radical feminism*, The Women's Press, London, 1979.

[14] 'Redstocking manifesto', 1969, in Leslie B. Tanner (ed.), *Voices from women's liberation*, Mentor, New York, 1970, p. 109.

[15] E.g. Michèle Barret, *Women's oppression today: problems in Marxist feminist analysis*, Verso, London, 1980; Ann Game and Rosemary Pringle, *Gender at work*, George Allen & Unwin, Sydney, 1983; Iris Young, 'Beyond the unhappy marriage: a critique of dual systems theory', in Lydia Sargent (ed.), *Women and revolution*, South End Press, Boston, 1981; Sylvia Walby, *Patriarchy at work: patriarchal and capitalist relations in employment*, Polity Press, Cambridge, 1986; Juliet Mitchell, *Psychoanalysis and feminism*, Allen Lane, London, 1974; Rowbotham, 'The trouble with "patriarchy"'.

bureaucracies, the pioneering 'femocrats', did 'patriarchy' mean anything more specific than the overwhelming masculinism of the cultures and structures within which they had to work?[16]

Part of the difficulty was that the term was too specific for the variety of uses to which it was put. What was needed was a superordinate term that was empty of specific content, just as, in Marxism, the terms 'mode of production' or 'relations of production' do not specify whether they are feudal, or capitalist. North American feminist Gayle Rubin had escaped the problems associated with 'patriarchy' by using the term 'the sex/gender system', almost before the debate got under way.[17] Australian feminist historian Jill Matthews contributed importantly to the debate when she formulated the term 'gender order', which then allowed for some gender orders to be characterised as patriarchal, some, perhaps, as egalitarian, and some, like ours in Australia, as downright misogynist (a term that gained worldwide attention in 2013 when uttered by Prime Minister Julia Gillard about the leader of the conservative — and deeply masculinist, not to say misogynist — opposition).[18] However, even as this solution presented itself, so that the term 'patriarchal' — adjective rather than noun — gained increasing acceptance, the Women's Movement was becoming less certain of the sisterhood of all women and therefore less inclined to seek totalising causes for the oppression of women.

The analysis presented in Chapter Seven is concerned with changing conditions of women's work, and it cheerily includes reproduction as one of the forms of women's work. Both the conditions of technologically assisted reproduction and the shape and character of the labour market have changed, almost beyond recognition, since I wrote that chapter. Indeed, feminist issues around women's work have added to a focus on the struggle for equal pay and conditions — first, anxieties around a 'work-life balance' and more recently, analyses of how women work and live in new

---

[16] E.g. Sara Dowse, 'The bureaucrat as usurer', in Broom (ed.), op. cit.; Sara Dowse, 'The Women's Movement's fandango with the state: the movement's role in public policy since 1972', in Cora V. Baldock and Bettina Cass (eds), *Women, social welfare and the state in Australia*, Allen & Unwin, Sydney, 1983; Suzanne Franzway, 'With problems of their own: femocrats and the welfare state', *Australian Feminist Studies*, vol. 1, no. 3, Summer 1986, pp. 45-57.

[17] Gayle Rubin, '"The traffic in women": notes on the "political economy" of sex', in Rayna R. Reita (ed.), *Toward an anthropology of women*, Monthly Review Press, New York, 1975.

[18] Jill Julius Matthews, *Good and mad women: the historical construction of femininity in twentieth century Australia*, George Allen & Unwin, Sydney, 1984, pp. 13-15.

economies characterised by shifts away from manufacturing to the production of services and knowledge in which any boundary between work and home is being obliterated.[19] Nevertheless, a distinction between primary and secondary labour markets is still pertinent, and the importance of technological change to even more aspects of women's lives than their paid employment prompts reconsideration of what it was like a generation ago. In an era which foresees the possibility of medical technicians digitally 'printing' organs to replace those that might have failed, the early stages of the development of *in vitro* fertilisation might appear distinctly ho-hum. But the ethical debates in each period of time echo each other closely, and women still have reason for complaint about their conditions of work — in relation to reproduction and in households, as well as in the quite desperately casualised labour market, for it is still women who provide most of the unpaid, usually unrecognised, 'caring work' in our society.

Chapter Eight turns to the dreams that we might have for a different way of being, living and relating to each other. After a nod towards two nineteenth-century Australian pioneers of feminist utopias — Henrietta Dugdale and Catherine Spence — it explores four late-twentieth-century works, concluding with a discussion of *The Dispossessed: An Ambiguous Utopia*, Ursula Le Guin's engaging and politically sophisticated exploration of a society in which sexual difference did not, or did not necessarily, equate with differences of power.

North American Le Guin's work has always been considered to be science fiction, and it is as a writer of science fiction that she has won a number of prizes. (Most recently, though, she has joined the list of recipients of the medal awarded by the National Book Foundation of America for Distinguished Contribution to American Letters, a recognition of her status beyond a single genre of writing).[20] Younger writer Canadian Margaret Atwood refuses to consider her works as fitting into that genre. She does not transport her characters to a different planet or solar system. Rather, she stays right at home, insisting that she is describing conditions already in existence. She has one of the characters in *Oryx and Crake* comment: 'Think of an adaptation, any adaptation, and some animal will have thought of it first'[21]; she

---

[19] Just for example, see Lisa Adkins and Maryanne Dever, 'Gender and labour in new times: an introduction', *Australian Feminist Studies*, vol. 29, no. 79, June 2014, pp. 1-11.

[20] Alison Flood, 'Elegant, popular and enduring', *Guardian Weekly*, 26 September 2014, p. 39.

[21] Margaret Atwood, *Oryx and Crake*, Bloomsbury, London, 2003, p. 164.

made a similar point about her earlier and most famous novel, *The Handmaid's Tale*, when she noted that all the elements of the social and sexual organisation in that fiction already existed somewhere on earth. In *Oryx and Crake*, Atwood has created a world in which the coastal aquifers have turned salty, the northern permafrost has melted, the vast tundra bubbles with methane, the mid-continental plains have developed permanent drought and the Asian steppes have turned to sand dunes.[22] It is a horror. But it is not so very far from the nightmares about climate-change that we all live with in the twenty-first century. It shines a glaring light on the science-fiction qualities of conditions around us. Atwood points to the capacities for technological invention made possible by the development of the World Wide Web and gene-splicing by introducing her readers to animals which are a combination of rat and skunk, wolf and dog; to pigoons — transgenic pigs grown as specially large hosts for human-tissue organs; to ChickieNobs — a modification of chickens which consist of almost nothing but breast-meat; and then to the possibility of making your own entertainment by, say, downloading a standard core plot and adding whatever faces you might choose, a naked *Pride and Prejudice*, for instance; or to smart wallpaper which has energy-sensing algae in it that make it possible to change the colour of the walls of your room to complement your mood.

The science-fiction qualities of life on earth in the twenty-first century acquire an especially vivid hue when a reader considers the change to sexual dimorphism in relation to sex and reproduction in both *Oryx and Crake* and Le Guin's *The Left Hand of Darkness*, a change that is entirely different from the change depicted in Marge Piercy's *Woman on the Edge of Time*, which follows brilliant pioneering feminist theorist Shulamith Firestone. As Atwood depicts it, one invention is a kind of people called 'crakers', distinguished most markedly by their practice of sex and reproduction. A female comes into heat, signalled to everyone by the bright blue colour of her buttocks and abdomen, 'a trick of variable pigmentation filched from the baboons, with a contribution from the expandable chromosomes of the octopus'.

> Since it's only the blue tissue and the pheromones released by it that stimulate the males, there's no more thwarted lust; no more shadow between the desire and the act. Courtship begins with the first whiff, the first faint blush of azure, with males presenting flowers to the females — just as male penguins present round stones ... or as the male silverfish presents a sperm packet ... Their

---

[22]   ibid., p. 24.

penises turn bright blue to match the blue abdomens of the females, and they do a sort of blue-dick dance number, erect members waving to and fro in unison, in time to the foot movements and the singing … [like] the sexual semaphoring of crabs. From among the floral tributes the female chooses four flowers, and the sexual ardour of the unsuccessful candidates dissipates immediately, with no hard feelings left. Then, when the blue of her abdomen has reached its deepest shade, the female and her quartet find a secluded spot and go at it until the woman becomes pregnant and her blue colouring fades.

A 'blue-dick dance': this is not the only example of Atwood's beguiling sense of humour. More seriously, she provides protection for the females. They all have 'ultra-strong vulvas — extra skin layers, extra muscles' — so that they, too, enjoy themselves. This celebration occurs only once every three years or so — a form of population control. And the whole arrangement has other beneficial consequences as well.

No more prostitution, no sexual abuse of children, no haggling over the price, no pimps, no sex slaves. No more rape … It no longer matters who the father of the inevitable child may be, since there's no more property to inherit, no father-son loyalty required for war. Sex is no longer a mysterious rite, viewed with ambivalence or downright loathing, conducted in the dark and inspiring suicides and murders. Now it's more like an athletic demonstration, a free-spirited romp.[23]

It is exclusively heterosexual sex — an effect of sex being confined to reproduction, perhaps? These creatures, the crakers, represent the single most hopeful element in Atwood's predominantly dystopian trilogy, *Oryx and Crake*, *The Year of the Flood* (2009) and *MaddAddam* (2013). By the end of *MaddAddam*, they are able to reproduce with those poor relics of the human species left after the devastation wrought by the waterless 'flood' of the second novel. This emphasis on the centrality of (heterosexual) sex and reproduction to the possibility of a society which has eliminated differences in power between one sex and the other is extraordinarily similar to that in Le Guin's *The Left Hand of Darkness*, discussed in Chapter Nine. So very different are these two writers — Le Guin and Atwood — and yet, even a generation in time apart, a generation marked by vast differences in social, technological and ecological conditions, they seem both to have reached such similar conclusions.

If I were still teaching, I'd ask students to read both Atwood and Le Guin and tell me what they thought of these conclusions. Are these brilliant creative artists —

---

[23]   ibid., pp. 164-5.

the 'unacknowledged legislators of the world', said the poet Shelley — offering us a dream which has eliminated the differences in power between one sex and the other? A dream that has managed to combine both sexual difference *and* androgyny?

Androgyny appears here in Chapter Nine, too. This is the piece that I wrote most recently. It is also the one I have most enjoyed writing — partly, I think, because it recalls moments of such immense pleasure, to say nothing of intellectual excitement, from the late 1970s and early 1980s when I was teaching Women's Studies at the Australian National University, and partly because, almost at the end, the inimitable Daphne Gollan — libertarian-socialist, author of the sparkling autobiographical essay, 'The Memoirs of "Cleopatra Sweatfigure"'[24] — appears once again.

This chapter also charts a major shift in understandings of sexual difference. Readers of Virginia Woolf might remember that exquisite moment when Orlando wakes to discover that he — or, now, she — has become a woman, something which fails to prompt any signs of discomposure: 'The change seemed to have been accomplished painlessly and completely and in such a way that Orlando herself showed no surprise at it'.[25] Among adherents of Women's Liberation in the early 1970s were those whose desire to eliminate difference in power between women and men amounted to a desire for cultural androgyny, like Orlando, capable — not of *being* either sex equally well, but rather — of *doing* most things that either sex already did. 'I can do anything you can do/ Anything you can do, I can do better', we sang. The distinction between sex and gender, as outlined in this chapter, was useful to such a desire because, while it necessarily left physical sex intact, it could argue persuasively for major change in the cultural norms which defined the feminine as inferior. However, as this chapter explains, the Australian feminist philosophers of the body reinstated sexual difference in our understanding of human interaction, and therefore in our understanding of the operation of power differentials between women and men. So, too, it must be acknowledged, did our advancing years. Even so, we retain the hope that we learned from the feminist utopias, if from nowhere else, and the joy in misbehaving that allowed us to celebrate something as unlikely as a tampon.

---

[24] Daphne Gollan, 'The Memoirs of "Cleopatra Sweatfigure"', in Elizabeth Windschuttle (ed.), *Women, class and history: feminist perspectives on Australia 1788-1978*, Fontana/Collins, Melbourne, 1980, pp. 313-29.

[25] Virginia Woolf, *Orlando: a biography*, first published 1928, Triad/Panther Books, St Albans, 1977, pp. 86-7.

1

The sexual revolution as big flop: Women's Liberation Lesson One

This paper was first presented to the Network for Research in Women's History section of the Australian Historical Association Conference, University of Melbourne, 2008.

Foreplay

Some years ago, the Australian Research Council funded research towards a history of the Women's Liberation Movement in Australia.[26] Other projects interrupted what had initially been designed to be a smooth transition from research to writing. However, I am now engaged in writing that history, and, herewith, its beginning. I had expected that my story of the resurgence of feminism in Australia in the late 1960s and early 1970s would start by linking the origins of Women's Liberation with the sexual revolution that followed from the appearance of the Pill on the mass market in Australia in 1961. But I have now decided that the connection between the

---

[26] As I explained in the Acknowledgements, one aspect of the research carried out for that project was a series of interviews carried out by Research Assistants Kate Borrett, Liz Dimmock, Ruth Ford, Ann Genovese, Judith Ion, Tristan Slade, Lizzie Summerfield, Inara Waldron, Deborah Worsley-Pine and Sarah Zetlein. These interviews were then transcribed by Mary Lyons, a very considerable labour, sent back to the interviewees for any changes they wanted to make, and after that stowed in my filing cabinets, where they remain. Copies have also been lodged in the State Library of South Australia (which lent us recording equipment), but they cannot be accessed until I have completed the history of Women's Liberation in Australia.

Pill, the sexual revolution and Women's Liberation was not so simple. First, the sexual revolution had been brewing for longer than the few years between 1961 and, say, 1968. Second, there were two kinds of uneven development: the Pill did not simply 'appear' on the mass market: its dissemination occasioned controversy and conflict and took some time; and its distribution was patchy. Let me elaborate, briefly.

Explanations for all manifestations of what has been called the cultural revolution of the West — from the student movement to new concerns with ecology, including the sexual revolution and Women's Liberation — usually have three elements. One is economic growth and an associated expansion of domestic markets as, to quote Stella Lees and June Senyard, 'Australia became a modern society and everyone got a house and car'.[27] A second is the beginnings of a new communications revolution with the appearance of television. The third is expanding education, especially tertiary education. I have written such explanations myself. Now, I would like to add to that mix two other factors.

One comes from the work of sociologists Ann Game and Rosemary Pringle. Considering the making of the Australian family, focused on sex and the suburban dream, they argued that the 1950s and '60s saw not only an expansion of consumption but also its sexualisation, targeted specifically at women. Advertisers, journalists and educators developed and spread the view that women — housewives — were to form love relationships with their homes, to have an emotional investment in the wellbeing of their furnishings. They set about persuading the housewife that her sexuality, her allure, her attractiveness would be enhanced by her maintenance of a well-stocked pantry, or her acquisition of a Hills hoist.[28] As I have been schooled by reading Michel Foucault, I want to add to that analysis an equal and opposite understanding of precisely the same phenomenon, that is, the commodification of sex. Such advertising also led the housewife — and other women as well — to believe that the pinnacle of a happy life was sexual satisfaction, her most prized acquirement a good orgasm. Publications multiplied: Alfred Kinsey's *Sexual Behaviour of the Human Male* appeared in 1948, followed by his *Sexual Behaviour in the Human Female* in

---

27 Stella Lees and June Senyard, *The 1950s — how Australia became a modern society, and everyone got a house and car*, Hyland House, Melbourne, 1987.

28 Ann Game and Rosemary Pringle, 'Sexuality and the suburban dream', *Australian and New Zealand Journal of Sociology*, vol. 15, no. 2, 1979; 'The making of the Australian family', in Ailsa Burns, Gill Bottomley and Penny Jools (eds), *The family in the modern world: Australian perspectives*, George Allen & Unwin, Sydney, 1983.

1953 — works which shocked the United States and inspired Hugh Hefner to launch *Playboy* magazine in 1953.[29] Masters and Johnson's *Human Sexual Response* followed in 1966, and their work culminated with a book called simply *The Pleasure Bond* in 1975. Bookshops created whole new sections of shelf-space for the plethora of new sex manuals. 'All You Need is Love', we sang, along with the Beatles. Germaine Greer's demand that women cease being eunuchs and develop an active sexuality of their own[30] was merely a logical extension of these two developments, both of which had been underway since the end of the 1940s.

By the 1960s, women's enormously enhanced desire for sexual satisfaction could lead them to engage in freewheeling sexual encounters, just as men did — *if* they had reliable contraception. Former professional soldier Barry Billing, at home from Vietnam, encountered the marches in protest against Australia's participation in the war he was fighting. 'Everyone gets horny', he recalled, and afterwards 'the testosterone's up and the birds are hot'. He discarded his uniform to go on marches 'looking cool' because, then, he said, 'you'd get a root'.[31] The Pill did not cause women's heightened libido. But as reliable contraception, it did make it possible.

The sexual revolution was never going to be sexual liberation for all women, though; the laws of uneven development appear clearly. The importance of campaigns for the legalisation of abortion during the first years of Women's Liberation testify to the numbers of women still not using the Pill. As a doctor's prescription was necessary to obtain the Pill, its appearance reinforced the authority that doctors — still predominantly male — could exercise over what could be seen as women's sexual morality; some doctors refused to prescribe the Pill for women who were not married; some doctors refused to prescribe it for any women. When researchers for the history of the Women's Liberation Movement interviewed former Legislative Councillor Anne Levy, she told them about being on the Board of the Family Planning Association in Adelaide, and the opposition that they encountered from the medical profession: they didn't want the Family Planning Association giving out the Pill, only family doctors should be allowed to do that. 'We had lots of fights with the

---

[29]   See, for example, Barbara Ehrenreich, *The hearts of men: American dreams and the flight from commitment*, Pluto, London, 1983.

[30]   Germaine Greer, *The female eunuch*, first published 1971, Flamingo, London, 1993.

[31]   Barry Billing, quoted in *The Weekend Australian*, 5-6 January 2008.

A[ustralian] M[edical] A[ssociation]', she noted.[32] The Pill was also subject to a 17 per cent luxury tax throughout the 1960s, limiting its availability to those who could afford it. Melbourne author Joyce Nicolson told these researchers that in the early days of Women's Electoral Lobby, with only about six months to the federal elections, they went to election campaign meetings. 'We all got up and asked questions about contraception' and asked for the 'luxury' on contraceptives tax to be removed.[33] It was, on the Whitlam government's third day in office in 1972.[34]

Even then, not all women — not even all feminists — saw the Pill as contributing to sexual revolution. Sydney feminist Catharine Lumby, a generation younger than Anne Levy, was 'getting ready to enter First Form at Newcastle Girls High' in 1973.

> In 1973, nice girls kept their legs together and their options open … Lounging on the hockey field … the good girls dreamed of surfer boyfriends with peroxide-blond hair and a Sandman panel van. Actually daring to get into a panel van was a different matter … Girls who got into panel vans ended up pregnant and expelled. As far as we knew, they deserved it.[35]

Achieving orgasm?

When Melbourne feminist Laurie Bebbington went from school to Melbourne University in 1972, she was elected to the newly created position of Women's Officer in the national Australian Union of Students. The first and major imperative for that position was, it emerged, to collect and distribute information in four key areas. One was 'sexuality' which was, she explained 'health, really. Women's health and women's sexuality together'. She told our researchers,

> I remember reading in 1971, before I even got to university in 1972, this revolutionary article by Germaine Greer in a Monash University paper about the clitoris. And quite literally I think many women at university in the early seventies didn't know about the clitoris.[36]

---

[32] The Hon. Anne Levy, AO, interview with Deborah Worsley-Pine, 25 July 1996.

[33] Joyce Nicholson, interview with Ruth Ford, 9 October 1997.

[34] Marilyn Lake, *Getting equal: the history of Australian feminism*, Allen & Unwin, Sydney, 1999, p. 234.

[35] Catharine Lumby, *Alvin Purple*, Currency Press, Strawberry Hills, NSW, 2008, p. 21.

[36] Laurie Bebbington, interview with Ruth Ford, 1 December 1997.

Sydney feminist, postgraduate student Lyndall Ryan was but one of many in Women's Liberation to have encountered American Anne Koedt's electrifying piece, 'The myth of the vaginal orgasm' and its unequivocal assertion: 'It is the clitoris which is the center of sexual sensitivity and … is the female equivalent of the penis';[37] 'it knocked me out', Lyndall told our researchers.[38] Anne Summers, a student at Adelaide University at the time, printed 'all these extra copies of the cover of the pamphlet "The Myth of the Vaginal Orgasm"', she said,

> [a]nd I was going around the campus putting them up on trees, advertising where you could get them. And there was this group of Engineering students walking behind me ripping them off. They were just outraged that you would use the word 'vagina' and 'orgasm'.[39]

Some women missed it, though. In about 1972, I was part of a conversation in which a feminist postgraduate student in the Canberra Women's Liberation group, a young woman who had had several heterosexual affairs that I knew about, asked how far away her clitoris was from her vagina. If reproductive control was — as so many of us believed — vital to the liberation of women, then understanding how our bodies worked was vital, too.

In Canberra, Women's Liberation acquired a copy of the Boston Women's Health Book *Our Bodies Our Selves*, first published in 1971, typed the chapter on 'Sexuality' onto a stencil — these were the *samizdat* days of Women's Liberation — and roneoed off about a hundred copies to distribute. Another Canberra feminist wrote an article on masturbation for the Australian National University student newspaper; it occasioned some stir when it was published in February 1973 because its author had, by then, stopped tutoring in Philosophy and become Women's Advisor to Prime Minister Gough Whitlam.[40] In Bathurst, Kay Schaffer was one in a group that organised a conference on 'Women's Changing Roles' in 1974. No fewer than 250 women turned up, she said, from all over the central west: 'from Dubbo and Orange and Forbes and Wagga'. The session that gained the most attention was on 'Female

---

[37] Anne Koedt, 'The myth of the vaginal orgasm', in Leslie B. Tanner (comp. and ed.), *Voices from Women's Liberation*, Signet Books, New York, 1970.

[38] Lyndall Ryan, interview with Ann Genovese, 25 September 1997.

[39] Anne Summers, interview with Ann Genovese, 30 April 1998.

[40] Susan Magarey, recollection of a conversation with Elizabeth Reid in London, early in 1974.

Sexuality', to which women from Sydney presented 'a kit of contraception material, contraception advice'. Kay and her friends thought this 'particularly important for the girls at Bathurst College because they had no access to the Pill. The two Catholic doctors in town would not prescribe it'.[41]

And then there were the consciousness-raising groups. Melbourne feminist Jean Taylor, a young mother in the early years of Women's Liberation, described them. In a consciousness-raising group there would be about a dozen women, she said, which meant that at any meeting there would be about eight or nine, an 'ideal number' for a group if 'you want to get things done and still maintain intimacy'. She went on to explain:

> The main things that differentiate a consciousness-raising group from an ordinary discussion is that we did very in-depth stuff on a topic around our personal lives, and then we would put it into a political context … [Y]ou'd hear other women talking about … their relationship with their mother or how they were told about their first period. Some of the stories were hysterical. Most of our groups we'd laugh. It would be really, really funny. And by that time you'd have built up a whole — that intimacy, that friendship that was built up in, I'd say, every CR group was absolutely unique.[42]

Some consciousness-raising groups moved from talking to something more physical. One in Sydney was once treated to a lesson in how to treat period pain with an exhibition of sisterly massage of the afflicted belly.

Sometimes such discussions put what Adelaide feminist Yvonne Allen described as 'enormous stresses' on her relationship with her husband. 'All that resentment that had been sort of not able to be expressed suddenly found expression. Everything was legitimised. And I had a language … to talk about these things'.[43] They were not always an occasion of strife, those discussions. Rather, they could lead to new sexual possibilities for women. 'It looks like a classic Women's Liberation story', Sue Sheridan told our researchers about her own life: 'Got involved in Women's Liberation, ended a marriage and started having sexual relationships with women. It's almost like a cliché, but it … didn't feel like a cliché'.[44]

---

41   Kay Schaffer, interview with Kate Borrett, 18 June 1996.

42   Jean Taylor, interview with Ruth Ford, 12 December 1997.

43   Yvonne Allen, interview with Deborah Worsley-Pine, 4 July 1996.

44   Sue Sheridan, interview with Sarah Zetlein, 29 February 1996.

For women like Sue Williams, who had already decided she was gay and disliked the role-playing she found in the gay scene at the Elephant & Castle in Adelaide, Women's Liberation was an emotional and intellectual delight. 'It turned my life absolutely upside down', she said. 'It was painful but it was incredibly stimulating, and it was emotionally very exciting'.[45] Sydney feminist Sue Wills was also already gay and said, 'I guess Women's Liberation didn't appeal to me because it didn't appear to have anything to say about lesbians'. But then she encountered the early issues of Sydney Women's Liberation's newspaper, *MeJane*, and, she said, 'an article by Jill Roe that started off with a wonderful sentence something like "in the interstices of society lurks the lesbian", or something like that. So that's how I got involved'.[46]

Consciousness-raising among lesbians could revolve around rules for lesbian relationships. Melbourne feminist Jan Chapman Davis was a mother of four and becoming aware of her Aboriginality when she first contacted Women's Liberation to help her with her divorce. Once she had become involved with Radical Lesbians, however, she encountered a new set of rules which concerned monogamy versus polygamy: 'And there was a big push for polygamy', she told us. 'Monogamy wasn't on ... "We shall be polygamous. Everyone's our sister. We love everyone", when the reality was that we certainly didn't'.[47] Here, perhaps, there is just a trace of sexual liberation's moment at the end of the 1960s and early 1970s.

Post-coital tristesse
(*post coitum omne animal tristis est*: Galen, 130 AD)

Some people in the Libertarian Push in Sydney could be seen as forerunners of the sexual revolution. After all, the Push, which dated from the beginning of the 1950s, held that women were equal to men ('if they "came up to scratch" intellectually'). Germaine Greer had been one of the Push women for a time, while she was tutoring at Sydney University. So Push men were willing to accept some aspects of her attack on the current state of heterosexual sexual relationships. But they objected strongly to her attack on Freud. They insisted that there was no difference between a male and

---

[45]   Sue Williams, interview with Deborah Worsley-Pine, 19 August 1996.

[46]   Sue Wills, interview with Tristan Slade, 26 September 1997; the quotation 'in the interstices of our social fabric hides the lesbian ... ' that inspired Sue is from Jill Roe, 'Lesbians and women', *MeJane: a women's liberation newspaper*, no. 3, July 1971, p. 4.

[47]   Jan Chapman-Davis, interview with Ruth Ford, 29 October 1997.

a female orgasm. They even wrote papers on the subject. But some Push women had to resort to backyard abortions to remain the freely relating individuals of the Sydney Push's — thoroughly masculine — expectations. And when Push women — finally — began to discuss Push men's sexual performance, their descriptions were less than enthusiastic: they described them as '"workmanlike", "threadbare" and with a "lack of foreplay"'.[48]

In Melbourne, the 'Push' was a definition confined to Carlton, according to Joyce Nicholson. It was just like life depicted in Helen Garner's novel, *Monkey Grip*, she said. 'I mean, everyone slept around with everyone else'. And Helen Garner's heroine suggests as early as page one of that novel what was wrong with sexual liberation for women. Her lover, 'knowing perhaps in his bones that nothing would be the same again', says to her, 'I wish I could — you know — *turn you on*'. He does, that time. But it is nevertheless the end of the affair.[49]

It was not only people in a 'push' involved in the sexual revolution. There were the academics, and there was the Left. Adelaide feminist artist Annie Newmarch dates her involvement with Women's Liberation to the time when she went to the very new Flinders University in the early 1970s. 'During my time doing Philosophy', she said, 'I fell in love with who I shouldn't have, and had a baby'; her lover was at the time married to someone else.[50] In Sydney, Lyndall Ryan was, she said, 'probably having on and off, you know, sort of one night stands or whatever with various blokes around the Left'.[51] Anne Summers was also in Sydney, by then, having left her husband, John Summers. She said she used to go to the pub every night, 'trying to pick up blokes'. She had, she told us, 'a lot of one-night stands, or one month stands, or whatever. A lot of very short term relationships, but nothing serious'.[52] Wary of the Left, she would have been, after watching the Students for Democratic Action in Adelaide:

> You could certainly see, you know, a lot of sexual and other sorts of exploitation
> on the left, and it was true that men would have all the glory and the women

[48]   Anne Coombs, *Sex and anarchy: the life and death of the Sydney Push*, Viking, Melbourne, 1996, pp. 259-61, 269, 270.

[49]   Helen Garner, *Monkey grip*, McPhee Gribble Publishers, Melbourne, 1977, p. 1, emphasis in the original.

[50]   Annie Newmarch, interview with Deborah Worsley-Pine, 22 August 1996.

[51]   Ryan, interview with Ann Genovese, op. cit.

[52]   Summers, interview with Ann Genovese, op. cit.

would be making the tea and making the flags and running the Gestetner and all of that.[53]

Lyndall said that she thought the girls made the tea 'because they wanted to get off with the boys'.[54] Anne went on, at least temporarily, to a relationship with a woman, Kris Melmuth, which lasted more than a month.[55] Maybe the girls did want to get off with the boys. But they clearly did not enjoy themselves enough to go back for much more from the same individual.

Lesley Lynch, another Sydney feminist, had been a child bride, married to Colin Gray at the age of twenty in the mid-1960s. In the days of the sexual revolution they kept their distance because, she said, 'even then we had a very clear sense … sexual liberation was going to bring a great deal of exploitation with it'.[56] Carol Treloar went to the Women's Health Conference in Brisbane in 1975. There had been, she observed, 'a sexual free-for-all between [university] students and staff', and, she went on, 'I think many of us were starting to see that, you know, the women had got the raw end of that'.[57]

Conclusion

Not long ago, Catharine Lumby published a book called *Alvin Purple* in which she maintained that the film of that name, on Australian screens in 1973, but R-rated, 'reflects and refracts so many of the cultural, political and sexual anxieties and realities of its time'. It is all there, she writes, 'the nudge-nudge humour, the anxiety about where female sexual desire fits into heterosexuality, the electricity of burgeoning cultural and political change'.[58] But not for everyone. Joyce Nicholson was having her first experience of a demonstration in Bourke Street in Melbourne at the time when this film was screening. Young women from Women's Liberation were directing the march. They would shout through their loudspeakers 'What do you want?' and the marchers would reply 'We want equality!' 'When do you want it?' 'Now!' And as

---

[53] ibid.

[54] Ryan, interview with Ann Genovese, op. cit.

[55] Anne Summers, *Ducks on the pond: an autobiography 1945-1976*, Viking, Ringwood, 1999, p. 331.

[56] Lesley Lynch, interview with Ann Genovese, 26 October 1997.

[57] Carol Treloar, interview with Deborah Worsley-Pine, 1 August 1996.

[58] Lumby, op. cit., pp. 3-4.

they reached the movie-theatre, the young women shouted, 'Fuck *Alvin Purple*!' 'I remember', said Joyce, 'we all shouted "Fuck *Alvin Purple*!"' Well, I'd never used the word "fuck" in my life'. But by now, she was well beyond nudge-nudge humour and anxiety about female desire. Joyce had been brought up very strictly and never even thought of sleeping with anyone but her husband until she was forty-five. 'Then', though, she told us, 'I began to do it with great enthusiasm'.[59] For her, sexual liberation came with and from Women's Liberation, not from either the Pill or the sexual revolution.

---

[59] Nicholson, interview with Ruth Ford, op. cit.

2

Sisterhood and Women's Liberation in Australia

This paper was presented to the Australian Women's History Symposium at the University of Adelaide in 2012, and then published in Outskirts *online journal, vol. 28, 2013, co-edited by Catherine Kevin and Zora Simic. I am grateful to those editors for their encouragement, and to Alison Bartlett, editor of* Outskirts, *who assured me that copyright for anything published in* Outskirts *remains with the author.*

Made in America: two moments of origin

In 1969, Martha Ansara, an American, was in her early twenties, living in Boston with her three-year-old son, and splitting up with her husband. 1969 was a big year for Ansara. She moved first to California with her new Australian boyfriend, and then, with the same boyfriend, to Australia. In Sydney, she made left-wing friends through Bob Gould's Third World Bookshop, in particular with Sandra Hawker and with two Australians who had recently returned from the United States: Margaret Elliot and Coonie Sandford.[60] Together they formed a group and discussed the pamphlets that Ansara had brought with her and their own experiences. Towards the end of that year they decided to hold an open meeting about Women's Liberation. The official story is

---

60   Sue Wills, 'The politics of women's liberation', PhD Thesis, University of Sydney, 1981, p. 20.

that those three women composed a leaflet headed *Only the Chains Have Changed* to distribute during a protest march against the war in Vietnam on 14 December 1969, calling a meeting about Women's Liberation for January 1970. Many years later, Ansara confessed that, being a young mother, she had been exhausted and had fallen asleep, so the leaflet was the work of Hawker and Sandford and Ansara's film-making journalist boyfriend.[61]

The meeting should have been a failure, Ansara was to recall: 'Nobody in their right mind holds meetings in January. I knew nothing, you know'. But even though it was January — when everyone goes to the beach — the meeting was packed. This was, Ansara remembered, a 'new phenomenon': 'we were swept up, I guess, in the sort of new wave of interest in this imported phenomenon'.[62]

Early in 1969, Warren Osmond, a tutor in Politics at the University of Adelaide, had been reading anti-war publications which made a great fuss over the Miss America Protest of 7 September 1968. New York Radical Women organised about 100 women onto buses to travel to Atlantic City where they picketed the pageant, performed guerrilla theatre on the boardwalk, and tossed '"instruments of torture to women" — high-heeled shoes, bras, girdles, typing books, curlers, false eyelashes, and copies of *Playboy*, *Cosmopolitan* and *Ladies Home Journal* — into a "Freedom Trash Can"'.[63] Just for the record, they did not, despite the endlessly reiterated myth, burn these objects: the city prohibited any burning because its boardwalk was flammable. In an article published in the Adelaide student newspaper, *On Dit*, Osmond drew a parallel between the Miss America Pageant and Adelaide University's 'Miss Fresher' beauty contest, part of the Orientation Week celebrations at the beginning of the academic year. Was it not, he asked, 'Just about time for a new feminism?'[64]

A year later, in March 1970, a group of about fifty young women calling themselves Women's Liberation picketed the 'Miss Fresher' contest at Adelaide University. Anna Yeatman, another Politics tutor, said that they were protesting against being seen simply as objects of male desire, 'sex slaves', 'to be gaped at by

---

[61] Martha Ansara, interview with Tristan Slade, 29 September 1997.

[62] ibid.

[63] Alice Echols, *Daring to be bad: radical feminism in America 1967-1975*, University of Minnesota Press, Minneapolis, 1989, pp. 93-4.

[64] Sylvia Kinder, *Herstory of the Adelaide women's liberation movement 1969-1974*, Salisbury Education Centre, Adelaide, 1980, p. 31.

pathetic, goggling men'. The media (briefly) went into a frenzy: Channel Nine's newsreader interviewed Yeatman on television, and the evening newspaper, the *News*, with uncharacteristic prescience, headed its report, 'Women's liberation is quickly shaping as a major world issue of the seventies'.[65] Women's Liberation — made in America — had arrived in Australia.

A movement for the liberation of women

It was nothing if not ambitious. One of the movement's earliest publications, called *MeJane*, signalled a newspaper that would leave Tarzan out of the picture altogether. 'Our changes will be total', its editorial declared: 'they will not be immediate, but we want to start now, changing life styles, changing the family and above all, changing ourselves'.[66]

It would be different from other political movements which involved men as well, and women behaving like men. In May 1970 Anne Summers travelled from Adelaide to Melbourne to a conference on 'Female Conditioning' which she found entirely antipathetic. 'There was', she noted,

> much talking and shouting, there were heated exchanges between the protagonists of various 'lines' and those espousing minority views were frequently patronized or even jeered at. One woman abused several of us for wearing make-up … others were castigated for knitting during the sessions …[67]

Martha Ansara and senior Communist Party member, Mavis Robertson, went to that conference, too. There were, Ansara remembered, 'these weird young ladies in black jackets who were Maoists, I think, who were just thought police'. They criticised and castigated: 'This is backward'. Mavis Robertson scoffed: 'I wonder if they're going to be doing underarm inspections next to see if we shave under our arms'.[68] Eighteen months later, though, a report on a Women's Liberation conference in Melbourne in August 1971 noted two seasoned campaigners praising 'the radical approach of today … with its rejection … of male-type structures'; they considered that such an

---

[65]   *News*, 23 March 1970, n.p.

[66]   'Editorial', *MeJane*, no. 1, 1 March 1971.

[67]   Anne Summers, 'Where's the Women's Movement moving to?', *MeJane*, no. 10, March 1973, reprinted in Jan Mercer (ed.), *The other half: women in Australian society*, Penguin Books, Ringwood, 1975, p. 406.

[68]   Ansara, op. cit., p. 6.

approach was more likely to be successful than older forms of feminist activism with their 'too frequent courting of male support'. The different approach 'led so many to realise how their previous separations had been imposed upon them by values which were for the benefit of others rather than themselves'.[69]

Banishing the men

'Others rather than themselves': this meant men. It took a little while to decide that men could not be part of the Women's Liberation Movement. In Adelaide, Anna Yeatman argued for men to continue to be involved in Women's Liberation, rejecting any idea that 'men themselves' could be identified as 'the source of male dominated social organisation and the male chauvinist value system'.[70] During the summer of 1970-71 in Adelaide, Women's Liberation meetings were held at the home of Julie and Bob Ellis, perpetuating the involvement of men. Short-lived it was, though, as — according to historian of Adelaide Women's Liberation, Sylvia Kinder — the works of North American feminists Shulamith Firestone and Kate Millett became more widely available in Australia during 1971.[71] In Sydney, the process was quicker and more pragmatic. Martha Ansara described what took place at Glebe Point Road.

> It seemed to me that because women's voices had been so overwhelmed by the voices of men, and because, in fact, our agendas conflicted, that you would not have men at the meetings. It didn't make any sense. Well, you know, this just got debated and debated, and the communist women in particular … couldn't see any reason why the comrades couldn't all be equal together. So we said, 'Okay. We'll hold an open meeting'. That open meeting … was enough to do the trick. The men came in and they hogged all the conversation, and they were opinionated. They used all those tactics … of overwhelming people, and that was it. They were out.[72]

It was an experience replicated many times; I myself recall a similar moment at an early Women's Liberation meeting in Canberra. A husband who believed himself entirely supportive stood in the doorway with one arm stretched upwards along the doorframe so that (a short man) he occupied a taller space; we all sat in a circle on the

---

[69] *MeJane*, no. 5, November 1971, n.p.

[70] Anna Yeatman, 'The liberation of women', *Arena*, no. 21, 1970, p. 21.

[71] Kinder, op. cit., pp. 48-9.

[72] Ansara, op. cit.

floor, as we were accustomed to doing, but in this corporeal configuration, at his feet, and he lectured us on what Women's Liberation '*should* do'.

As early as July 1971, experienced campaigner Joyce Stevens — like Mavis Robertson, one of Martha Ansara's communist women — had given up on the notion of comrades all being equal together. She told *MeJane* that women would need to get used to 'the unpalatable fact that women are by word and deed oppressed on the basis of their sex and … the vehicles of this oppression are men'. Then, in an observation so radical that it took some time to gain widespread acceptance, she added:

> All men benefit from the oppression of women indirectly through the male domination and privileges of society generally and individually through the life styles set aside for women, whether the women [*sic*] be his mother, wife, daughter, girlfriend or sister (or any combination of these).[73]

The movement for the liberation of women was to be a movement *of* women as well as a movement *for* women.

Small-group egalitarianism

Women's Liberation quickly developed a characteristic 'approach to meetings', participants breaking up into 'small (rap) groups' which 'promoted an openness and width of participation impossible in large numbers'. Such an approach, *MeJane* claimed, enabled 'industrial workers, housewives, teachers, students — all women' to accept and relate to each other.[74] This was important: they were relating as equals. Indeed, in one small group at the 1971 Melbourne conference, the housewives — traditionally dismissed on the Left as, at best, a 'reserve army of labour' — demonstrated a sophisticated appreciation of their own political potential and its wider implications that made some of the early feminist theorists sound both narrow and naïve.

> They discussed the potential power of housewives, as consumers, to support their sisters in industry: when women workers make it known that a certain company exploits its female staff even more unmercifully than the average — housewives can stop buying that company's products. Such action need not take on the proportion of an organised national boycott to have a pinprick

---

[73] *MeJane*, no. 3, July 1971, p. 6.

[74] *MeJane*, no. 5, November 1971, p. 4.

effect on the company and to let the women in the industry feel bolstered by the support.[75]

Small groups, without men, and — above all — committed to equality among the participants in each group were necessary, Sydney feminist Sue Wills has pointed out, for 'allowing women to develop self-confidence'.[76] Women's Liberation was developing an analysis of power that reached from the most traditional and public to the most intimate and private — challenging conventional distinctions between public and private as well as showing a household to be quite as much a political arena as a house of parliament. As Queensland-born Women's Liberationist Eileen Haley explained:

> Most people think of themselves as having a 'private life' in which politics does not operate. Politics is something that goes on 'out there'. Feminism shows this distinction as non-existent. It exposes the 'private life' areas as a political arena. It also shows how the dominant political system invades that private life continually in very deeply felt ways.[77]

Power governs all relationships, everywhere, from the ballot-box to the bedroom. This was one of the most resonant understandings of late twentieth-century feminism: that 'the personal is political'. The power relations of personal life affected interactions between women in Women's Liberation groups, too. By the time of the third national Women's Liberation Conference over the June long weekend in 1972 in Sydney, small groups had become the order of the day, and the principle of refusing hierarchies held sway.

Structurelessness and consciousness-raising

Anne Summers had a better time at the June 1972 gathering. A year or so later she spelled out the general rule in Women's Liberation about opposition to any kind of hierarchy, indeed to any kind of formal organisation. 'From its inception Women's Liberation has been anti-organization', she wrote:

> in the sense that we have no elected officers, no formal membership, no rules or platform to which people must adhere, and no theories determining the

---

[75] ibid.

[76] Wills, op. cit., p. 46.

[77] Eileen Haley, 'The long haul', *Politics*, vol. 8, no. 2, November 1973, p. xxxvi.

relationship of factions or opposition groups to the movement as a whole. We have justified this stance by pointing out that formal organizations [*sic*] is always oligarchical in that it inevitably produces an elite of leaders who cling to their powerful positions more tenaciously than they adhere to the principles of the organization they purportedly represent.[78]

Many if not most of the small groups springing up around Australia included consciousness-raising in their discussions. Martha Ansara described it: 'we formed a group and the first thing we did was we followed this consciousness-raising procedure, and we discussed our own lives'.[79] In consciousness-raising groups, participants learned that an isolated problem or an individual misery was neither isolated nor individual. Rather, each was a feature of a structural or systemic organisation of relations of power, of politics, of the politics of what, at that time, Eileen Haley called 'male supremacy'. An individual woman's personal life was, Sue Wills noted, 'political reality in microcosm'.[80] But to reach such perceptions, the women involved needed to learn to trust each other with narratives about themselves, about moments in their individual lives that they thought they would never describe to anyone, about aspects of their relationships with their mothers, fathers, husbands, lovers, daughters, sons that they had never thought to articulate, much less share. Trust of this order formed strong bonds, and with this came sisterhood.

'Sisterhood is Powerful' (Robin Morgan)

'We call on all our sisters to unite with us in struggle', exhorted the manifesto of Redstockings[81], the group that Shulamith Firestone and Ellen Willis founded in New York in February 1969.[82] *Sisterhood is Powerful* announced Robin Morgan's collection of articles conceived of as an action by feminists 'committed to a Women's Revolution', published in 1970.[83] Across the Pacific in Australia, women read these words, adopted the concept, and themselves felt united and, accordingly, powerful. It

---

[78] Summers, 'Where's the Women's Movement moving to?', p. 408.

[79] Ansara, op. cit., p. 4.

[80] Wills, op. cit., p. 386.

[81] 'Redstockings Manifesto', in Robin Morgan (ed.), *Sisterhood is powerful: an anthology of writings from the Women's Liberation Movement*, Vintage Books, New York, 1970, p. 600.

[82] Echols, op. cit., p. 139.

[83] Robin Morgan, 'Introduction', in Morgan, op. cit., p. xvi.

was a transformation: Deborah McCulloch, Women's Adviser to radically reforming South Australian Premier Don Dunstan, observed that before the Women's Liberation Movement, 'most of my contemporaries grew up in a culture which said … you don't spend any time with women, you didn't like women … you always complained about them, and the ideal and the norm was male'.[84] Now it was different. 'The concept of sisterhood became the theory of unity', wrote Sylvia Kinder.[85] When someone congratulated Edna Ryan, doyenne of Women's Electoral Lobby in Sydney, on the career of Susan Ryan, Minister of Education and Minister with responsibility for women in the first two governments of R.J. Hawke — assuming that Susan, no relation of Edna, was Edna's daughter — Edna responded: 'She's not my daughter, she's my sister'.[86] 'Sisterhood', Canberra feminist journalist Helen Shepherd affirmed, 'was like a petrol pump: it kept you going and going'.[87]

There were echoes, of course, of the Labour Movement's assertion of solidarity in the brotherhood of man, and men's struggle against exploitation in the capitalist labour market. But the solidarity of women in sisterhood went much further, for women's grievances extended from the labour market to workplaces that were also their homes, in which their bosses were their fathers, their brothers, their husbands, even their sons, and their grievances included the domestic labour in their double workload, difficulties preventing them from controlling their reproductive capacities, their unfulfilled desire for sexual pleasure, being required to take exclusive responsibility for children and their care, and — having just lived through 'the decade of domesticity'[88] — anxieties about feeling *un*-natural for registering these conditions *as* grievances. Sisterhood had a reach far beyond that of the brotherhood of man.

In a paper that she took to the Marxist Feminist Conference in Sydney in June 1977, Canberra Women's Liberationist Biff Ward described the 'initial exhilarating

---

[84]   Deborah McCulloch, interview with Deborah Worsley-Pine, 12 April 1996.

[85]   Kinder, op. cit., p. 13.

[86]   Julia Ryan, anecdote about her mother, Edna Ryan, and politician, Susan Ryan, told to Susan Magarey.

[87]   Helen Shepherd, anecdote about saying that sisterhood was like a petrol pump, told by Elizabeth Reid to Susan Magarey at a meeting of the Academy of the Social Sciences in Australia, Canberra, 21 November 2012. Elizabeth Reid, subsequently Women's Adviser to Prime Minister Gough Whitlam; Helen Shepherd, subsequently a distinguished journalist; and Susan Magarey were all early participants in the Canberra Women's Liberation group.

[88]   Lynne Segal, *Making trouble: life and politics*, Serpent's Tail, London, 2007, p. 65.

flush of feminism' which was 'based on four things, which together gave a feeling of personal elation and closeness to other women, which we call sisterhood'. The four things were acceptance, support, change and development. Acceptance came from consciousness-raising, 'sharing … our experiences as women'. Support was 'the key aspect of sisterhood': 'Other women heard, accepted, what we said, and we thereby felt validated and supported'. Then change: 'Feminism changes people', she observed. 'Sisterhood encompassed that.' Finally, 'sisterhood meant group/collective development of feelings, ideas, strategies, praxis'.[89] The emotion rises like steam from the page: exhilaration, elation, bonding, sisterhood. And Biff Ward was by no means alone.

Melbourne feminist Sue Jackson described that moment of exhilaration to interviewer Ruth Ford:

> I don't know if you've seen photographs of it, from that time, and everyone from Margaret Whitlam on through, all the women of that time, there's a look on the face. That wide-eyed sort of bright and hopeful look and it was that feeling you know. There was a feeling of incredible anger, of course, when you're understanding all the various ways … in which women were oppressed. But at the same time, this sense of joy and power coming from this working together and working it out and the scales being taken from the eyes.[90]

Joy and power from working together was a powerful mix. 'The bonding was like with the Women's Movement forever', recalled Adelaide feminist Anne Dunn.[91] 'Oh … the buzz of it all', exclaimed Treena Everuss, remembering the early 1970s in Adelaide; what she liked especially was

> the relationships I was forming with women. It was the whole social life that it offered you … And the friendships and everything that I made, more than friendships. That was — I just loved that as well, because that was what I was looking for. So it was fulfilling that for me as well.[92]

'We knew that the whole society had to change', said Sue Jackson,

---

[89]   Biff Ward, 'The way forward for the revolutionary Women's Movement: understanding trashing and sectarianism', paper for the Marxist-Feminist Conference, Sydney, June 1977, in the Edna Ryan Papers, National Library of Australia, MS 9140, box 13, folder 73.

[90]   Sue Jackson, Interview with Ruth Ford, 3 November 1997.

[91]   Anne Dunn, Interview with Deborah Worsley-Pine, 19 August 1996.

[92]   Treena Everuss, Interview with Deborah Worsley-Pine, 2 July 1996.

and that involved every kind of structure and mode of relating, and everything. And individuals had to re-pattern themselves, and the whole thing. We knew how big it was. The amazing thing is — we thought it would happen.[93]

This was, Australian-born Lynne Segal in England observed, 'the feminist dream of a common language, of shared values or goals'.[94] This was a politics of affinity.[95] North American pioneer of Women's Liberation, brilliant political analyst Jo Freeman, wrote of the 'sweet promise of sisterhood': 'It claimed to provide a haven from the ravages of a sexist society; a place where one would be understood'.[96] Women who had once thought of each other as rivals for patriarchal prizes now formed political solidarities with each other — and more, closely bonded friendships, sometimes even sexual relationships. The fabric of the whole social order quivered.

But there were problems.

Sisterhood is Powerful: it kills sisters (Ti-Grace Atkinson). Structurelessness — again.

In her exposition of the principles of organisation — or refusal of it — in Women's Liberation, Anne Summers explained that 'in trying to overcome these deficiencies in other modes of organization we have in our own political methods tried to prefigure the kind of social relations which would prevail in the kind of society we are trying to create'.[97] These were entirely appropriate for small groups primarily engaged in consciousness-raising. But even participants in Women's Liberation could find general meetings that were structureless and leaderless distinctly irritating. Kay Daniels, a founding — indeed, a leading — participant in Women's Liberation in Hobart, reported on the June 1972 Conference in Sydney in tones of exasperation. 'Some', she commented,

> who weren't sufficiently mellowed by sun and sisterhood found the non-organisation immensely irritating and time-wasting … The interminable

---

[93] Jackson, op. cit., p. 4.

[94] Segal, op. cit., p. 13. On the dream of a common language, see also Adrienne Rich's title, *The dream of a common language: poems 1974-1977*, Norton, New York, 1978.

[95] See, for example, Donna Haraway, 'A manifesto for cyborgs: science, technology and socialist feminism in the 1980s', *Australian Feminist Studies*, vol. 2, no. 4, Autumn 1987.

[96] Jo Freeman ['Joreen'], 'Trashing: the dark side of sisterhood', *Ms.*, April 1976, p. 51.

[97] Summers, 'Where's the Women's Movement moving to?', p. 408.

introductions around the circle made me feel like a brownie on my first day out. Disagreement was softened and total irrelevance suffered to an incredible extent.[98]

Lack of political efficacy irritated Martha Ansara, wanting to get things organised for action to take place. 'If you want to get something done', she observed, 'you do need to divide up the tasks and have clear line of authority and so on'.[99] But in Women's Liberation, there was, instead, 'unbelievable anarchy':

> I found it very difficult because you could meet, for instance, have a meeting, be involved in a group that was organising for International Women's Day, and some new mob of people would come in and throw everything that you decided open to debate, and more than that, they didn't have children, they could go on and on all night if they wanted and wear you out. So I found it very difficult and very chaotic. You know, very wasteful of our time and energy in the way that decisions were made under the guise of not being hierarchical.[100]

In time, it became clear that there were greater difficulties to encounter in the refusal of leadership and structure than provocation of impatience. Again, we were to learn from the United States of America where, as early as 1970, Jo Freeman wrote what became an extremely influential article titled 'The Tyranny of Structurelessness', initially circulated anonymously under the pen-name 'Joreen'. 'Contrary to what we would like to believe', she announced, 'there is no such thing as a structureless group'. Any group of people coming together for any length of time, for any purpose, will 'inevitably' structure itself 'in some fashion'. The concept of 'structurelessness' then 'becomes a smokescreen for the strong or the lucky to establish unquestioned hegemony over others', a 'way of masking power' — the power of informal elites within the group. These, because they are informal, and seldom recognised, 'have no obligation to be responsible to the group at large'. Unstructured groups, in an unstructured movement, are, ultimately, she argued, 'politically inefficacious, exclusive and discriminatory against those women who are not or cannot be tied into the friendship network'.[101]

---

[98]   Kay Daniels, 'Womens [*sic*] liberation national conference June 10-12, a personal report', *Liberaction*, no. 3, 1972, pp. 4-5.

[99]   Ansara, op. cit.

[100]   ibid.

[101]   Jo Freeman, 'The tyranny of structurelessness', reprinted in Rosalyn Baxandall and Linda Gordon (eds), *Dear sisters: dispatches from the women's liberation movement*, Basic Books, New York, 2000, pp. 73-5.

Anne Summers agreed with Freeman that '*de facto* elites have arisen in the small leaderless groups of an unstructured movement'.[102] Sylvia Kinder concurred, adding the note that the absence of structures and leaders engendered 'stars'.[103] And Biff Ward's paper at the Marxist Feminist Conference in Sydney in 1977 explicitly addressed — with considerable anguish — the question of 'trashing', one of the effects that Freeman identified of structurelessness. Sisterhood, Ward argued, was being 'replaced' — destroyed — by trashing. 'Trashing' is defined in *A Women's Thesaurus* as '[p]olitically motivated, destructive criticism or character assassination, often in the guise of honest conflict'.[104] Ward's paper conveys all the hurt and anger attendant upon personal disagreement descending into personal attack. Trashing, it tells us, destroys and prevents development of the kind that sisterhood fostered. Instead of acceptance and support, trashing 'produces fear and inertia and bitterness'. It 'stops people changing any more since they need to spend so much energy on merely surviving at the point they have reached, personally and politically'. The way out of the impasse that trashing produced, the paper concluded, reaching back to Women's Liberation's first principles, was to remember the belief 'that the means is the end; that we create the revolution in our own image; how it is made determines the future society'. We have 'hurt and maimed each other with our own trashing', and therefore, Biff Ward noted, 'I believe that we can never work too much on understanding how repression of individuals works'.[105]

Martha Ansara printed many copies of 'The Tyranny of Structurelessness' for her group, Words for Women, to distribute, she said. But she didn't think it did any good.

Difference

Despite sisterhood, there were major disagreements within the Australian Women's Liberation Movement. They were there from the beginning, as is hardly surprising in an 'imagined community' encompassing women from such a variety of walks of life.

---

[102] Summers, 'Where's the Women's Movement moving to?', p. 408.

[103] Kinder, op. cit., p. 52.

[104] Mary Ellen Capek (ed.), *A women's thesaurus: an index of language used to describe and locate information by and about women*, Harper & Row, New York, 1987, p. 480.

[105] Ward, op. cit.

Merely in Sydney, Sue Wills demonstrates, there were a large number of small groups, each one conforming (more or less) to one of three quite distinct orientations. These were:

(a) groups based on locality — e.g. Balmain, Glebe, and other suburban groups as well as the university campus groups;

(b) groups based on interest or ongoing projects — e.g., Working Women's Group, the Art Workers for Liberation Group, the Radical Therapy Group, and the collectives responsible for the production of *MeJane* and *Refractory Girl*;

(c) groups formed to organize specific activities which disappeared or transformed themselves after the event — e.g., the collectives formed to organize conferences, demonstrations, marches and the like.[106]

All of these groups could work quite happily separately, or in collaboration over demonstrations, marches and conferences, for example, and in participation in the less frequent general meetings which dealt with nitty-gritty matters such as paying the rent on the Women's Liberation House in Alberta Street. But there were moments when differences proved destructive. Let us consider just two briefly told examples. The first: in Sydney and Melbourne, general meetings of Women's Liberation were frequently subjected to long-winded hectoring addresses by young women from the Spartacist League; they contended that participating in class struggle was the only way to achieve the liberation of women. Ultimately, general meetings in both cities resolved to expel the Sparts, a drastic and, at least for some, a disturbingly un-sisterly decision.[107] The second: I was one of a small Canberra group which organised a residential conference on Feminist Theory at Mt Beauty in the Victorian Alps for the long weekend in January 1973. We called ourselves 'The Hevvies'; the self-mocking name was a deliberate ploy to ward off accusations of pretentiousness. We sent out a letter addressed to 'Dear Sisters' inviting people to propose papers. Ironically, though, given our sisterly aspirations for it, the Mt Beauty conference is best remembered as the weekend when the Hobart Women's Action Group ripped into Women's

---

106 Wills, op. cit., p. 46.

107 Transcript of tape of Meeting to discuss Motion to Expel Spartacist League from the General Meetings of Sydney Women's Liberation, 17 April 1977, transcribed by Sue Wills, June 1997, in the Sydney First Ten Years Collection, Mitchell Library, State Library of New South Wales; Jean Taylor, *Brazen hussies: a herstory of radical activism in the women's liberation movement in Victoria 1970-1979*, Dyke Books Inc., East Melbourne, 2009, pp. 215-16.

Liberation — that is, everyone else there — on the charge of discriminating against lesbians.[108]

These, I would emphasise, were disagreements over the campaigns and causes to which the Women's Liberation Movement could and should devote its energies. The Spartacist women may have wanted all the participants in the Women's Liberation Movement to join them, but even they knew that this was not a realistic wish. The Hobart women did not want everyone else to *be* lesbians; theirs was not an assertion that sisterhood meant that all women were, or should be, identical. The Hobart women were arguing only that *all* women *included* lesbians as well as heterosexual women.

The politics of identity

Differences of identity were present in the Women's Liberation Movement from its beginning: if nothing else demonstrates this vividly, then the very title, as well as the contents, of the collection of papers from the first of the Women & Labour Conferences — *Women, Class & History* — does so. But by the 1990s, differences of identity were acquiring a fresh and encompassing emphasis. Melbourne feminist Laurie Bebbington was irritated, she said, that some histories of feminism in Australia taught that the identities of the women who made up Women's Liberation were limited to the white and middle-class. She argued fiercely against such a view. Young women today, she told Ruth Ford in the 1990s,

> will categorise the Women's Movement, the Women's Liberation Movement back then [in the 1970s], as a movement of middle class women, you know, none of whom were Kooris or are from different ethnic background or anything of that sort. It was just not true. There was [*sic*] women across class, across race barriers, across ethnic origins … And across ages — and that was one of the things that was really exciting.[109]

Bebbington herself, it is worth noting, was still at school during the early years of the Women's Liberation Movement. Her irritation prompts attention to shifts in historical context.

---

[108] Transcript of discussion of the Hobart Women's Action Group Paper, 'Sexism in the Women's Liberation Movement', at the Mount Beauty Conference, January 1973, transcribed by Sue Wills, August 1997, in Sydney First Ten Years Collection, Mitchell Library, State Library of New South Wales, especially p. 30.

[109] Laurie Bebbington, interview with Ruth Ford, 7 December 1997.

Sisterhood as the solidarity of *all* women, as shared goals and values, shared political commitment, could slide into a very different concept. As the collectivist and inclusive 1970s yielded to the individualised, acquisitional, neo-conservative 1990s, the politics of collective struggle began to seem stale and dated, while identity politics acquired a new precedence and gloss. As a concept connecting with identity politics rather than the politics of collective struggle, the concept of sisterhood could come to mean that all women had to be the same; sisterhood could shift in meaning from solidarity over common causes to a unity based in a common identity. But since we were not, at that time, or ever, all the same, then recognising differences among women — differences of class, race, ethnicity, sexuality, age — could also, by reversing that initial slide, splinter the commitment to solidarity. It was not differences of identity among women that fragmented the political solidarity, the sisterhood, of late twentieth-century feminism; the differences were and always had been there. Rather, it was the context in which those differences acquired primacy, a far broader shift in focus from the group to the individual, from politics to lifestyle, from activism to identity. Commentators began to speak of Women's Liberation as failing in the promise that women could 'have' it all; a sharp contrast to the desire of 1970s Women's Liberation to be able to 'do' so much more than women were allowed or able to do at that time. In Melbourne in the 1990s, Jan Chapman Davis, a mother of four, a feminist, had only begun to learn about her Aboriginality during the 1970s. She told a story about an academic woman.

> Miss White Middle Class herself, she was sitting at the table … and I was talking about my life, and the kids and the problems that I have … And … she just turned to me and said, 'Oh, my goodness. You are oppressed, aren't you!' And it was a big put-down. Basically she was just having a go at me. And I was just, you know, been hearing all this 'sisterhood is powerful and love your sister' and there was this bloody snobby bitch being really nasty to me.[110]

For Davis, at this time, her identity as an Aboriginal woman, together with her identification with working-class deprivation (health, education), was assuming greater importance in her life than her identity as a feminist, together in sisterhood with the un-sisterly 'Miss White Middle Class'. Lynne Segal was to comment: 'The rise of what would at times prove a divisive identity politics was as much due to the

---

[110]   Jan Chapman Davis, interview with Ruth Ford, 29 October 1997.

39

success as the failure of Women's Liberation, as women explored both the potential strengths and the particular suffering of their multiple identifications'.[111]

A legacy?

By the time that Emma Grahame came to write the entry on 'Sisterhood' for the *Oxford Companion to Australian Feminism* in the late 1990s, she observed that 'the notion of sisterhood has become more problematic' as feminism has 'grappled with issues of sexuality, race and class' and their emphases on differences between women.[112] Ten years later, when Monica Dux and Zora Simic produced *The Great Feminist Denial*, rescuing basic feminist demands from 'four popular debates about the crises facing modern women and the culpability of feminism'[113] — caricatures, they decided — the term 'sisterhood' did not even appear in their index. When popular glossy *marie claire* interviewed Prime Minister Julia Gillard and six of her senior female ministers, in the wake of Gillard's world-famous speech accusing the leader of the opposition of sexism and misogyny in 2012, the collective term that the magazine invoked was 'handbag hit squad', not sisters.[114]

Of course, sisterhood was not confined to the Women's Liberation Movement. Women's Electoral Lobby, a national body which was prepared to structure its organisation, and was thereby more practically effective than Women's Liberation, invoked a solidarity of women as sisterhood. Marian Sawer's study of that predominantly 1980s phenomenon, the 'femocrat', was titled *Sisters in Suits*, acknowledgement that the female bureaucrats so labelled were feminists working for specifically feminist goals. And feminism has a broader and longer history than any story of the Women's Liberation Movement of the 1970s in Australia. But the sisterhood of the Women's Liberation Movement left a powerful legacy. In England,

---

[111] Segal, op. cit., p. 124.

[112] Emma Grahame, 'Sisterhood', in Barbara Caine, Moira Gatens, Emma Grahame, Jan Larbalestier, Sophie Watson and Elizabeth Webby (eds), *Australian feminism: a companion*, Oxford University Press, Melbourne,1998, p. 490.

[113] Monica Dux and Zora Simic, *The great feminist denial*, Melbourne University Press, Carlton, 2008, p. 179.

[114] 'Women on top', a report with photographs and extensive quotations of a gathering to which Jackie Frank (publisher/editor of *marie claire*) and Di Webster (features editor-at-large of *marie claire*) attended at The Lodge with Prime Minister Julia Gillard and six of her senior female ministers, *marie claire*, December 2012, p. 48. A full transcript of this meeting is at www.marieclaire.com.au.

Lynne Segal, in 2007, observed that almost every woman she spoke with considered that 'the most cherished gain from the past, was the enduring network of friends they had acquired through Women's Liberation'.[115] In Sydney, that astute political activist Joyce Stevens commented that what had kept 'avenues of discussion open, even when political differences have been ... profound' was 'the friendship network'.[116] Stevens's 'friendship network' formed as participation in the 'imagined community' of Women's Liberation was one of the principal elements in the emotional bonding which has sustained a commitment to the liberation of women into the twenty-first century. 'For me', said Martha Ansara in 1997, 'it was absolutely the foundation of my life, and my future life ever since. I never looked back'.[117] And nor have I.

---

[115] Segal, op. cit, p. 136.

[116] *MeJane*, no. 5, November 1971, p. 8.

[117] Ansara, op. cit.

3

'Holding the Horrors of the World at Bay': 'The Feminist Food Guide', 1972-75

This paper was first presented to the Australian Historical Association conference in Mildura in 2003, and published in History Australia, *vol. 1, no. 2, July 2004. My thanks to Frank Bongiorno, present co-editor, and to* History Australia *for permission to reprint it here.*

Dedicated to the memory of Kay Daniels

It could be expected that food and feeding would have been central concerns for the resurgent feminism of the 1970s. Housework certainly was. And child care. Food and feeding are integral to both. Moreover, men's resistance to sharing equally in either housework or child care has proved one of the more intransigent of the shifting imbalances in power between women and men.[118] So it would seem axiomatic that feminists would evince a major preoccupation with cooking and eating (and

---

[118] See, for example, Duncan Iremonger, (ed.), *Households work: productive activities, women and income in the household economy*, Allen & Unwin, Sydney, 1989; Bettina Cass, 'Gender in Australia's restructuring labour market and welfare state', in Anne Edwards and Susan Magarey (eds), *Women in a restructuring Australia: work and welfare*, Allen & Unwin in Association with the Academy of Social Sciences in Australia, Sydney, 1995; Barbara Pocock, *The work/life collision: what work is doing to Australians and what to do about it*, Federation Press, Annandale, 2003.

Figure 3: Kay Daniels, 1941-2001
Photograph courtesy of Susan Magarey,
gift from Kay Daniels

drinking), and welcome any signs of men engaging in anything beyond the glamorous and elite, or the consumerist, dimensions of the food world.

Not so, however. In most of the research carried out for the history of the Women's Liberation Movement that I am trying to write, there is almost no sign of any such concern; the exception is an issue of *MeJane* in 1974, announcing that food is a feminist issue.[119] Further, I recall, myself, the outrage among feminists in the early 1970s when Colonel Sanders began advertising its wares with the slogan 'Liberate Mum: take home some Kentucky Fried Chicken today'.[120] For Women's Liberation it was the power-relations in the kitchen that mattered, and they were seen as entirely separate from what was cooked, presented and eaten. And the overlap of Women's Liberation with various fragments of socialism meant that food was fuel, not a subject of investigation in public hostelries or experimentation at home.

It came as a pleasant surprise, then, to encounter consistent attention to food, to wine, and to dining out, in the pages of *Liberaction*, the monthly paper that the Hobart Women's Action Group produced from April 1972 until December 1975.

The Hobart Women's Action Group (HWAG) was small and most of its members were connected with the University of Tasmania. It consisted of Kay Daniels, a lecturer in the History Department; Shirley Castley, a social worker in the Tasmanian bureaucracy, and Kay's partner; Frances Bonner, a postgraduate student

---

[119] See also *Liberaction*, no. 26, p. 4.

[120] See also *Liberaction*, no. 17, pp. 9-10.

in Political Science; Lorraine Miller, a postgraduate student in English; Anne Picot, a postgraduate student in Classics; and Rosemary Pringle, a tutor in History.

Others came and went. Helen Prendergast reported on efforts towards equality in the Tasmanian public service, and on the possibilities, and lack of them, associated with Elizabeth Reid's job as Women's Advisor to Prime Minister Gough Whitlam.[121] Betty Picot (Anne's mother?) protested at the use of four-letter words by proponents of Women's Liberation, but then, apparently having been won over by a learned defence of Women's Liberation's language by Lorraine Miller, set about a campaign on behalf of HWAG to counter the ban on prams in buses in Hobart.[122] Jean Hearn protested at the report of a government committee supposed to investigate reform to the law of abortion.[123] Pat — who was not given a second name — protested about the difficulties that women encountered in trying to raise loans.[124] Anne Summers appeared in December 1972, visiting from Sydney, and leading a whole weekend's discussion of the subjects that she wanted to treat in her book, *Damned Whores and God's Police*, eventually published in 1975.[125] She appeared in Hobart again, disguised by the name 'Zowie', in a ten-page transcript of a taped conversation between two lesbians, Kay and Shirley, represented as 'Starr' and 'Dorry', and a straight woman, all in bed together, printed in *Liberaction* in March 1974.[126] Heather, another without a second name, reported on six months working in a soft-drink factory in Launceston.[127] Mary (Murnane?) from Sydney reported on the Women's Commission and its failure to give adequate attention to lesbians, then on the Porno Fest at Sydney University.[128] Andy Malone from Adelaide reported — not on picking apples in Huon Valley, which is what took her to Tasmania, but on problems for women gaining access to pool tables in pubs.[129] Jill — whom subsequent research has identified as Jill Roe — from Sydney protested about wages for housework campaigns.[130] David Widdup,

---

[121] *Liberaction*, no. 5, p. 4; no. 19, pp. 1-4.

[122] *Liberaction*, no. 4, p. 1, pp. 1-3; no. 5, p. 1.

[123] *Liberaction*, no. 5, pp. 1-3.

[124] *Liberaction*, no. 7, p. 5.

[125] *Liberaction*, no. 8, pp. 7-8.

[126] *Liberaction*, no. 23, pp. 1-10.

[127] *Liberaction*, nos. 9 & 10, pp. 3-4.

[128] *Liberaction*, no. 12, pp. 4-5; no. 13, pp. 1-2.

[129] *Liberaction*, no. 15, pp. 4-5.

[130] *Liberaction*, no. 17, pp. 3-5.

disguised as 'Minnie Drear', appeared several times in his feminine manifestation, 'the original androgynous mind'.[131] Elizabeth Reid appeared in November 1973, and subsequently as the cartoon figure 'SuperFem' in 1974.[132] ('Superfem' went on to mainland fame in the edition of *Refractory Girl* that the '*Liberaction* diaspora' edited in 1975.)[133] Marilyn Lake appeared in *Liberaction* twice. Frances Bonner tells me that she was a member of HWAG. Kay told me that HWAG packed Marilyn off to Women's Electoral Lobby (WEL). There is no necessary contradiction between the two statements: HWAG and WEL were quite close in their initial stages. Marilyn spoke at HWAG's first general meeting, addressing the question 'Who cleans the toot in your house?' She was protesting 'the nastiness of the customary female chores'. 'Even when partners can be persuaded to help in the house, they regard it as a special concession or favour', she argued.[134]

Housework, to be sure, but nothing about cooking or eating. Nevertheless, among the reading groups, the discussion groups, and the meetings that HWAG organised, there was a growing emphasis by April 1973 on confining their activities to producing *Liberaction*[135] and it is in *Liberaction* that we meet the Hobart Women's Action Group's 'Feminist Food Guide'.

Liberaction is exceptional among the productions of the *samizdat* period of the Women's Liberation Movement for being intellectual, witty, non-conformist, and camp. It was not uniformly so, of course; no publication that depends on contributions can maintain a single, monolithic style. But as the bulk of its contributions were written by Kay, Shirley, Frances, Lorraine, Rosemary and Anne — the '*Liberaction* diaspora', as they described themselves, and later, for reasons closely related to food, the 'rat pack' — it was possible for a distinctive style to develop. The intellectualism appears in the range of reference deployed in Lorraine's discussion of the words that women may not use, which swung from Chaucer to twentieth-century socio-linguistics[136], for instance. It appears in the incisive argument between

[131]   E.g. *Liberaction*, no. 13, p. 5; no. 7, pp. 6-7.

[132]   *Liberaction*, no. 19, p. 9; no. 24, p. 8.

[133]   *Refractory Girl*, no. 6, June 1974.

[134]   *Liberaction*, no. 3, p. 2.

[135]   *Liberaction*, no. 12, pp. 8-9.

[136]   *Liberaction*, no. 4, pp. 1-3.

Kay (a socialist) and Rosemary (an anarchist) over feminist activism.[137] It appears in Shirley's defence of rational thought, against criticism of thought as irretrievably male and therefore to be rejected.[138] It appears in Kay's demolition of Sheila Rowbotham's *Women, Resistance and Revolution*, her critique of Dennis Altman on sexism, and her enlightening analysis of aspects of the Australian government's budget in 1974.[139]

The non-conformity is evident almost from the beginning, in Kay's report on the Women's Liberation National Conference held in Sydney in June 1972. She lists some of the subjects of discussion: 'media, working women, child care, lesbians, social attitudes to women, women's studies'. By halfway through the conference, she had joined those who were convinced that they were 'getting more out of the in-between pub sessions'. She had cheered up by the end of the conference, though, enough to enlarge on 'women's lib virtues'.

> As a movement it is an anti-leader, anti-hierarchy, anti-bureaucratic organisation, because these approaches give us the only way we have to get at one of the real difficulties that lie behind getting women involved in the movement and in social issues generally — women's inability (albeit through conditioning) to accept responsibility. Women will work because they are used to working, but to accept the responsibility that comes with freedom and independence is another kettle of fish. Within the movement the same problem applies. There are those who think of the group as 'we' and who share the decisions and the obligations, and those who think of 'them' or 'you'. Women have to realise that they have to earn membership. I think that full participation at every level is the only way to break down the division between organisers and spectators, and this was done at the conference. In fact although a structureless meeting can itself indulge irresponsibility, encouraging full participation is what asking women to 'come out' really means.[140]

It is an acute analysis and sensible proposal for strategy, its bossy manner reflecting that of its contexts. It was also — for *Liberaction* — uncharacteristically earnest. For the tone developing in this paper was better represented by Rosemary's observation, after her own visit to the mainland: the Sydney *Women's Liberation Newsletter*, she

---

137   *Liberaction*, no. 7, pp. 2-4.

138   *Liberaction*, no. 11, pp. 4-5.

139   *Liberaction*, no. 13, p. 7; nos. 21 & 22, pp. 15-16; no. 29, pp. 1-2.

140   *Liberaction*, no. 3, pp. 4-5.

wrote, 'positively reeks of sisterhood and consciousness-raising which are spoken of in a mealy-mouthed and totally nauseating way'.[141]

It still took an outsider — or, rather, one who was an outsider to begin with, though she visited Hobart as Rosemary's partner during 1974 — to draw attention to the wit and the camp quality of *Liberaction*'s style. In August 1973, *Liberaction* carried a piece by Mary — identified by Frances Bonner as Mary Murnane — referring to 'the indigestible earnestness of Sydney', and complaining of 'the mental flatulence caused by reading the latest output of feminist literature from Sydney, Melbourne and Sorrento'.[142] In language that evoked the postgraduate student, Mary then expounded on the various shifts in her analysis of what *Liberaction* was doing. At one point, '*Liberaction* repelled seriousness because readers were intimidated by the thought of appearing mawkishly earnest in the midst of elegant flippancy'. But Mary had decided that this was just as bad as the 'liturgy of zealotry', and therefore 'just as effective in repressing thought and perpetuating self-congratulatory superiority'. 'However', she continued:

> I have begun to reassess. Another way of interpreting *Liberaction*'s tone would be to see it as the transformation of despair into wit — a well known Camp method of holding the horrors of the world at bay.[143]

Despite its Latinate prose, this is an extremely perceptive observation.

In her 'Notes on "Camp"', dated 1964, North American feminist critic Susan Sontag discusses Camp sensibility. Beginning with a glance towards a definition — 'the essence of Camp is its love of the unnatural: of artifice and exaggeration' — she moves through a series of illustrations organised under quotations selected from Oscar Wilde. 'The more we study Art, the less we care for Nature', just for example; 'It's absurd to divide people into good and bad. People are either charming or tedious'; 'Life is too important a thing ever to talk seriously about it'; and 'I adore simple pleasures, they are the last refuge of the complex'. Camp taste, she explains,

---

[141]   *Liberaction*, no. 15, p. 2.

[142]   Sorrento is a seaside town in Victoria where, according to Jean Taylor, two weekend conferences were held in a boarding house, one from 10 to 12 November 1972, the second from 30 March to 1 April 1973. She quotes from an essay about the experience of the second: '"When I got up in the morning and walked into the living room to see two sisters lying naked in bed with their arms around each other — wow, what an experience (it had a big effect on me) … Sisterhood does transcend all barriers'". See Jean Taylor, op. cit., pp. 179-80. Clearly, then, the central difference from HWAG was not one of sexual preference but rather of style.

[143]   *Liberaction*, no. 16, p. 2.

turns its back on the good-bad axis of ordinary aesthetic judgement. Camp doesn't reverse things. It doesn't argue that the good is bad, or the bad is good. What it does is to offer for art (and life) a different — a supplementary — set of standards.

'Style is everything', she asserts. 'The whole point of Camp is to dethrone the serious'. Camp and homosexuality are related but not identical, she maintains. She moves on to the relationship between Camp and good and bad taste. 'Camp asserts that good taste is not simply good taste', she asserts, but also 'that there exists, indeed, a good taste of bad taste'. Finally, she argues,

> Camp taste is, above all, a mode of enjoyment, of appreciation — not judgement. Camp is generous. It wants to enjoy ... Camp taste doesn't propose that it is in bad taste to be serious; it doesn't sneer at someone who succeeds in being seriously dramatic. What it does is find the success in certain passionate failures.
>
> Camp taste is a kind of love, love for human nature. It relishes, rather than judges ...
>
> The ultimate Camp statement: it's good because it's awful ...[144]

(It is probably useful to understanding Mary Murnane's preoccupation with Sontag to recall *Liberaction*'s extra-feminist context here: the establishment of Camp Inc. — Campaign Against Moral Persecution Inc. — in Sydney, to organise for gay rights and publish *Camp Ink*, in 1970, a crowded two years before the formation of HWAG.)[145] Sontag's conglomerate definition and illustrations 'fitted' the Hobart Women's Action Group and *Liberaction* quite neatly, and distinguished them both sharply from the newly formed *Refractory Girl*, for instance, and the anti-intellectualism of many Women's Liberation Newsletters. In response to Mary's analysis, Kay penned an attack on 'the heavy hand of women's lib orthodoxy' emphasising 'feelings', 'sincerity' and 'anger' while rejecting 'cold logic', 'hypocrisy' and 'politeness' as reinforcing the *status quo*. Such orthodoxy allowed humour, she continued, only 'if it is used in a girl-guide-picnic sort of way to induce feelings of sisterhood', but opposed irony and flippancy. 'One of the great pleasures of women's liberation', she proclaimed,

---

[144] Susan Sontag, 'Notes on "Camp"', in Susan Sontag, *Against interpretation and other essays*, Dell Publishing Co., Inc., New York, 1969, pp. 277, 288, 289, 291-2, 292, 293.

[145] See, for example, Garry Wotherspoon, *'City of the plain': history of a gay sub-culture*, Hale & Iremonger, Sydney, 1991, pp. 168-76.

is that one does actually see the world differently, and while this can be (& usually is) anger-making and traumatic, it can also be amusing and entertaining (and in that way too, liberating), the dead hand [of] orthodox appropriateness reflects a movement which is not only increasingly puritan and dogmatic, and unliberating, but which seems to be unsure of its own feminist consciousness so that it is in danger of prematurely truncating that consciousness and cocooning the movement in an alternate world of its own making — a world that reflects the deficiencies of the sub-culture from which it derives, the deficiencies of the feminine ideals which it espouses, and the deficiencies of a half-thought out ideology.[146]

Camp and *critically* unorthodox together. Was it this distinctive quality that enabled 'the rat pack' and *Liberaction* to relax into something as rude, irreverent, humorous, serious — and as utterly different from the rest of the Women's Liberation Movement in Australia — as 'The Feminist Food Guide'?

It appears first in December 1972, claiming a commitment to changing the dining-out world.

Women eating out together without male escorts are seen as not only deprived [*sic*] but also timid, incapable of ordering a meal, afraid of complaining about poor food, poor service, etc. — mouse packs in fact! H.W.A.G. has put hands, feet, and tongu[e]s into ACTION to sink this mythology — the mice have turned into rats.[147]

They attempted no fewer than four public eating places for this first report. One was 'the newly-opened Pennyfarthing Lane', which they chose because they wanted to introduce a visiting feminist to Hobart's feminist past, 'the brothel-type atmosphere'. They booked private rooms, which meant that '[w]e moved from Molly to Flo and ended up in Ada'. Their second venture was to the Ball and Chain. There they found that 'by the time the main course arrives, you don't notice it. The reason is simple: it's easier to catch a drink-waiter than a wench'. Then, they reported, 'Having exhausted the colonial offerings, the reading group moved on to sample what the Old World had to offer in the way of cuisine in Hobart'. This meant two restaurants, the Don Camillo and the Monna [*sic*] Lisa.

---

146 *Liberaction*, no. 19, pp. 8-9.

147 *Liberaction*, no. 8, p. 8. 'Mouse Packs' was a term used in a women's magazine to refer to 'groups of single girls going out together without the saving grace of male company', *MeJane*, no. 3, July 1971, p. 4.

The services that they encountered improved. From 'non-existent' it moved to 'slow', then to 'usually prompt', to not needing comment at all. The food also improved. Their first meal consisted of 'microwave heated roast beef, tinned carrots, frozen beans, ice-cream scoops of mashed potato, all floating in plasma'. Even so, they approved of the garlic prawns, but considered the other entrees — '[v]ariously described as day-break and crayfish' — to be too expensive and smothered in tomato sauce. At their second outing, the main courses were too small and tough. Their third 'brought on one of the reading group's vociferous rows (where *do* you get the worst salad in Hobart?)'. That meal divided the rat pack between those who approved 'the scallopine vino bianco, the cognac pancakes, the white mice [*sic*]' and those who 'pointed out the potatoes smothered in oil, the too-salty chicken soup, and the overall similarity of the main courses'. The last meal included in this report was treated briefly: 'erratic but it has got the Houghton's White Burgundy, and a good veal-lemon dish'.[148]

At their second venture for this report, their revolutionary zeal overflowed onto the dance-floor, 'cigars firmly clenched between the teeth', in a conga-line. They were disappointed to find that those who joined them were the husbands and boyfriends also dining out, while the wives and girlfriends remained sitting at their tables. Clearly, even if it had to include men, dining-out was to be a total experience.

As this initial report makes clear: there were two other elements about the rat pack besides a 'Camp' style that made 'The Feminist Food Guide' possible. One was the absence of children — except for one occasion when the rat pack noted their own identification with children.[149] Another was personal control of their own incomes, and having incomes. As Frances Bonner reminded me recently: 'The scholarships Lorraine, Anne and I lived on were far more generous than anything offered now (& untaxed) so we could more or less keep up with the salaried Kay, Shirls, Rosemary & Marilyn'.[150] However, even with decent scholarships and salaries, they could not spend all their dining dollars in restaurants. By December 1972 they were reporting on pizza and salads as well as fine dining, and promising 'a run-down on lunches round town for the working girl' in the new year. 'You eat pizza at Peppone's at your own risk', they warned.

---

[148] *Liberaction*, no. 8, pp. 8-9.

[149] *Liberaction*, no. 25, p. 8.

[150] Frances Bonner to Susan Magarey, email communication, 16 September 2003.

A starving W. Libber attacked her mushroom pizza in a frenzy of delight only to bite into a Throatie. She was assured it was a fresh Throatie, not chewed, and 10c would be taken off the bill.[151]

One salad was 'reasonable' — 'you could taste the oil, vinegar, and garlic', though it needed more salt and pepper. But another produced the line that Lorraine was most happy at having penned: 'naked limp lettuce shuddering at the bottom of the bowl'.[152] This report concluded: 'P.S. Why eat your Xmas pud? Apply it straight to the hips'. A month later, they noted that they had neither the funds nor the capacity for anything more than a sandwich.[153]

The 'Feminist Food Guide' for March 1973 was largely a reflection on the Women's Liberation 'Theory' Conference, organised by a group of four in Canberra: Biff Ward, Daphne Gollan, Eileen Haley and Susan Magarey (myself). We called ourselves 'The Hevvies', defensively, to ward off attacks at intellectual pretentiousness for wanting to talk about theory. We needn't have worried: Shirley noted acerbically: 'Theoretical discussions were few and far between and discussions of feminism were kept pretty much at the experiential level'.[154] The conference was held over the Australia Day weekend at a chalet at Mt Beauty in the Victorian Alps. Only four members of HWAG attended: Kay and Shirley, and Lorraine and Frances who had taken up with each other towards the end of the previous year. They were to deliver a paper on sexism in the Women's Liberation Movement, charging the movement with discriminating against lesbians. It caused a huge ruction among the 100 or so participants in the conference. And that ruction came as the climax to a series of instances of the rat pack's distinctive style. They all wore black T-shirts, I recall, and arrived with the spoils of visits to various Victorian wineries on the way, something the other less sophisticated participants had simply not thought of. 'The Feminist Food Guide' noted that their 'flamboyant life-style' had drawn comment when they arrived, and criticism for 'cliquey-ness' later, when they brought some of their wine to the meals in the chalet, 'to make more palatable the institution-type food'.[155] One lunchtime feature of that institution-type food was 'spaghetti sandwiches'.

---

[151] *Liberaction*, no. 9, p. 7.
[152] ibid.
[153] *Liberaction*, no. 10, p. 5.
[154] *Liberaction*, no. 11, p. 5.
[155] ibid., p. 7.

By May 1973, Frances was living in Canberra. When Lorraine visited her there, the result was a 'Feminist Food Guide' which first reported that they had been laid low by over-indulgence so 'were last heard in heated argument over the merits of Dexsal vs. Eno', then went on — with impeccable logic — to a 'Feminist Guide to Lavatory Paper'.[156]

'The Feminist Food Guide' attracted criticism. One correspondent who signed herself 'Fed up Feminist' accused the Guide of not being feminist because it was focusing on the food, and 'not even mentioning [the restaurants'] … attitudes towards women eating alone …'[157] To this Lorraine responded, 'It's sad to see that yet another reader has more Dedication to the Cause than sensitivity to tone — IT WAS FLIPPANT, DEAR'.[158] In November 1973, Jill Roe wrote about the importance of Marie Coleman's appointment as chair of the Statutory Social Welfare Commission in the Australian government, far more important — in her view — than Elizabeth Reid's 'token' appointment, but concluded by noting, 'Also I'm sick of the feminist food guide'.[159] Anne Picot responded suggesting that Jill had confused the terms 'significant' and 'powerful' in her comments on Coleman and Reid, but said nothing about her views of the food guide. A third, Lyndall Ryan, wrote telling the rat pack that they picked 'lousy restaurants', that they 'never seem to visit Chinese, Indian, Mexican, Lebanese restaurants, *even on your interstate trips*'. She had taken against their apparent predilection for French food: 'Quite frankly I dislike French food you seem to think every restaurant in the country should serve to perfection. If you want decent frog food in this country you have to cook it yourself'. She had taken against their reported treatment of waiters and restaurateurs: 'Quite frankly in perusing past feminist food guides, I have always been on the side of the waiters'. Clearly well underway, she then moved into her peroration:

> [D]on't expect me to take you to some decent restaurants when you come to Sydney. You see restaurants as an ego trip, as a place to persuecute [*sic*] waiters and your friends. I have too much respect for both peoples to inflict you on them. Your idea of going to a restaurant seems to be to behave like super males so that both the chef and the waiters will cringe before you and treat you like

---

[156]   *Liberaction*, no. 13, p. 9.

[157]   *Liberaction*, no. 15, pp. 9-10.

[158]   *Liberaction*, no. 16, p. 8, emphasis in the original.

[159]   *Liberaction*, no. 19, p. 6.

Catherine the Great. If that isn't an ego trip, what Is [*sic*]? And someone is
always having an ego trip in the feminist ffod [*sic*] guide.[160]

In response, *Liberaction* noted of this letter that '[f]or once none of the errors, typing,
spelling, grammar, veracity, etc. are ours'. Yet another clash of the flippant and the
earnest, perhaps? 'The Feminist Food Guide' did go on to make the point, though,
that it was not that they preferred 'ritzy' joints, but that, following the establishment
of Wrest Point Casino in Hobart, the trend has been towards opening 'elaborate
and very expensive eating places, which often concentrate on an international style
menu'.[161]

For all the criticisms, the menus that appear in most of the 'Feminist Food
Guides' do provoke nostalgia — another characteristic of 'Camp' — for the days
of food before the onset of 'lean cuisine', or maybe a present, and risky, enthusiasm
for a Dr Atkins diet. Some meals began with pâté, moved on to Lobster Thermidor,
chicken kiev, steak tartare, grilled flounder or Coquilles St Georges, Filet de Boeuf
Medallion au vin rouge, and ended with Bombe Alaska.[162] One began with Beluga
caviar with cream (at $6!), followed by 'fresh tender scallops cooked with raisins in a
wine sauce' and Lobster Newburg.[163] Yet another listed 'Fritto Misto, Fillet Mirabon
(anchovies & stuffed olives) and Fillet Maison, all beautifully cooked', a menu which
showed, the rat pack asserted, that 'good but not expensive meals can be turned on
in Hobart'.[164] In June 1974, the rat pack visited 'another of the Sydney-styled ethnic
restaurants'. This one, called Omar Khayyams, presented satays, lamb or beef, 'spiced
by freshly ground cumin, cinnamon, coriander, and ginger for the lamb and with
fenugreek for the beef', then, spoiling it all, eaten with peanut sauce.[165]

As such accounts usually make clear, the rat pack's dining-out was informed
by a knowledge of food and how to cook it that was extensive and practised. Frances
Bonner says that most of the 'Feminist Food Guides' were written by Lorraine Miller;
Lorraine must have been a splendid cook. Many from the days of Women's Liberation
know personally that Kay — standing in her grandmother's footsteps, Jill Roe says

160 *Liberaction*, no. 20, pp. 9-10, emphasis in the original.
161 ibid.
162 *Liberaction*, no. 16, p. 7; no. 18, p. 6.
163 *Liberaction*, no. 20, p. 10.
164 *Liberaction*, no. 24, p. 10.
165 *Liberaction*, no. 26, p. 10.

— was an inspired cook, a talent that was rare and distinctly ahead of its time in the early years of the Women's Liberation Movement.

Such knowledge gives an added piquancy for the account in 'The Feminist Food Guide' of dinner in Launceston with Elizabeth Reid in November 1973.

> The deep sea bake reflected an old local cook's saying 'when they win's be up, and they boaties be down, add another Murphy to the pot', and spuds is what it mostly was. The minute scallops could hardly be described as fresh … The Beef Wellington however, when it came was incredible; an obscenely large object looming over the edge of the plate, consisting of pounds and pounds of overcooked fillet in uninspired pastry, coated with a gravy euphemistically called Sauce Espagnol — the dish was immediately christened The BOOt [*sic*].[166]

A horror, indeed. One of the horrors of the world to be held at bay by the transformation of despair into wit.

---

[166] *Liberaction*, no. 19, p. 7.

4

And now we are six: a plea
for Women's Liberation

*An outline of this paper was first discussed at a meeting on
14 September 1976. It was first published in March 1977
in* Refractory Girl, *a journal which has ceased publication.*

The Women's Movement reached Canberra six years ago, when a Women's Liberation group was formed in June 1970.[167] The first Women's Liberation *Newsletter* appeared in October that year. The group, varying in size from about six to about fifty, continued to meet and to issue a monthly newsletter for the following five years. For three years, from February 1972 until January 1975, our centre of activities was the Women's Liberation House in Bremer Street, Griffith[168] and participants in the group later secured the present Women's Centre in Lobelia Street.[169] This now houses the Women's Information Service, the Abortion Counselling Service, and a feminist bookshop; it provides meeting and office facilities (telephone, typewriter, duplicator and filing cabinets) for Women's Electoral Lobby, the Women's Refuge, and the Rape Crisis Centre; it is the place at which we celebrate the publication of

---

[167] 'The movement in Canberra — Report June 1972', duplicated paper in *Newsletter* file, Lobelia Street, O'Connor.

[168] Canberra Women's Liberation [CWL] *Newsletter*, no. 18, March 1972; no. 47, February 1975. *Canberra News*, 8 March 1972.

[169] Minutes of meeting, 16 April 1975, CWL Minute Book 1974-5, Lobelia Street, O'Connor.

Beryl Henderson's translation *Abortion: The Bobigny Affair*[170], for instance, or the achievement of a national Women and Politics conference, or the arrival of a barrel of wine and some cases of empty bottles. The movement has grown large. It has diversified. It has become a vital necessity to a number of women in this city. Yet the predominant temper in the Women's Movement in Canberra during 1976 has reflected neither complacency about this state of affairs, nor the excitement, anger, and sense of urgency which contributed to achieving it. Rather, the prevailing mood has been bewildered, irritated, and weary. And the Canberra Women's Liberation group has disappeared. Its last *Newsletter*, Number 57, appeared in June 1976. The last meeting recorded in its minute book was held on 12 November 1975.

'Women's Liberation' was a label which implied a particular cluster of expectations and commitments within the Women's Movement. Its disappearance from our groups, activities and writings is not simply a shift in semantic fashion. Nor is it merely the absorption of one group into the far larger community formed by the Women's Movement. On the contrary, it represents the loss of those expectations and commitments which were essential for many of us to our continuing engagement in the feminist struggle.

The Women's Liberation group in Canberra always had some things in common with other, older women's groups which drew together people with similar interests. We raised money, for instance, by setting up stalls in Garema Place during the Friday night shopping hours and selling our products — not the cakes, pots of jam and fudge of the Country Women's Association, but T-shirts and underpants with the Women's Liberation symbol screen-printed on them, and leaflets about our ideas and activities. The group also had much in common with other groups formed as the Women's Movement grew. Like the Abortion Law Reform Association, it proselytised. The group's first public meeting in November 1970 drew an attendance of 130 and flooded the subsequent weekly meetings with new enthusiasts.[171] A second public meeting in April 1971 brought a month of two concurrent meetings each week.[172] And, like Women's Electoral Lobby, the group worked for specific practical reforms. Three of the five points listed in the manifesto drafted in about September

---

[170] *Abortion: the Bobigny affair: a law on trial: a complete record of the pleadings at the court of Bobigny 8 November 1972*, 'Introduction' by Simone de Beauvoir, trans. Beryl Henderson, Wild & Woolley Pty Ltd, Marrickville, NSW, 1975.

[171] CWL *Newsletter*, no. 2, November 1970.

[172] CWL *Newsletter*, no. 8, May 1971, *Canberra Times*, 7 April 1971.

1970 concerned equal pay, equal opportunity for work, and reform of the education system.[173] The Family Planning Clinic established in 1971, the women's group in the Australian Clerical Officers' Association and the women's group in the Secondary Teachers' Association both formed in 1972, and the Women's Refuge opened in March 1975 — all grew out of the work of the Canberra Women's Liberation group.[174]

But unlike either traditional women's groups or new groups formed within the Women's Movement, the Women's Liberation group saw all its efforts as directed ultimately towards the total transformation of the whole society, indeed of all societies. 'Women's Liberation' meant commitment to social revolution. The *Newsletter* for February 1971 carried quotations from the Women's Liberation conference in Sydney the previous month which made this clear to any new participants in the group. Juanita had declared that '[a]ny movement seeking a change in women's roles attacks the family structure upon which capitalism rests and poses demands which capitalism cannot meet … The struggle for Women's Liberation is revolutionary because of this'. Ann and Lyndall were concerned 'with every male-dominated society, whether it be capitalist, communist or socialist'. They spoke about forms of 'cultural oppression'; 'it is here', they observed, 'that the oppression of women goes beyond the traditional class barriers. And it is here that we have to start to smash those myths for unless we can change the whole *cultural orientation* of women, no revolution is going to bring us the liberation we are seeking'.[175] Each represented a difference in analysis, critique and strategy, but all represented unequivocal commitment to social revolution. For the Canberra Women's Liberation group, that commitment was the imperative behind all our efforts to build a mass Women's Movement and all the particular reforms we worked for. This was the imperative which distinguished 'Women's Liberation' from the other constituents of the growing Women's Movement.

The distinction crystallised early in 1972. In February that year, in Melbourne, the 'Meeting of Ten' laid the foundations of Women's Electoral Lobby. WEL's first

---

[173] 'Canberra Women's Liberation', duplicated sheet in *Newsletter* file, Lobelia Street, O'Connor.

[174] 'The movement in Canberra — Report June 1972', minutes of meetings, 12 June 1974, 6 November 1974, 5 February 1975, 5 March 1975; CWL Minute Book 1974-5; CWL *Newsletter*, no. 20, May 1972; no. 49, April 1975.

[175] CWL *Newsletter*, no. 5, February 1971, emphasis in the original. This speech is reproduced with the title 'The theory of women's liberation', in Ann Curthoys, *For and against feminism: a personal journey into feminist theory and history*, Allen & Unwin, Sydney, 1988; see especially p. 10.

broadsheet proclaimed that reforms like equal pay, equal opportunities, day care, contraception, abortion, and prevention of ecological ruin were too urgent to wait; they should be advanced by women acting as 'a voting bloc which will decide these elections, not in terms of party politics, but in terms of particular issues'.[176] The people who joined WEL in increasing numbers, as new branches established themselves throughout Australia during 1972, saw such reform as ends in themselves. Moreover, they had no misgivings about working through established political, economic and social institutions to effect them. They sought the reform of society through, and within, its existing framework. Participants in the Canberra Women's Liberation group supported the reforms WEL wanted. But we saw them as essentially palliative, as alleviations of oppression, inch marks of progress, not as constituting qualitative change itself. Further, we saw the use of traditional channels, and methods of exerting pressure, as implying acceptance of their legitimacy. We were apprehensive of being contained by achieving participation in the existing socio-political structure and of being bought off with conceded reforms. We restated this, with some heat, at a meeting on 7 April 1972, when Thelma Hunter read us the paper earlier given to a Political Science seminar at Australian National University, in which she criticised the 'conflict view of politics' held by 'revolutionary feminists'.[177] And when WEL-ACT was formed in the following month, it was composed largely — though by no means wholly — of women who were not involved in the Women's Liberation group.

This did not mean that there was antagonism between the two groups. Rather, there was continuing mutual assistance, its major achievement being the Women's Refuge. But WEL and Women's Liberation remained distinct, despite such co-operation, because Women's Liberation was committed, not only to reform but also to revolution.[178]

The precise nature of the social revolution we aimed for was the subject of continuing, sometimes anxious, often inconclusive discussion. Ideas changed with

---

[176] Women's Electoral Lobby [WEL] *Broadsheet*, no. 1, February-March 1972.

[177] Thelma Hunter, 'Reform and revolution in contemporary feminism', *Politics*, vol. 8, no. 2, November 1973. CWL *Newsletter*, no. 19, April 1972; see also Thelma Hunter, *Not a dutiful daughter: the personal story of a migrant academic*, Ginninderra Press, Charnwood, 1999.

[178] This point was restated in a session led by Gail Wilenski [Radford] and Wendy Fatin, called 'Reform and revolution', at the Women and Politics Conference, Canberra, 3 September 1975; see Julia Ryan, Women's Movement Notes, book II, pp. 26-7.

different experiences, developments in the society we inhabited and accumulated reading. But they generally fell into one of two broad areas of preoccupation.

One was characterised by a fairly conventional structural-functionalist view of societies, illuminated by Robin Morgan's contention that 'capitalism, imperialism, and racism are *symptoms* of male supremacy — sexism'.[179] It focused attention on the nuclear family as being simultaneously both the epitome of the hierarchical and exploitative relationships in sexist society, and the foundation of society's structure. It emphasised three of the four 'key structures' that Juliet Mitchell identified as making up 'woman's condition': production, reproduction, and socialisation (the other is sexuality).[180] It stressed the first three of Shulamith Firestone's 'Revolutionary Demands' — '*(1) The freeing of women from the tyranny of reproduction by every means possible, and the diffusion of the child-rearing role to the society as a whole, men as well as women*'; '*(2) The political autonomy, based on economic independence, of both women and children*'; '*(3) The complete integration of women and children into society*'. (The fourth is '*The sexual freedom of all women and children*'.)[181] It led to such analyses and critiques of the relationships between domestic unit and whole society as Julia Ryan's 'Capitalism and the Family'[182], and to experiments in living in domestic groups that tried not to centre on the nuclear family unit.

The other was characterised by the redefinition of the 'political', which Eileen Haley explained like this:

> Most people think of themselves as having a 'private life' in which politics does not operate. Politics is something that goes on 'out there'. Feminism shows this distinction as non-existent. It exposes the 'private life' areas as a political arena. It also shows how the dominant political system invades that private life *continually* in very deeply felt ways. The 'politics' which inhabits both areas welding them into a single system is that of male supremacy.[183]

---

[179] CWL *Newsletter*, no. 5, February 1971, emphasis in the original; Morgan, op. cit., p. xxxix.

[180] Juliet Mitchell, 'Women: the longest revolution', *New Left Review*, no. 40, November-December 1966.

[181] Shulamith Firestone, *The dialectic of sex: the case for feminist revolution*, Paladin, London, 1972, pp. 193-5, emphasis in the original.

[182] Julia Ryan, 'Capitalism and the family', *Refractory Girl*, no. 7, November 1975, pp. 18-19.

[183] Eileen Haley, 'The long haul', *Politics*, vol. 8, no. 2, November 1973, p. 330.

It focused attention on the pervasiveness of women's oppression, made ever more detailed in the consciousness-raising groups which met frequently during 1971 and 1972. It emphasised the 'political' nature of individual efforts to change personal relationships, in particular the changes embodied in the concept of sisterhood, and in the Reichian notion of the autonomous, freely relating sexually expressive human being. It stressed the revolutionary implications of a movement which 'is not a movement one "joins" … It exists in your mind'.[184] It led to analyses and critiques of female-male, female-female, and male-male relationships, to changes in people's existing personal relationships which sometimes took some years in resolution, and to the exhilarating growth of friendships among people involved in the group.

For roughly four years both areas of preoccupation dominated the group's ideas about the revolutionary transformation of society. And both were closely meshed. A meeting in November 1972, for instance, decided that we should be working for two revolutions — one to be 'external', brought about by the achievement of socialism, the other 'internal'.[185] During discussion at a meeting in March 1974, Julia Ryan pointed out the contradiction for Women's Liberation between the prospect of 'seizing power' and the necessity of 'retaining the qualities which make women more human than men'. Biff Ward resolved this by saying: 'We aren't on about gaining power. We are not in favour of anyone having power. This is the really revolutionary thing'.[186] At a meeting the following month, Sara Dowse observed that '[r]evolutionary groups must behave as if the revolution has occurred — otherwise there is no model', though she also noted, '[y]et this often exposes them to a double strain'.[187]

Occasionally the mesh separated into opposed camps; at the 'Hevvies' Theory Conference at Mt Beauty in January 1973, a workshop on capitalism and the family was sabotaged for several participants who had brought to it a perspective shaped chiefly by the first area of preoccupation, by three participants insisting that only personal 'gut' experiences deserved discussion.[188] More often the mesh enriched both clusters of ideas. Lorraine Tilley reported that at the Workers' Control Conference in Newcastle during Easter 1973, the women pointed out to the predominantly

---

[184] Morgan (ed.), op. cit., p. xxxvi.

[185] Julia Ryan, Women's Movement Notes, book I, p. 18.

[186] ibid., pp. 86-7.

[187] ibid., p. 96.

[188] ibid, pp. 33-4.

male gathering that 'the basic assumption of workers' control is that people can make decisions, communicate and relate to each other in a positive way *without* the impositions of what amount to obstacles to worthwhile discussion' (the paraphernalia of 'points of order', time bells, etc.)[189] At a meeting in September 1974, when Biff asked, 'Are we big enough to say that feminism has something to teach socialism?', Daphne Gollan replied: 'We ... don't just have to relate feminism and socialism — we can change the whole concept of socialism'.[190]

Both strands of ideas were discernible in our discussion of questions that were being considered in Women's Liberation groups throughout Australia during the years 1972-74. The relationship between common experience based on gender and that based on class[191]; the implications of the Women's Movement's autonomy for, on one hand, links with socialist groups, and on the other, the logic of lesbian separatism[192]; recognition of the economic deprivation of all women relative to the men in their social class with, on one side, the cry for wages for housework, on the other, a demand for more women to be able to enter the workforce without abandoning the value systems they had developed to counter the 'dominant reality'[193] — all these were issues which occupied other Women's Liberation groups as well as ours. They

---

[189]   Lorraine Tilley, 'Impressions of the workers' control conference', CWL *Newsletter*, no. 31, June 1973, emphasis in the original.

[190]   Ryan, Women's Movement Notes, pp. 120-1.

[191]   ibid., p. 44. See also Linda Rubinstein and Martha Kay [Ansara], paper distributed at the 'Hevvies' Theory conference, Mt Beauty, 27-29 January 1973; Joyce Stevens, 'The autonomous Women's Movement and revolutionary social change', Janey Stone, 'A strategy for the women's liberation movement', Helen Anderson, 'The choice before us', National Women's Conference on Feminism and Socialism, 5-6 October 1975, duplicated papers.

[192]   Ryan, Women's Movement Notes, pp. 72-8. See also 'National conference — Sydney 10-13 June', CWL *Newsletter*, no. 22, July 1972; 'Sexism and women's liberation or "Why do straight sisters sometimes cry when they are called lesbians?"', paper distributed at the 'Hevvies' Theory conference; Anne Summers, 'Where's the Women's Movement moving to?', *MeJane*, no. 10, March 1973, pp. 7-8; Pat Vort-Ronald, 'Women and class', Jocelyn Clarke and Laurie Bebbington, 'Lesbian oppression and liberation', National Women's Conference on Feminism and Socialism, duplicated papers.

[193]   Julia Ryan, 'Tweedledum and Tweedledee — some comments', Ts. in Julia Ryan's Women's Movement file. Report on alternative trade union conference September 1973 in Ryan, Women's Movement Notes, book I, pp. 68-9. See also Barbara Taylor, 'Our labour and our power, *Red Rag*, no. 10, Winter 1975-76; Jean Curthoys, Mia Campioni, Pat Vort-Ronald and Liz Jacka, 'A discussion on the political economy of housework', First Australian Political Economy Conference, Sydney, 18-20 June 1976, duplicated note.

recur, unresolved, in discussions today. But during 1972-74, the Canberra Women's Liberation group discussed them largely within the terms of our two principal areas of preoccupation, drawing analyses and arguments eclectically from both.

The left-wing orientation of each of these two strands in the group's thinking about revolution were identified and labelled as early as November 1972. Eileen had presented a paper called 'New thoughts on sexuality' which defined two approaches to the subject within the Women's Movement: one — represented by Juliet Mitchell and Dana Densmore — held that sex ('the opium of the people') doesn't matter much; the other — represented by Germaine Greer, Shulamith Firestone and Reichian feminists — maintained that sex (the basic form of all energy) matters a lot. In the discussion afterwards, Daphne pointed out that the difference between the two approaches was very like the classical argument between the organised Marxists and the anarchists.[194]

From that time on, awareness of the orientation of one area of preoccupation to an undifferentiated (i.e. non-sectarian) form of socialism, and of the other to an equally undifferentiated form of anarchism, grew. Each carried with it a different view of 'the revolution'. One was of a socialist revolution, as traditionally projected by the Left, infused with feminism to ensure that the socialist society should also be an un-sexist society. This revolution belonged to the future. Its form could not be specified for, as Mitchell had noted, '[c]ircumstantial accounts of the future are idealist and worse, static. Socialism will be a process of change, a becoming … [T]he form that [it] takes will depend on the prior type of capitalism and the nature of its collapse'.[195] The other was of an anarchist revolution achieving, by the disintegration rather than the overthrow of the state, full individual freedom and collective responsibility in a self-managed society. This revolution belonged to the present. It was being achieved within the Women's Liberation group, if not throughout the Women's Movement, by its structureless, leaderless ability to act collectively, and beyond the Women's Movement by the persuasive experience of self-determination. It was, as Peggy Kornegger wrote, 'a vision, a dream, a possibility which becomes "real" as we live it'.[196] As discussion of the socialist and anarchist orientations within the Women's

---

[194] CWL *Newsletter*, no. 26, November 1972. Ryan, Women's Movement Notes, book I, pp. 13-17.

[195] Mitchell, 'Women: the longest revolution', pp. 36-7.

[196] Peggy Kornegger, 'Anarchism: the feminist connection', *The Second Wave*, Spring 1975, p. 37.

Movement become more explicit, the two strands of ideas that they encompassed grew more distinct, and finally separated.

This did not divide the Canberra Women's Liberation group doctrinally. Instead it developed as a sequential shift in emphasis, first to socialism, then to anarchism. Each shift was marked by a national conference; the Feminism and Socialism conference in Melbourne in October 1974, and the Feminism-Anarchism conference in Canberra in October 1975.

The Melbourne conference was an overwhelming testimony to the strength of the Women's Movement. Over 600 women gathered to listen to more papers than could even be summarised, much less discussed, in the time available, and at the plenary sessions there were queues for the microphone. But the brief statements made at the plenary sessions, and the less breakneck discussions in the workshops, indicated deep rifts within the movement between people who saw themselves as working-class and those who saw themselves as middle-class, and between people who were members of left-wing groups and the others whom they tried to instruct on the 'correct' assessment of the position of women.[197] Moreover, the organisation adopted to cope with the numbers, particularly of the plenary sessions when everyone packed into a single lecture theatre with tiered seats to listen to speakers with restricted time on the microphone, was authoritarian and alienating. Discussing it on the way back to Canberra, some of the Canberra Women's Liberation group concluded that Juliet Mitchell's dictum — 'We should ask feminist questions, but try to come up with some Marxist answers'[198] — simply hadn't worked. And the antagonising *mode* in which interchange of views had taken place had been reflected in the antagonising *tenor* of those views. Perhaps the next step was to concentrate on the mode, to hold an anarchistic conference on feminism and anarchism.

Fewer people came to the Canberra conference, though 300 was not a negligible number.[199] It was loosely structured, discussion groups forming around particular sets of issues agreed on by participants on the spot. This mode of self-organisation, with its spirit of co-operation, was reflected in the tenor of the discussions. One large

---

197   See Lillian Rosor, 'Working class women' and Sparticist League, 'Towards a Communist Women's Movement', National Women's Conference on Feminism and Socialism, duplicated papers.

198   Juliet Mitchell, *Woman's estate*, Penguin, Harmondsworth, 1971, p. 99.

199   Estimate made by Elizabeth O'Brien, who collected the registrations. This account of the Feminism-Anarchism conference was compiled from recollections of participants.

group, for example, spent most of a morning talking about what 'anarchism' is, a question which could not even have been asked in a competitive gathering dominated by a hierarchy of specialists. Another group started with the question, 'Can [the concept of self-management's] perspective, hitherto seen as proceeding through the elimination of class oppression, accommodate the aims of those struggling against an oppression antedating and not encompassed within the class struggle?'[200] That group went on to connect elements of Marxist, anarchist and feminist theory into an analysis, unfortunately unrecorded, of sexist society. Yet another group formed itself to discuss the sexual politics of heterosexual relationships. The whole reinforced the idea with which the conference had been planned: the importance of embodying our theory in our actions here and now. It revived enthusiasm for the task of constructing an informed theory of feminist revolution. And it gave fresh vigour to the determination that the Women's Movement must act in accordance with its own analysis and strategies, not in response to opportunities made available by the state. This last, ironically for the state, was a point made at the government-funded Women and Politics conference held a month earlier in Canberra, by a feminist in the federal bureaucracy[201], and reiterated at the Feminism-Anarchism conference in October. It arose from the particular conjuncture in Australia at that time.

The return of a Labor Party majority at the federal elections of 1972 and 1974 brought greater federal government responsiveness to demands for reforms concerning women than there had been throughout the previous twenty-three years of Liberal-Country Party coalition rule. The Labor government's efforts, Ann Game, Rosemary Pringle, and Anne Summers all argued, made little appreciable difference to the lives of most women in Australia.[202] But they did foster the rapid expansion of the Women's Movement, hence politicising many women previously untouched by

---

[200] Daphne Gollan, 'The Women's Movement and the revolutionary critique of capitalism', paper distributed at Feminism-Anarchism conference, Canberra, 11-12 October 1975, also printed as 'The Women's Movement — revolutionary?', *International*, no. 44, October 1975.

[201] Sara Dowse, 'Power in institutions — the public service', paper given to the Women and Politics conference, Canberra, 1-5 September 1975.

[202] Ann Game and Rosemary Pringle, 'Women and the Labor Government 1972-75', duplicated paper read to the First Australian Political Economy Conference; Anne Summers, 'The Women's Movement', *Nation Review*, 7-13 March 1975, reprinted in Henry Mayer and Helen Nelson (eds), *Australian politics: a fourth reader*, F.W. Cheshire, Melbourne, 1976, p. 171.

feminist arguments. And they did heighten the expectations of a great many women that their lot would improve.

The Canberra Women's Liberation group experienced these events firstly in the readiness with which the government responded to the proposal, made by a combined committee from the group and WEL, for a house and funds for a Women's Refuge.[203] Secondly, several participants in the group were recruited into the bureaucracy to help administer policies specially concerning women. Thirdly, the establishment of the International Women's Year [IWY] secretariat in December 1974, the meetings of the IWY national advisory committee, and the national IWY-funded conference on Women and Politics, all in Canberra, brought people in the Canberra Women's Liberation group into contact with women from all parts of the country more frequently and extensively than ever before.

We had an elating sense of the possibility of achieving large-scale reform, of exercising some collective power, and of solidarity with women not only throughout Australia but also across the globe. The underbelly of anxiety about how the reforms would work, about what the power would effect, and about the persisting divisions in solidarity (working class vs middle class in Australia, developed nations vs third world nations at the IWY conference in Mexico) did not seriously undercut our conviction that we were moving forward.[204]

Such experiences had important consequences for the group's ideas about revolution. Our involvement in reforms assisted by government funds clearly signalled modifications in our attitude to working through government institutions and to the importance of achieving reform. But we had not forgotten the revolution.[205] The combination of engagement in reform with the shift in orientation to anarchism produced an amalgam of both in our view of the revolution.

This was probably articulated first in the draft of a paper which Biff Ward gave in February 1975 to a small gathering initiating plans for the Feminism-Anarchism

---

[203] Minutes of meeting, 6 November 1974, CWL Minute Book 1974-5. Reports of refuge meetings, 22 July 1974, 9 October 1974, as well as reports of meetings with Department of the Capital Territory, 18 October 1974, 6 November 1974, all in Ryan, Women's Movement Notes, book I, pp. 118-19, 148-51, 153-6, 162-5. It should be noted that at this time the Australian Capital Territory, and therefore Canberra, was run by a department of the federal government rather than having self-government.

[204] See, e.g., CWL *Newsletter*, nos. 48, 49, 51, March, April, June 1975.

[205] Minutes of meeting, 16 April 1975, CWL Minute Book 1974-75.

conference. The paper traced the development of the Women's Movement in ten spheres, separating each into three aspects under the headings 'theory', 'practice' and 'reality'. The first, for instance, looked like this:

Theory	Practice	Reality
1.Consciousness-awareness raising	Rap sessions/small groups	Self awareness. Charges of elitism. Introversion

The paper did not claim simple triumphal progress, as the 'Reality' of the fourth sphere shows:

Theory	Practice	Reality
4. Minimal reforms produce mass consciousness-raising	Child-care, refuges submission, etc.	Endangers existence of movement's critique

But it was confidently optimistic. The last sphere, and the most recent stage of development in the Women's Movement, appeared like this:

Theory	Practice	Reality
10. The means is the end	Self-managed movement. Collectiveness/Support	Old rubbish/putting our-selves down/ Being competitive/ putting men first. Jubilation/achievement/getting there is living the revolution.[206]

'The Means is the End' and 'getting there is living the revolution', combined with the conviction that '[m]inimal reforms produce mass consciousness raising', were the chief components of what could be called the anarchist-reformist concept of the revolution which had become dominant among participants in the Canberra Women's Liberation group towards the end of 1975. People from the group marched to a public rally in November that year, after the governor-general's coup had thrust a federal election upon the nation, to support the Labor Party whose policies had facilitated the growth of the Women's Movement.[207] In the months following the Liberal-Country Party coalition's return to government in December 1975, people from the group gave priority to preserving the gains already made. And, as disbelief in the changed political climate faded during the winter of 1976, people from the

---

[206] Biff Ward, 'The politics of feminism', duplicated paper in Ryan, Women's Movement Notes, book II, also given at the Women and Politics conference.

[207] *Canberra Times*, 27 November 1975.

group increasingly looked to the feminists in the federal bureaucracy for guidance in preserving the movement in an increasingly alien environment.[208] If 'means were ends', then it was essential to sustain the reforms already achieved as examples of the far greater reforms required. If 'getting there was living the revolution', we must preserve the various centres in which people could encounter women engaging in uncompetitive, un-hierarchical self-management. Few could avoid resentment and disappointment as the scale of growth dwindled. But the Women's Movement gave vent to no outbursts of rage at frustration of heightened expectations: its expectations remained high.

Yet for some of the participants in the Canberra Women's Liberation group by mid-1976, when our last *Newsletter* appeared, the anarchist-reformist view of the revolution was more profoundly troubling than the feminist-socialist mode had been in late 1974. We had agreed with Sara Dowse when she told the Women and Politics conference on 4 September 1975 that women may be able to forge a strength from their physically and spiritually scattered weakness by operating 'on many fronts at once', that the patriarchal 'system' might 'be "brought down" just as much by a thousand blows [as] by one well-directed powerful punch'.[209] But now, instead of attempting to support and co-ordinate those blows, the Women's Movement in this city seemed fragmented, groups and individuals isolated, sometimes antagonistic.[210] Some participants in the now defunct group appeared to have carried the 'personal is political' argument to the extreme of opting out of the feminist struggle altogether, turning inwards to sole concern with dwellings and personal relationships. Some had become heavily involved in what looked like alternative social services, making themselves into an unpaid labour force to supply welfare needs largely ignored by the state. Many appeared to have developed a mendicant attitude to government, trimming demands to accord with those that could be advanced within the bureaucracy. Indeed, when a combined WEL and Women's Liberation *Newsletter* for December 1975/January 1976 appeared, the old distinction between these two elements in the Women's Movement seemed to have evaporated, and not because WEL had developed a new commitment to revolution. On another occasion, in

---

[208] Small group discussion, 20 July 1976, personal recollection.

[209] Dowse, 'Power in institutions', pp. 7, 6.

[210] See, for example, *Out from under: a journal of women and power*, April 1976 (only one issue appeared) and Ryan, Women's Movement Notes, book II, pp. 32-4.

August 1976, when a small group discussing differences in approach between the Women's Movement and the male Left produced the dictum 'The old distinction between reform and revolution is obsolete and irrelevant'[211], the Women's Movement in Canberra seemed to have shrivelled into an informal branch of the federal bureaucracy. The same discussion in August 1976 dismissed the socialist revolution promulgated by the male Left as pie-in-the-sky, another kind of opium for the female masses. We appeared to have travelled a great distance from the discussions of 1972-74, and some of us were disturbed at the terrain we appeared to have arrived in.

What was this so-called revolution we were engaged in? Was it simply the extension of reforms already initiated, assisted by increasing diversion of government attention and funds to changes in the education system, the health and welfare services available to women, the provision of child care, etc., etc., etc.? Were isolated individuals, fashioning their own lives in accordance with a concept of self-determination, really offering models for the self-managed society? Did the failure of Marxist analysis and the struggle for socialism to encompass a form of oppression far older than capitalism really make the current crisis of capitalism irrelevant to the struggle for women's liberation? What, then, of the men, the other half of the human species? Could the feminist revolution occur without the fundamental transformation of the totality of capitalist society?

Answers to most questions like these would vary. But for everyone who has ever been involved in Women's Liberation the answer to the last must surely be an unequivocal 'No!' Sexism might be an older, more fundamental, and more universal oppression than capitalism and imperialism. No doubt sexism could survive in socialist society. But the present manifestation of sexism occurs in capitalist-imperialist form.[212] To combat sexism is necessarily also to combat capitalism.

Several of us believe that it is necessary now to revive the expectations and commitments that characterised Women's Liberation. We're not on a nostalgia trip. Certainly, there are some things to be retained from our recent absorption in reform. The importance of consciousness-raising through refuges, women's health centres, and rape crisis centres can never be underestimated. Nor can the pragmatic benefits of involvement with government bureaucracies: increased understanding of the current

---

[211]   Small group discussion, 3 August 1976, personal recollection.

[212]   Sheila Rowbotham makes the same point, indirectly, in *Hidden from history*, Pelican Books, 1975, p. x.

condition of capitalist society, and heightened attention to the issues from which we can fruitfully draw strategies for the transition from capitalism to self-managed feminist socialism. There are, too, some things to be preserved from our anarchism. Our awareness of the importance of the mode — the manner in which we approach, indeed enact, our ideas — will reinforce our opposition to hierarchical or authority-differentiating organisations like vanguard parties. And our insistence upon individual self-determination and collective co-operation must sustain our commitment to the totality of the self-managed society. There is also something to be rescued from the socialism that we threw out with the bath-water of the Left groups' mode. Recognition of the continuing oppression of one class by another in all societies must commit all of us, whatever the male-defined class to which we find ourselves allocated, to the struggle of the working class in all societies for socialism. But the very feature of the Women's Movement's ideas that we select, now, as characterising the struggle for women's liberation compels us to work towards a new and more encompassing theory of revolution than one confined to the abolition of female oppression, and to develop more strategies than are provided by the model of protest movements in democratic societies, for its achievement.

Men have never hesitated to assume that they could speak for the entire human species. Why should we feel unable to develop a theory and strategy for revolution for all humanity? If we do not demand more than the state can give, what is a movement for? If we cannot show the chronically warring left-wing factions a compelling strategy for transition to socialism, why hope for a feminist revolution at all? If we will not require men to recognise the necessity for the feminist revolution, how can we demand an end to sexism? We must, of course, heed Juliet Mitchell's warning against voluntarism.[213] But that does not mean that we should do nothing but hold coffee parties till capitalism crumbles. Our present confusion may have grown out of bewilderment and weariness. But it is, nevertheless, thoughtful, imaginative and energetic. Above all, it is impatient.

---

[213]   Mitchell, *Women: the longest revolution*, p. 34.

5

Feminism as cultural renaissance

This paper was first presented to a Women's Studies Association Conference at the University of Queensland in 2003, then published in Hecate: An Interdisciplinary Journal of Women's Liberation, *vol. 30, no. 1, 2004. I am grateful to Carole Ferrier, editor of* Hecate, *for permission to republish.*

'Truly, it felt like Year One', wrote English novelist Angela Carter; 'towards the end of the sixties it started to feel like living on a demolition site — one felt one was living on the edge of the unimaginable'. There was 'a yeastiness in the air that was due to a great deal of unrestrained and irreverent frivolity', and 'an air of continuous improvisation'. 'I can', she wrote, 'date to that time and to that sense of heightened awareness of the society around me in the summer of 1968 my own questioning of the nature of my reality as a woman. How that social fiction of my "femininity" was created and palmed off on me as the real thing'.[214]

To begin what is predominantly — but not exclusively — a white story: in January 1971, at Australia's first Women's Liberation conference in Sydney, postgraduate students Ann Curthoys and Lyndall Ryan spoke of forms of 'cultural oppression': '[I]t is here', they proclaimed,

> [t]hat the oppression of women goes beyond the traditional class barriers. And it is here that we have to start to smash those myths for unless we can change

---

[214] Angela Carter, 'Truly, it felt like Year One', in Sara Maitland (ed.), *Very heaven: looking back at the 1960s*, Virago, London, 1988, pp. 209, 211, 212, 213.

Figure 4: Sue Williams and Chris Westwood doing 'Berlington Bertie', Women's Dance, Adelaide, 1978

Photograph by Carrie Anconie who has generously given permission for it to be reprinted in this book

> the whole cultural orientation of women, no revolution is going to bring us the liberation we are seeking.[215]

The language was that of the new New Left[216] and the popular movement against Australia's participation in the United States' war against the Vietnamese people

---

[215] Reported in Canberra Women's Liberation *Newsletter*, no. 5, February 1971, pp. 3-4.

[216] The distinction between the New Left and the new New Left was a distinction between such anti-Stalinists who had abandoned their membership of the Communist Party of Australia in the 1950s and 1960s, and the largely Althusserian structuralist Marxists of the late-1960s and 1970s who would never have thought of joining the CPA. It was also, clearly, at least partly a generational distinction. Examples of each among historians are R.A. Gollan, *Radical and working class politics: a study of Eastern Australia, 1850-1910*, Melbourne University Press, Melbourne, 1960, and R.W. Connell and T.H. Irving, *Class structure in Australian history: documents, narrative and argument*, Longman Cheshire, Melbourne, 1980.

Figure 5: Ann Curthoys on the cover of
MeJane, **vol. 1, no. 1, 1971**
Copied with permission from Ann Curthoys

— except for its emphasis on 'culture'.[217] That emphasis pointed to a dimension of the movement for the liberation of women that is seldom recognised. Look at Chris Westwood and Sue Williams: they've abandoned their skirts and stockings, not to make coffee for men at the anti-war meeting, but rather to sing — and on stage, not at home in the bathroom — in drag. Young singer/songwriter, Robyn Archer sang on a subject previously unmentionable in public, 'The menstruation blues'. Ann Curthoys made more than speeches; she made a spectacle of herself swinging from a tree on the cover of *MeJane*, volume 1, number 1.[218] All over the country, but especially in the cities, women took to their pens, typewriters and gestetners; to their easels and kilns; to their guitars; to their classrooms, and — breaking all the rules about separate spheres — to the street and stages.

Such activism *could* be seen as an extension of the Youth Movement of the late 1960s, with its insistence on its counter-cultural distinction from the mainstream. Such activism *could* be seen as an extension of the cultural revolution of advanced industrial capitalist nations and its debates over what would come to be called 'Euro-

---

[217]   See, for example, Theodore Roszak, *The making of a counter culture: reflections on the technocratic society and its youthful opposition*, University of California Press, Faber, London, 1970 (1969).

[218]   Sue Williams, 'A decadent dancing delight for women who waltz', Burnside Town Hall, Adelaide, 1977; Robyn Archer, 'The menstruation blues', in Robyn Archer, *The ladies' choice, 1973, the Robyn Archer songbook*, McPhee Gribble, Melbourne, 1980; *MeJane*, no. 1, Sydney, March 1971.

communist marxism'.[219] The chronological overlap of the new New Left, the Youth Movement and the Women's Liberation Movement makes the association inevitable.

But the disorderly conduct associated with Women's Liberation distinguishes it from such chronology, if only because the women continued to erupt through the bounds of convention over and over again, throughout the 1970s and beyond. The 'Coming Out Ready or Not' show put together by the Australian Women's Broadcasting Co-operative to go to air on Saturday afternoons signalled in its very name what Julie Rigg and Julie Copeland noted as 'that new tone we can hear in women's voices: a boldness and enthusiasm for the possibilities of change'; it was launched on International Women's Day in 1975, in Sydney.[220] *Refractory Girl* had been coming out in Sydney since 1972 and in Brisbane *Hecate* launched itself, with the assistance of a grant from the Australian government's International Women's Year funds, as one of the first international journals of academic feminism in 1975. The South Australian Women's Art Movement's vision arrived in 1976.[221] The Sydney Women Writers' Workshop got themselves together when, 'with a bit of a bang', they organised a reading at Bondi Pavilion in May 1978.[222] Sisters Publishing, a co-operative of five women-publishers based in Melbourne, established itself to national fanfare in 1979.[223] It was as late as 1989 when Jackie Huggins took time out from writing her Honours thesis in Women's Studies at Flinders University to erupt onto the stage as 'a Cherbourg Girl' in Anne Dunn's *Black and White Women's Show* in Adelaide.[224]

---

[219] Roszak, op. cit.; Andrew Wells, 'Marxism and Australian historiography', *Thesis Eleven: A Journal of Socialist Scholarship*, no. 11, 1981, p. 103.

[220] Julie Rigg and Julie Copeland (eds), *Coming out! Women's voices, women's lives: a selection from ABC's Coming Out show*, in association with the Australian Broadcasting Corporation, Nelson, Melbourne, 1985, p. 1.

[221] Catherine Gough-Brady, '"You don't want to be an artist, do you babe?": Social change and the women's art movement', BA Hons. Thesis, Adelaide University, 1992, p. 1.

[222] Anna Couani and Pamela Brown, 'Sydney women writers' workshop', *Lip*, 1978-79, p. 188.

[223] See Rosemary Dobson (ed.), *Sisters poets 1*, Sisters Publishing Ltd, Carlton, 1979, with the Sisters Editorial Board at the beginning. See also Hilary McPhee, *Other people's words*, Picador, Sydney, 2001, pp. 159-61; Louise Poland, 'The devil and the angel? Australia's feminist presses and the multinational agenda', *Hecate*, vol. 29, no. 2, 2003.

[224] The Feminist Theatre Group, directed by Anne Dunn and Eva Johnson, *Is this seat taken?*, The Space Theatre, Adelaide Festival Centre, 1989.

Further, the Women's Movement's cultural transformations were notable precisely because they were *extensions* of those earlier Left and anti-war movements. The women took the men's arguments to logical conclusions entirely beyond those envisaged by the antecedent movements. 'Liberation' was supposed to refer to the working class or the third world or young men, not to women. Women's Liberation's claims and visions were all-encompassing; the liberation of women meant total transformation of whole societies, and elimination of power differences between white and black, first and third world, employer and worker, even parent and child, and — the new, unanticipated coda which the Women's Liberation Movement introduced — between men and women. Moreover, because Women's Liberation was a movement of women, women began to talk with each other, to form political solidarities with each other, and also, instead of rivalries around patriarchal prizes, friendships; sometimes even sexual relationships. A politics of affinity?[225] The fabric of the whole social order quaked.

Cultural disruption is a dimension of second-wave feminism that gains little, if any, attention in any of the histories written to date.[226] So I have no ready-to-hand analysis to follow. Yet historical scholarship shows such exhilarated rule-breaking by women to be by no means unprecedented. The scholar I want to invoke, here, is North American doyenne of early modernity, Natalie Zemon Davis. In a wonderful essay titled 'Women on Top' published in 1975, she detailed ways in which people — men as well as women — challenged the hierarchical order of pre-industrial societies with widespread forms of cultural play in literature, art and festivity depicting sexual inversion and offering examples of the unruly woman. In an argument that ran counter to the orthodoxy of the day, and to an orthodoxy subsequently established around the name of Bakhtin, she maintained that the comic and festive inversion, which other scholars considered as ultimately reinforcing assent to that hierarchical order, could

---

[225] A recommendation for a politics of affinity for feminists would appear in Haraway, op. cit.

[226] For example Echols, op. cit.; Susan Brownmiller, *In our time: memoir of a revolution*, Aurum Press, London, 2000; Ruth Rosen, *The world split open: how the modern Women's Movement changed America*, Viking Penguin, New York, 2000; Judith Ezekiel, *Feminism in the heartland*, Ohio State University Press, Columbus, 2002; Beatrix Campbell and Anna Coote, *Sweet freedom: the struggle for Women's Liberation*, Pan Books, London, 1982; Juliet Mitchell and Ann Oakley (eds), *What is feminism?*, Basil Blackwell, Oxford, 1986; Marilyn Lake, op. cit.

Susan Magarey

also undermine such assent 'through its connections with everyday circumstances outside the privileged time of carnival and play'. 'I want to argue', she wrote,

> that the image of the disorderly woman did not always function to keep women in their place. On the contrary, it was a multivalent image that could operate, first, to widen behavioural options for women within and even outside marriage, and, second, to sanction riot and political disobedience.

The image of the 'women-on-top' she proposed 'might even facilitate innovation in historical theory and political behaviour'.[227]

Davis herself is careful to make her argument specific to her researches in early modern Europe. With the advent of industrialism, modern states, classes and systems of private property and its exploitation of racial and national groups, she observes, then the symbolisms of disorder change.[228] I would like to be far more cavalier with her idea. I want to suggest that by the end of the 1960s in Australia — towards the end of the longest economic boom in the history of the advanced industrial capitalist West — the symbolism of good order and social hierarchy was once again strongly gendered, with women seen as confined to Hegel's nether world, the domestic sphere in which her labour was categorised as consumption (rather than production) and in which such labour was highly sexualised.[229] The gap between such symbolism and the movement of so many women, including wives and mothers, into the labour market constituted one of the major contradictions provoking the resurgence of feminism in 1970. That symbolism and its association with the demure and domestic was one of the primary targets of the feminist cultural renaissance of the 1970s and 1980s, and the feminist cultural renaissance, in itself, constituted an onslaught on the conventions of marriage and domesticity, the symbolism or good order and propriety expressed by women and men being in their proper and separate spheres. To translate Natalie

---

[227] Natalie Zemon Davis, *Society and culture in early modern France: eight essays*, Stanford University Press, Stanford, 1975, p. 131. My thanks to John Docker for reminding me of this essay, and to Lynn Martin for lending me his copy of the book. On Bakhtin, see M.M. Bakhtin, *Speech genres and other late essays*, trans. Vern W. Gee, Caryl Emerson and Michael Holquist (eds), University of Texas Press, Austin, 1986, p. xv.

[228] Zemon Davis, op. cit., p. 150.

[229] See, for example, Ann Game and Rosemary Pringle: 'The making of the Australian family', *Intervention*, no. 12, 1979, pp. 63-83, and 'Sexuality and the suburban dream', *Australian and New Zealand Journal of Sociology*, vol. 15, no. 2, 1979, pp. 4-15; Magarey, 'Questions about "patriarchy"', pp. 182-4.

78

Zemon Davis slightly, girls behaving badly sanctions 'riot and political disobedience' throughout the population; it might even facilitate 'innovation in historical theory and political behaviour'.

Any consideration of Women's Liberation as cultural renaissance will need to attend to a host of events, processes, manifestations. There was the wonderful moment in 1976 when seventy-nine-year-old feminist, Beryl Henderson, a woman who would marry for the first time a year later, 'made some passing remarks about etymology' on the 'Coming Out Show'. The radio manager decreed that what she had said was offensive and prohibited the customary replay on the regional network. The Women's Broadcasting Collective responded with charges of censorship and what was then broadcast was not some substitute program but five minutes of what broadcasters call 'tone' instead. Here are Beryl's words, the words that the radio manager found offensive:

> Women's Liberation has gone beyond the worlds I dreamed of … in their freedom, their language … I don't enjoy their language … I've always felt it a shame that something which is really delightful should be used as a swearword … Actually 'fuck' is a very nice word. It's an Anglo-Saxon word. 'Cunt' is the worst thing you can call someone, yet as a man will say, it's really a very nice thing, isn't it.[230]

(Perhaps not, for some twenty-first-century white male football players.) There was the Daylesford Embroidered Banner Project of 1981-82 about which Christine Stoke said:

> My belief is that the capacity to define oneself and one's priorities is the essential beginning of any productive activity. I base it on the experience of feminism which represents a continuing struggle to become one's own subject.[231]

There were the singer/songwriters, from Robyn Archer and 'The old soft screw' to the Ovarian Sisters from Hobart and their album titled *Beat your Breasts*, which included the delightful send-up 'The IPD', the intra-uterine device converted to fit a man. The chorus of 'The IPD' went:

> Oh it's the IPD, the IPD!
> It may not feel too good to you

---

230 Rigg and Copeland, op. cit., p. 79.
231 Christine Stoke, 'The Daylesford embroidered banner project', *Lip*, 1984, p. 8.

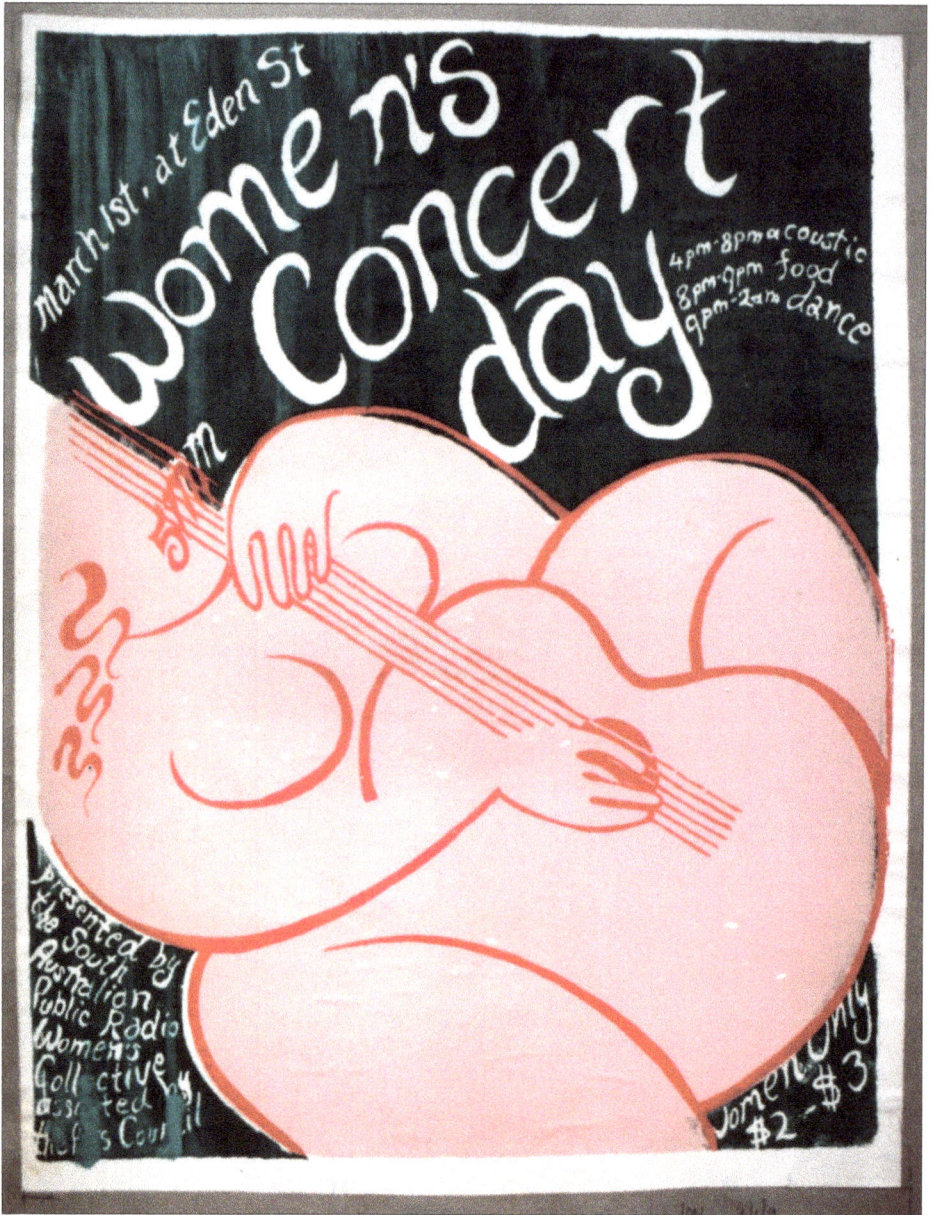

Figure 6: Poster, no artist identified

Courtesy of Susan Magarey

But it's not hurting me.
So every time the pain begins to fill your eyes with tears,
Remember I put up with it for years.[232]

There were the novelists, beginning perhaps with Kerryn Higgs's prize-winning work, *All That False Instruction*.[233] There were the feminist playwrights, actors and singers, from Fools Gallery's *Standard Operating Procedures* to another Canberra group's review which included a chorus of young woman dressed in imitation of Barbara Cartland, each twirling a tiny, fluffy pink dog on the end of a lead and singing to Dusty Springfield's music, 'Stand By Your Gran'.[234] There were the poets, collected by Kate Jennings in *Mother I'm Rooted* in 1975.[235] There were the endlessly inventive posters. Film-makers took longer to become widely visible. Early work by Sarah Gibson and Susan Lambert heralded films that appeared in the mainstream: directed by Margaret Fink and Gillian Armstrong, *My Brilliant Career* (based on the novel by Miles Franklin first published in 1901) came out in 1986, and the first film by Tracey Moffat, *Nice Coloured Girls*, was made in 1987.

Let us look at one of these disruptive manifestations more closely by considering some (presciently post-modern) elements of one of the productions of the Adelaide Feminist Theatre Group, a collective associated with such other productions as *The Carolina Chisel Show* and *Redhead's Revenge*.[236] This one is called *Chores!* The first script was written collectively by six women who, in their own words, 'sat around and made jokes and had ideas for a year of Sunday afternoons', then staged their show first

---

[232] Archer, op. cit., p. 20 and 'The old soft screw', in *The Robyn Archer songbook*, pp. 14-15; The Ovarian Sisters, *Beat your breasts*, Candle Music Company Pty Ltd, Hobart, 1980.

[233] Elizabeth Riley, pseud., *All that false instruction*, Angus & Robertson, Sydney, 1975. See also Harriet Malinowitz, 'Introduction' and Kerryn Higgs, 'Afterword', in Kerryn Higgs, *All that false instruction*, Spinifex, North Melbourne, 2001; this has been called the first lesbian novel in Australia.

[234] See Andrea McLaughlin, '"Acting on it": feminist theatre: politics and performance', *Lip*, 1984, pp. 76-7. This reference does not give a date for the performance season; Fool's Gallery was an amateur theatre group in Canberra, and *Standing operating procedures* was largely based on Mary Daly, *Gyn/Ecology: the metaethics of radical feminism*, Beacon Press, Boston, 1978. I saw the musical review that included the hilarious send-up of Barbara Cartland in both Canberra and Adelaide, but I have not been able to find any documentation about it.

[235] Kate Jennings (ed.), *Mother I'm rooted: an anthology of Australian women poets*, Outback Press, Fitzroy, 1975.

[236] *The redhead's revenge*, The Space Theatre, Adelaide Festival Centre, 3-13 May 1978.

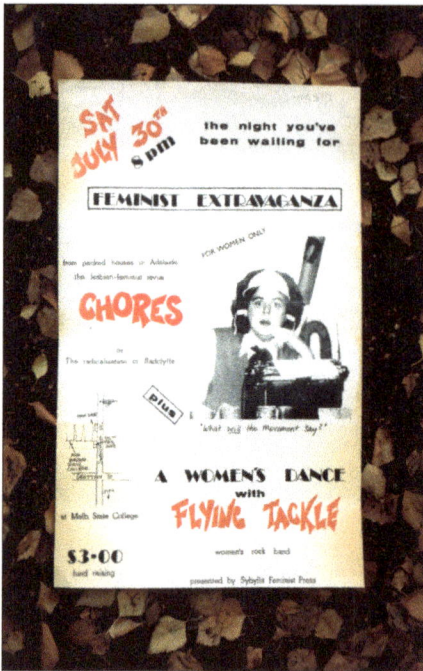

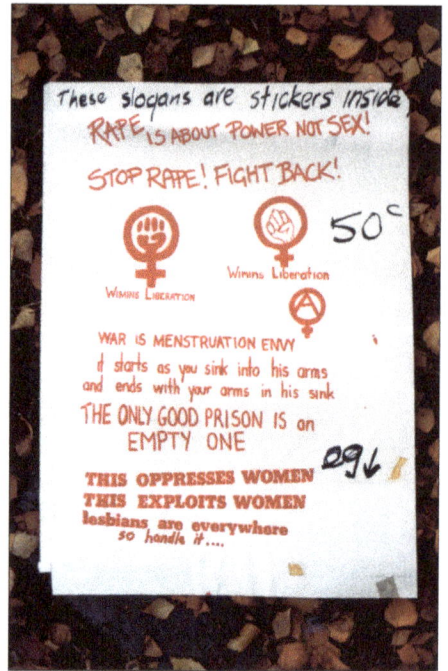

Figures 7 and 8: Posters, no artist identified
Courtesy of Susan Magarey

for the Women's Movement in 1977. The title signalled its ostensible concern, which was how to organise domestic labour in a feminist collective household. But the writers distanced it from the household in which most of it was written by making it an historical fantasy, set in 1911. It reflects some of the emphases in the syllabuses of tertiary education courses in history and English Literature in the 1970s. Its characters are not such first-wave feminists of Australia as Catherine Spence, Louisa Lawson, Rose Scott, Maybanke Wolstenholme, Vida Goldstein or Alice Henry, but instead fantasies of the English suffragettes, Christabel and Sylvia Pankhurst, Annie Kenney, Emily Wilding-Davis, and, to add spice to this mix, someone who probably never met any of the suffragettes, Radclyffe Hall, who arrives on stage boasting of being the author of a famous lesbian bestseller, *The Well of Loneliness*, a work not published until seventeen years later, in 1928. As that spice might suggest, the central concern of the piece turns from questions of who is to do the housework to who is going to get into bed with whom in this collective household.

Figure 9: Andy Malone and Sue Higgins (later Sheridan) performing in *Chores!*, Adelaide, 1977
Photograph courtesy of Sue Sheridan

Chores! is a musical, using well-known songs ranging from Gilbert & Sullivan to Rodgers & Hammerstein, from Mario Lanza to Bill Haley and early rock and roll. This produced satire of love songs, as when 'I have often walked down this street before', one of the romantic moments in *My Fair Lady*, becomes:

> I have often walked in this house before
> But it never seemed to smell so awfully foul before.
> Bulging rubbish bins — empty money tins —
> Can this be the place where *I* live?

Or 'Amazing Grace' becomes this:

> Amazing Grace and Sally Forth
> Are really fun to know.
> They like each other very much,
> And what they feel, they show.

When Sally sits on Grace's knee
It makes me feel so good.
I am so very glad to see
Amazing sisterhood.

It also produced a moment when the happily married Emmeline Pethick-Lawrence confounds historical realism, and the original meaning of her song, by singing it straight, but in a context which transforms its sense from straight to gay: 'Never knew I was pissed until I kissed her'. Sylvia Pankhurst does the same, addressing Annie Kenney, singing, 'Don't throw bouquets at me ... People will say we're in love', but hers is a triple whammy because her song also satirises feminism's attack on romantic love.

Chris Westwood, later to be Director of the South Australian State Theatre Company for a time, characterised these productions of what could be called the *samizdat* era of Women's Liberation as 'pro-am', mixing the talents of those who were or would become professionals in the entertainment industry with those of amateurs. For some they may have been training. In the productions of the Adelaide Feminist Theatre Group it is possible to glimpse Penny Chapman, who would become for a time producer of television drama with the Australian Broadcasting Commission. Janet Seidel, who wrote the music for *Chores!*, is now a professional blues singer. And Jenny Pausacker, who played Emily Wilding-Davison, typing with two of those little bits of cotton that Annie Kenney kept bringing back from the cotton factory in her ears, is now — not a marketer for tampons, but rather — a well-recognised and awarded writer of fiction.

The press hated *Chores!* when another group performed it for the general public in Adelaide.[237] They complained about it all being '[a]n in-joke for women gays', and 'too self-indulgent and narrow in its scope to appeal to a wider audience'. Perhaps this would have to be expected. It is another instance of the women behaving badly, just one more instance of feminism's cultural renaissance. What is probably most remarkable about it is how well-known the English suffragettes and their stories must have been among the production's audiences, both feminist and general public, for, despite the press, *Chores!* was so successful that it was revised and taken off to Melbourne to be performed again. It is, I think, heartening, in the early twenty-first

---

[237] A carbon copy of the text used for the second production of *Chores!* is in the possession of Susan Sheridan, Professor Emerita of Flinders University.

century when the Australian government is clearly committed to reducing women once again to the 'nether world' of housework, to recall the exuberance of Women's Liberation's cultural renaissance, its disorderly rule-breaking, and, above all, its belief in change.

6

Does the family have a future?

Invited address presented at Prospect 2000: A Conference on the Future, arranged by the Western Australian Division of the Australian and New Zealand Association for the Advancement of Science, Perth, May 1979, and published in S.T. Waddell (ed.), Prospect 2000, *ANZAAS W.A. Division, Perth, 1979, pp. 24-39.*

At the beginning of May 1979, four women appeared in a magistrate's court in Sydney, charged with having shot and killed a man. One of the women, aged forty-nine, was the man's wife. The other three, aged variously nineteen, seventeen and sixteen, were his daughters.

Neighbours gave evidence at the hearing: one said that she had seen the man beating his wife, sometimes as often as three times in one day; another said that he had seen the man knock his wife down and kick her. He had been present once, said this witness, when the man told his family, 'If I killed you all I would only have to go to jail once'. A detective told the court of the women's attempt to escape the repeated assaults by fleeing to a country town: the man followed them, armed with a rifle, and forced them to return home. He kept a loaded rifle in the bedroom, iron bars behind doors throughout the house, and threatened that he would be the first to sleep with his daughters.

The women did not complain to the police because they feared that any investigation would bring immediate retribution at home. Instead, one evening in January, when the man had beaten one of his daughters and thrown a glass at her, the wife mixed two crushed sleeping tablets into his food. Then, when he was snoring in front of the television, the four women resolved to kill him. The sixteen-year-old fired the shot. Afterwards, one of the daughters put her arm around her mother and said: 'It's all right, mum, we don't have to get belted any more'.[238]

Such violence was not unique to that family. The defence cited as a precedent the decision made about a similar case in Victoria in the previous year. And information about a variety of forms of brutality, in the most private of our social institutions — the family — is beginning to weigh upon the shelves of public libraries, upon the desks of public servants, and upon the minds of public welfare workers.

The widespread occurrence of wife battery, for instance, has only recently, and slowly, gained recognition. But during the last five years (that is, during the mid-1970s), groups formed within the Women's Movement have been establishing women's refuges to answer a need great enough for there now to be over seventy of these institutions throughout the country.[239] People involved in one of them estimated that roughly 75 per cent of the women driven to a refuge for help have suffered some form of physical violence at the hands of their husbands.[240] The Director of Research at the Mental Health Authority in Victoria exclaimed in amazement at the amount of suffering that deserted wives had experienced before their husbands left them. 'We found', he said, 'that a quarter of them were regularly and severely beaten, and our definition of that is that they were beaten to a stage where they had to go to a doctor or to a hospital or to bed as a result'.[241]

It is not only women who are the victims of violence in the family. One child, an eleven-year-old, told a Victorian police surgeon:

> When I do things wrong I know I should be punished but I don't think I
> should be hit so hard with the big stick. I don't like being hit with the big stick
> all the time because sometimes it makes me vomit.

Another, an eight-year-old, said to the same doctor:

> Boy, mum does a lot of terrible things to me. Do you know that one night she
> belted me so hard that I couldn't hardly breathe. My nose was bleeding and I
> kept falling on the floor and that. You know when mummy hits me, I have very

---

238 *Canberra Times*, 1 May 1979, 2 May 1979.

239 Anne Deveson, *Australians at risk*, Cassell Australia Ltd, Stanmore, NSW, 1978, p. 106.

240 Sue Edwards, Co-ordinator at the Women's Shelter, Hobart, quoted in ibid., p. 121.

241 Dr Jerry Krupinski, quoted in ibid., p. 86.

> bad dreams all night. I usually dream of horrible things like something awful
> going to happen and I get very scared and I wake up screaming.[242]

Again, Australians have only recently become generally aware of the child abuse syndrome. We do not have national statistics to compare with the spine-chilling numbers collected in the United States or Britain.[243] But a survey carried out in South Australia in 1975 found that over a three-month period, 211 children were injured and 867 children were considered to be at risk. Nearly 70 per cent of those children had suffered serious, possibly permanent injury. If we extrapolate from those figures on a population basis, we reach the estimate that some 14 000 children in Australia are injured each year — that is, 38 children each day.[244]

Yet children are not victims only. And this has been recognised in the public domain for longer. Research carried out in Britain in the 1950s and 1960s showed that some, though certainly not many, of a sample of people under twenty years old who had been convicted of crimes of violence had been charged as a result of family disputes.[245] One Australian mother commented recently: 'I'm my son's property, he bashes me up'.[246]

The family in Australia, it would seem, is quite literally a battleground. Our tidily self-contained suburban houses and gardens appear to be an arena of physical violence of a kind and extent usually associated only with a very old-fashioned kind of war.

Yet in Australia, perhaps more than in any other post-industrial capitalist country, we seem to regard such conflict as remote from our own experience, like road accidents, unlikely to happen to us. If we did not, might we not pause before hurtling into the ring ourselves? For that is what we have been doing. Until midway through the 1960s, this country had shown two trends which are unusual in the Western world — an increasing marriage rate (65 per cent of women were marrying before they reached the age of twenty-five; 95 per cent before the age of forty), and

---

242   Information supplied by Dr John Birrell, quoted in ibid., p. 140.

243   Arlene Skolnick, *The intimate environment: exploring marriage and the family*, Little, Brown and Co., Boston, 1973, pp. 291-2.

244   ibid., p. 125.

245   Donald J. West, *The young offender*, Penguin, Harmondsworth, 1967, pp. 20-1.

246   Lyn Richards, *Having families, marriage, parenthood and social pressure in Australia*, Penguin, Ringwood, 1978, p. 283.

a reduction in the median age of marriage (twenty-three for men, twenty-one for women). These marriages were, it is true, producing smaller families: in 1976 the crude birthrate dropped below 17 per thousand in the population for the first time since the Great Depression. But on average a woman in Australia still bears two or three children during her lifetime. Moreover, while the divorce rate increased by half again between 1972 and 1975, with 42 per cent of those marriages having lasted fewer than ten years, the number of remarriages was also increasing.[247] Such figures suggest that agitation about 'the death of the family' might well be — in Australia, at any rate — mere sound and fury, signifying nothing.

We appear to be faced with a paradox. On one hand, there is evidence suggesting a widespread confidence in the satisfactions of family life. On the other — evidence suggesting extensive and very acute unhappiness within families. To object that such a paradox simply reflects a gap between expectation and experience is not to dismiss it. It is still necessary to explain why such a gap exists.

Does it matter? Does such a subject warrant serious consideration in a forum concerned with the future of our nation? What have the ups and downs of domestic life to do with the great events being worked out in the theatre of public affairs, with the development of industry and technology, with the future of employment and leisure patterns, with the shifts in politics and government?

The answer to questions like those is, simply — a great deal. In Australia the predominant form of domestic group — whatever its size or shape or temper — is the fundamental unit of social organisation. It is within the domestic group that we take decisions determining the size of both the present and the future pool from which the workforce is drawn. It is primarily the domestic group which determines consumption of the nation's resources — 'Shall we put in oil or gas heating, or shall we get a pot-belly stove?' 'Petrol's getting too expensive; why don't we sell the car and get four bicycles?' It is primarily the domestic group that determines consumption of the commodities which the workforce produces — from tins of baked beans through refrigerators to four-bedroomed houses. It is (traditionally at least) primarily the domestic group that shapes the beliefs and values, the desires and fears, the loves and hates of the next generation of voters. It is the size of domestic groups, and their number, that we count in order to determine domestic and economic policy. We sanctify the domestic group with religious ceremony and sanction its existence

---

[247] ibid., pp. 15-18.

in the law. The character of the predominant form of domestic group is vitally and fundamentally important to the whole society. Some have depicted it as a microcosm of society — 'a little commonwealth', 'a little utopia'. Accordingly, the contradiction between evidence of confidence in family life and evidence of acute distress in families should prompt us to look for conflicting forces in the whole social formation that we constitute.

The kind of domestic group that we are concerned with is the nuclear family: the co-resident, economically co-operative unit consisting of a man and a woman whose socially approved sexual relationships have produced two or three children whom the couple nurture, protect, provide for, and teach until they are grown up. If we exclude people living in various kinds of institution, the nuclear family has probably been until recently the predominant form of domestic group in settler Australian society.[248]

It is also part of the prevailing image of the ideal domestic group that we still commonly encounter in the marketplace, the media, and the various instrumentalities of the state. But it is not the whole image: its other dimension represents the relationships assumed to exist between each member of the nuclear family. These are patriarchal.[249]

The husband is the head of the family, the locus of authority. A man responding to questions designed by the Royal Commission on Human Relationships summarised this when defining a 'good father': 'They are the head of the house', he said, and then, 'You are the controlling influence when it comes to the law being laid down ... or such and such is going to happen or won't happen. I try to be a disciplinary authority that's only used, you know, as a last resort ... '[250] The wife, even if she wields power within the family and even if she is not economically dependent, is subordinate to him. As the economist Margaret Power has reminded us: 'A recent poll, conducted by

---

[248]   Anne Summers, *Damned whores and God's police: the colonization of women in Australia*, Penguin, Ringwood, 1975, pp. 19-20. Summers did not, in that publication, note that this was an observation particular to settler society; nor did I when I first quoted her.

[249]   For a definition and discussion of 'patriarchal' see Kate Millett, *Sexual politics*, Rupert Hart-Davis, London, 1971, pp. 25-6; Sheila Rowbotham, *Woman's consciousness, man's world*, Penguin, Harmondsworth, 1973, p. 117; Roisin McDonough and Rachel Harrison, 'Patriarchy and relations of production', and Annette Kuhn, 'Structures of patriarchy and capital in the family', both in Annette Kuhn and Ann Marie Wolpe (eds), *Feminism and materialism: women and modes of production*, Routledge and Kegan Paul, London, 1978.

[250]   Richards, op. cit., p. 219.

Australian National Opinon Poll, showed that Australians of both sexes still believe in a society in which women are housewives and childminders'.[251] The children, at least while they are minors, are subordinate to both. The relationships of the ideal image are static: a recent study of family relationships in sixty families remarked that

> [t]he image of marriage as a container — full or empty — recurred throughout these accounts. A container is unchanging, static, not a developing thing, and to those who explained the need for children in terms of their importance to the marriage, marriage too was static.[252]

The image's relationships are also stable, contented and loving. Choice of partner in marriage is governed by romantic love and individual interest[253], and this is supposed to guarantee that 'all the significant emotional needs of each family member are satisfied within the ... family circle'.[254] The image of the ideal nuclear family is an image of a social unit which is 'natural' — wholly in harmony with the dictates of human biology and psychology — a social unit which is therefore universal.[255]

The belief that this image accurately represented reality was probably strongest and most prevalent during the twenty-odd years following the Second World War. This was a period of prosperity, the greatest prosperity in the history of the advanced industrial countries, indeed of the world.[256] With full employment, women — who had entered the workforce in huge numbers during the war — became once again predominantly home-makers, a shift which continued even after the period of post-war reconstruction, when women joined the workforce in proportions which increased from 23 per cent of the total workforce in 1954 to 32 per cent in 1970. This was the period of the baby boom, mass migration to the suburbs, and an emphasis on domesticity for women (including working women) and occupational involvement

---

[251] Margaret Power, 'Women and economic crises: the Great Depression and the present crisis', Women & Labour Conference paper, Macquarie University, May 1978, p. 5, published in Windschuttle, op. cit., p. 502.

[252] Richards, op. cit., p. 104.

[253] Bettina Cass and Heather Radi, 'The family: old and new — bread and circuses', paper presented to the Wrong Way — Go Back Conference, in association with the Bicentennial History of Australia project, Sydney University, February 1979. I am indebted to Cora Baldock for the opportunity to read this paper.

[254] Skolnick, op. cit., p. 13.

[255] ibid., pp. 7, 9.

[256] E.J. Hobsbawm, *The crisis and the outlook*, Socialist Society, Student Union, Birkbeck College, London, 1975.

for men.[257] All of this seemed to refute an earlier generation of social scientists who had forecast the erosion of the family in urban industrial societies.

The 1950s was also the period when the dominant mood of the social sciences was confidence and certainty; sociologists, anthropologists and psychologists felt no need to question the assumptions about the nature of the family and its relation to the rest of society which were embedded in the questions that they set out to answer, and hence in the answers that they constructed. Thus, even a group of sociologists challenging Parsonian orthodoxy by arguing that the 'modified extended family' was the norm in modern society did not challenge the 'naturalness' or centrality of the nuclear family as the basic unit of household organisation and socialisation. Similarly, anthropologists encountering domestic arrangements which looked very different from the standard image of the nuclear family translated them, often ingeniously, into an underlying nuclear type. Their work confirmed the prevailing belief that all societies, at all times, had — despite surface differences — consisted of collections of identical ideal nuclear family units.[258]

By the late 1960s, however, the long period of affluence in the advanced industrial countries had begun to generate its own difficulties.[259] Firstly, the increasing complexities of technical production required increasing and more specialised skills of productive workers. They also alienated the worker from his or her work even more than had the productive processes of an earlier stage of our industrial development; workers were no longer alienated merely from the product of their labour, but from production altogether. They only supervised what the machine produced. Secondly, for production to expand at the rate of the 1950s, it was necessary for consumption to expand as well. Accordingly, increasing numbers of people were employed in extending the market — 'For each new product a new advertisement, new copy-writer, new lay-out girl, new transmission operator, a new need in the buyer ... '[260] They worked in areas such as the growing communications industry, and sought to expand the consciousness of the population in order to expand the variety and

---

[257]   Arlene Skolnick, 'The family revisited: themes in recent social sciences research', *Journal of Interdisciplinary History*, vol. 5, no. 4, Spring 1975, pp. 706-7; Sol Encel, Norman Mackenzie and Margaret Tebbutt, *Women and society: an Australian study*, Cheshire, Melbourne, 1974, pp. 72-3.

[258]   Skolnick, 'The family revisited', p. 707.

[259]   The analysis in this paragraph is drawn from Mitchell, *Woman's estate*, pp. 29-33.

[260]   ibid., p. 29.

quantity of products that the population would consume. But, as English feminist Juliet Mitchell pointed out:

> Expanding the consciousness of many (for the sake of expanding consumerism) *does* mean expanding their consciousness. And the products of this expanded consciousness are more elusive than those of the factory conveyor belt. The ideologies cultivated in order to achieve ultimate control of the market (the free choice of the individual of whatever brand of car suits his individuality) are ones which can rebel *in their own terms*. The cult of the individual can surpass its use by the system to become that radical revolt of 'do-your-own-thing'. The cult of 'being true to your own feelings' becomes dangerous when those feelings are no longer ones that the society would like you to feel … The media that enables you to *experience* the feelings of the world, brings the Vietcong guerilla into your own living room along with the whitest wash of all.[261]

And, to add another example to Mitchell's, the command to develop your personality (in your choice of clothing, for instance) can become — for a twenty-four-year-old housewife, a former clerical worker who had left school at the age of sixteen — a direct conflict between her chosen domestic labour and her observation:

> You know it does get boring. And I can understand because we've been educated a lot higher than housework, you know. I think that's the downfall. If you're educated that way you should keep your mind occupied.[262]

The contradiction between the need for greater skill in the workforce and the greater alienation of the skilled worker, the contradiction between the need for expanded consciousness among consumers and the likelihood of consciousness expanding into life-conditions beyond those concerned with consumption — both contradictions achieved their clearest focus in the late 1960s in the various institutions of tertiary education that mushroomed throughout countries like ours to supply those needs.[263] So, not surprisingly, it was largely in, and from, the institutions of higher learning that the radicalism of the late 1960s erupted in the struggles for black power, student power, the rights of youth (including, in the USA and Australia, draft resisters), and finally in the Women's Liberation Movement.

---

[261] ibid., p. 31, emphases in the original.

[262] Richards, op. cit., p. 153.

[263] Mitchell, op. cit., p. 28; Power, op. cit., p. 7.

All of these changes found a reflex in the social sciences which began to question the assumptions and biases underlying the whole structure of their theory and research, and to pay more attention to the theories emphasising conflict and change. This development modified considerably studies of family life. Psychologists began to understand children as more complex and self-determining than previously, and to construct more indeterminate and conflict-ridden models of the process of socialisation. Anthropologists began exploring variation in both the social facts of family life and the ideologies that surround it, and hence to raise doubts that such concepts as 'marriage', 'family', 'kinship' and 'household' refer to anything in one society that can be compared precisely and empirically with the institutions of another society. Sociologists began investigating family violence, and recalling the views of an earlier generation of social theorists, including Max Weber, who took it for granted that conflict was a normal part of family life. 'Intimate relations', they argued, 'inevitably involve antagonism as well as love, and it is precisely this intertwining of strong positive and negative feelings that distinguishes intimacy from secondary or segmental relationships'.[264] Psychiatrists, particularly those associated with R.D. Laing and what became known as the anti-psychiatry movement, began concluding from their observation of the interaction of whole families that 'the concept of a psychiatrically "normal" family is coming to seem as abstract and empty as the concept of a "universal" nuclear family that is the same everywhere'.[265]

Such work called into question the extent to which the image of the ideal nuclear family which I described earlier had ever, or anywhere, fitted the realities of the relationships and processes labeled 'family life'. Domestic groups, such work tells, are far more varied — from one culture to another; within one culture, from one period to the next; and within one culture and period, from one group to another. The nuclear family is no more 'natural', no more determined by human biology and psychology, than any other of our social institutions. Domestic groups are not abnormal if they are not harmonious. Nor if they are not particularly stable. We have yet to determine whether they would be if they were not patriarchal.

Yet all of this work seems to have made little impact upon the ideal image of the nuclear family which is so widely and strongly held in Australia that we take it

---

264   Skolnick, 'The family revisited', p. 715.
265   Skolnick, *Intimate environment*, p. 66.

for granted. Australian sociologist Lyn Richards, who undertook research on 'why people marry and have children, what problems they meet when they do so' for the Royal Commission on Human Relationships in 1976, published some of her findings in a book called *Having Families*. The chapter headed 'Why Marry?' is divided into two sections: one is called 'They had to get married', the other 'I was ready to settle down'. In the first she discusses the response of a small proportion of the people she interviewed who were pregnant when they married. She concluded:

> But all would have married. More important, it cannot be said that *any* couple faced with premarital pregnancy was pushed into marriage by direct social pressure. The pressure in all cases was less direct and in important respects preceded pregnancy — marriage for all of them was inevitable anyway.[266]

In the second section, discussing the reasons given for marriage by people whom she interviewed who were not premaritally pregnant, Richards quoted one reply — 'But you will marry'. And commented:

> That was the assumption behind almost all comments, even of the few who had not wanted to … Asked, 'Before you decided to marry your husband/wife, were you wanting to get married about then anyway?' Only a quarter said no. And they almost all nevertheless expected to sometime …[267]

But few of the three-quarters who had wanted to marry at about the time they did could say why. Most of them clearly regarded it as a novel question, and on consideration gave replies that amounted to: 'It was the thing to do'.[268]

So, too, was having children, as a subsequent chapter shows. 'For almost all the respondents', Richards noted, 'there had been no consideration of the alternative'.

Such evidence may not argue that expectations of relationships in the nuclear family are wholly romantic. But nor does it argue that there is widespread scepticism or wariness of the nuclear family as an institution likely to bring boredom, loneliness, misery or strife. Further, though this might be because all the people whom Richards interviewed *were* married, there was no suggestion of people preferring to remain single, or childless, or both, or to experiment with other forms of domestic arrangement. Rather, the most common expectation of life was of life in a nuclear family, and the

---

[266] Richards, op. cit., p. 68, emphasis in the original.

[267] ibid., p. 80.

[268] ibid.

most common expectation of what that would be like was probably best summarised by one of Richard's respondents. She said, and without any intended irony:

> It's one of those things, *it's a bit like death*, you know, I don't think you can go into training for … One tends not to think a lot about it except that it's all beaut and starry and what have you.[269]

The image of the ideal nuclear family that we have held since the 1950s is, then, still alive and well and with us. And this is so despite recent investigations by social scientists which challenge belief in it as accurate description. It is so despite even direct experience that contradicts such belief. The woman whom I just quoted went on to say:

> The one thing we should know more about I guess is that it's … a terribly difficult thing to put two people together and expect them to, er, put up with each other for hours and hours a day seven days a week, it's a bit much to expect.[270]

The paradox with which I began is resolved by such evidence into a gap between ideal and reality. This has undoubtedly always existed. But there is evidence now to suggest that the gap is probably widening, and will continue to do so — unless the prevailing image of the ideal domestic unit should change. For the processes at work in our society now, and likely to continue over the next twenty years, are being accompanied by profound changes within households. And these cannot avoid impinging on precisely those relationships which are idealised in the image of the ideal family group.

Many of these processes concern women. In an important article published in 1978, sociologist Bettina Cass summarised some 'highly significant structural changes which have altered the life-conditions of women in the twentieth century', particularly in the period since the Second World War. These are:

1. The widespread dissemination and use of contraception (and abortion) which has enabled women to control their fertility and reduce their family size from an average issue of six children in 1901 to three children in 1942, with a continuing reduction in family size since then.
2. The increased longevity of women, as well as men, and the decrease in child mortality. Not only do women bear fewer children in order to have

---

269   ibid., p. 87, emphasis added.
270   ibid., p. 84.

a living issue of two or three, but they have a long span of life ahead when their child-bearing and early child-rearing years are complete. Early marriage, a concentrated period of child-bearing, and return to the workforce at ages thirty to thirty-five has become a typical pattern.

3. The dissemination of education, of longer years of schooling, to more groups in the community, particularly to women, whose retention rate in the secondary schools has increased substantially in the post war period. In 1954, 6.8% of girls aged seventeen were still at school, in 1970, 23.7%. In addition, women in their late twenties and thirties are returning to secondary and tertiary education in the 1970s, taking up opportunities not available to them in their adolescence.

4. The increased opportunities for women's employment which were opened up with the post-war expansion of the tertiary sectors of the economy. Women's workforce experience is a factor in their release from isolated, housebound activities ... It is not only an independent source of income, but an independent set of group-affiliations which are the precursors of women's individualistic action (in one sense) and collectivist action in relation to women's needs.

5. Women with higher levels of education, with careers or professional occupations, are the group most likely to postpone marriage, to choose not to marry at all or when married, to have fewer children. In other words, the conditions exist for more women to move out of the set of material conditions (dependence, subordination, child-bearing and rearing in nuclear family units) within which most women have been immersed and still are immersed.[271]

Such changes clearly have important ramifications for both the structure and the nature of relationships within the nuclear family. But before spelling them out, we might usefully consider how they are being affected by changes in the economy. For the period which, in advanced industrial countries, set full employment and unprecedented affluence side by side with the struggles for black power, students' rights and the liberation of women — that period is now over. The economies of the first world are now undergoing a severe crisis. Its effects in Australia, Ted Wheelwright estimates, will be — 'less export-led growth in the next twenty years than in the last

---

[271] Bettina Cass, 'Women's place in the class structure', in E.L. Wheelwright and Ken Buckley (eds), *Essays in the political economy of Australian capitalism*, vol. 3, Australia and New Zealand Book Company, Sydney, 1978, p. 37.

twenty'; closer integration into the world capitalist economy (perhaps 'by dismantling much farther its manufacturing industry, and becoming a "service" economy serving foreign capital and the needs of the industrialized countries for raw materials and markets for finished goods'); and consequently

> built-in structural unemployment for those with the least market power — the young, women, migrants and aborigines.[272]

It would be rash indeed for anyone as ignorant of economics as I am to venture modifications to Wheelwright's forecast. But there are questions that we need to ask about such predictions — one relating to what the developed world has been calling the energy crisis, the other three to the structural changes which Cass summarised — questions that we need to answer if we are to attempt any guesses about the future of the family in our society.

Firstly, then, will not the increasing cost of energy to the developed world affect domestic groups by making domestic labour more labour-intensive? And can we expect that, as petrol prices increase, fewer domestic groups will have more than one, or even one, car? Might this not isolate the already isolated suburban dwellings of nuclear families even more, from centres of employment, shopping centres, kin and friends?

Secondly, if women continue to live for longer and to spend fewer years of their lives bearing and rearing children, what are they to do if structural unemployment prevents them rejoining the paid workforce? Answers to the second question could be found in the first — women will spend more of their time scrubbing, polishing, baking, preserving, washing, ironing and preparing meals; in other words, structural unemployment and increasing energy costs might lead to the deification not of motherhood but of the housewife. Someone once asked why women should be thought to have married a house. Perhaps we may yet see. But in case we should seriously entertain the possibility of this happening, we should be warned of the social costs that such a combination of developments would entail: listen to these four Australian comments on house-bound isolation:

> 'Who am I? I don't know …. I'm just — I'm really just Michael's mother and Jeff's wife you know, and that would be all, I suppose'.

---

[272] E.L. Wheelwright, *Capitalsm, socialism or barbarism? The Australian predicament. Essays in contemporary political economy*, Australia and New Zealand Book Company, Sydney, 1978, pp. 22-3.

'Well it was either stay at home and go off my head and getting all neurotic and bitchy, which I was'.

'Well I was tense in myself. I can remember getting very close to battering her at times'.

'I think I remember one big nightmare, some days better and some days absolutely shocking'.[273]

English sociologist, Ann Oakley, noted that the *International Year Book of Neurology, Psychiatry and Neurosurgery* now recognises something it calls, simply, 'housewife's disease', and pointed out that

> [a] United States study of psychological-stress symptoms finds the highest symptom rates among fulltime housewives (compared with employed housewives and employed men). The fulltime housewives had high symptom rates for fainting, hand trembling, inertia, nervous breakdowns, heart palpitations, and dizziness. Retired men showed similar rates, suggesting that restriction to the home, with its concomitant social isolation, is a critical factor.[274]

However, there are countervailing considerations, which prompt the third and fourth questions.

Thirdly, then, figures published by the Australian Bureau of Statistics for May 1978 show that while women still constitute only just over a third of the total labour force, the majority of employed women — 62 per cent — are married.[275] Moreover, these women amount to over 40 per cent of all women who are married.[276] Among these women, and in sharp contrast to the proportions in the male workforce, the proportion in part-time work (42 per cent) is not much less than the proportion in full-time work (58 per cent).[277] That 42 per cent is the one major increase in the workforce in the last few years: 'Between May 1972 and May 1977 only 30 per cent

---

273   Quoted in Richards, op. cit., pp. 158, 162, 169, 170.

274   Ann Oakley, *Housewife*, Penguin, Harmondsworth, 1976, p. 232.

275   Women's Bureau, Department of Employment and Youth Affairs, *Facts on women at work in Australia 1978*, Australian Government Publishing Service, Canberra, 1979, p. 7.

276   Meredith Edwards, 'Taxation and the family unit: social aspects', paper delivered to a seminar organised by the Taxation Institute Research and Education Trust, Sydney, May 1979. I am indebted to Meredith Edwards, and Sara Dowse, for the opportunity to read this paper.

277   Women's Bureau, op. cit., p. 19.

of the growth in jobs was in full-time jobs; 70 per cent was in part-time jobs'.[278] And, as Margaret Power commented, 'It is not surprising that employers use part-time work to reduce labour costs. This cheapening of the labour process will be greater if women part-time workers are employed'.[279] There is some, though very scrappy, evidence that employers appreciate the extra intensity of work that can be gained from married women in part-time employment. Might this not suggest that at least some married women, even with the inequities and disadvantages that they encounter in the workforce, have more market power than Wheelwright allows?

Fourthly, and finally: Cass's observation of the increasing dissemination of education particularly to women can be expanded. The Australian Bureau of Statistics reports that

> [t]he gap between the numbers of males and females progressing from school
> to tertiary education is currently minimal. Of males who left school in 1975,
> 50.6% were doing tertiary courses in May 1976. The proportion of females
> who left school in 1975 and who were doing tertiary courses in May 1976 was
> only slightly lower — 49.8%.[280]

People gaining tertiary education are the people who are responding to advancing technology's need for an increasing level of skill in the labour force, and also to a consumption-orientated economy's need for a consciousness expanded to want not only to be able to consume *more* products but also to be able to *choose which* products to consume. These are the people who enter the professional and technical occupation groups, which absorb a considerably higher percentage of the female than the male workforce.[281] There are also the people who, again as I noted earlier, are most likely to expand their consciousness beyond the requirements of consumerism, to want to choose not only which brand of plastic bread to eat, but also — and consciously — whether or not to marry, to have children, and if they do, how to distribute domestic labour, consumption and authority within the domestic groups that they form, and whether or not to change either the shape of the domestic group, or their involvement with it, or both, as they grow older. If women participate in

---

278   Power, op. cit., p. 6.

279   ibid.

280   Women's Bureau, op. cit., p. 26.

281   ibid., p. 21; see also David Cox, 'Working married women and youth unemployment', Women's Advisory Unit, Premier's Department, South Australia, Adelaide, October 1978. I am indebted to Mary Sexton for the opportunity to read this paper.

equal, or even greater, numbers in both tertiary education and the professional and technical occupation groups, is it really likely that the economy could afford to force them out of the workforce? And, returning to the first two questions, is it likely that these women would consent to life as housewives, maids-of-all-work, in increasingly isolated, empty, labour-intensive domestic dwellings?

I said that it would be rash for me to attempt to modify Wheelwright's economic forecast for the next twenty years. But perhaps, towards the end of such a tissue of speculation, the time has come to be rash. It seems to me unlikely that increasing structural unemployment will disadvantage white Australian women — the majority of women in Australia — as much as it will disadvantage the unskilled. Rather, it could be argued that at this moment in their development, capitalist economies need both skills and consciousness and do not care whether they are male or female. In Australia there are a few indications — the equal pay decision of 1972, introduction of paid maternity leave by both federal and state governments, the establishment of offices of equal employment opportunity — which support such a supposition.

Some women undoubtedly will suffer with increasing structural unemployment: those who simultaneously share their initially limited educational experience with all women, and their lack of market power with all the unskilled — the young, the migrant, the Indigenous.[282] For these women, the structural changes which Cass identified as altering the life conditions of women in the twentieth century could grind back into first gear as Australian society gradually polarises into two camps — people with jobs and people without. Whether they do or not may depend chiefly upon their older, skilled, white Australian sisters.

For them, particularly those who are married and in part-time work, Cass's changes will probably continue, more and more rapidly. And these changes may bring with them an increasingly sharp division between women who can find work — the privileged — and women who cannot — the deprived. But, and this seems equally possible, they may not. Australia, like Britain, may witness a spread of white-collar unionism, and a growth in industrial militancy among the skilled which strengthens their allegiance to the unskilled and unemployed, encouraging the development of a hegemonic working-class consciousness.[283] A parallel development

---

[282] Power, op. cit., pp. 6-7.

[283] Royden Harrison, seminar in History, School of General Studies, Australian National University, May 1976.

among women — facilitated by the exploitation of married women in part-time work, who have nothing to lose from job-sharing[284] — would be the spread of what Cass calls 'sex-class consciousness'[285], and what I would prefer to call consciousness of gender solidarity, and hence of gender-based militancy.[286] The consequences of such a development form a subject of discussion within all the component groups of the great umbrella which is usually called the Women's Movement. Such discussion continues, unresolved. But one potential result seems clear: the changes which Cass outlined would continue, at a gathering pace, for all women.

Their impact upon the predominance of the nuclear family as the most common form of domestic group in our society has registered already. The last decade, notes economist Meredith Edwards, has shown marriages lasting for shorter periods, increasing proportions of one-parent families, larger numbers of young men and women leaving their parents' homes for reasons other than marriage, and hence 'a greater diversity of household types than existed just twenty years ago'. The statistics collected in the 1976 census show, she writes, that 'the family, defined in the traditional way as head, spouse and children, comprised only 29% of family types'.[287] Richards commented:

> The demand that we 'save the family', if it means preservation of the old family structures, was in the light of demographic evidence like a call for the return of the dinosaur.[288]

Nevertheless, even as a small uniform island in a sea of varieties — ranging from people living alone, through single parents, childless couples, to small- and large-scale communal groups, all having considerably shorter life spans than groups founded on promises to remain together 'until death do us part' — the nuclear family is probably still the single most common form of domestic group in our society now. Moreover, even if it, too, is becoming a stage in, as distinct from a condition of, people's lives, it seems likely to remain with us for the next twenty years. Richards concluded that

---

284   See Cox, op. cit.

285   Cass, 'Women's place in the class structure', pp. 33-5.

286   One example of gender solidarity over women's conditions of paid employment was the Grunwick strike in England in 1977. See Beatrix Campbell & Val Charlton, 'Grunwick women, why they are striking — and why their sisters are supporting them', *Spare Rib*, no. 61, August 1977.

287   Meredith Edwards, op. cit., pp. 4-5.

288   Richards, op. cit., p. 302.

'if "saving the family" means ... ensuring that most people will go on marrying and having children, the demand is superfluous. They will anyhow'.[289]

Even so the effect of the changes which Cass summarised upon relationships between members of nuclear family units will be, already is, profound. For an increasing number of both women and children, home and family is the focus of their existence for only a small portion of each day — now, roughly about as many hours as it is for men. Women return to work, or to education and work. Children spend as much of their time in school, watching television, or playing with friends, as they spend in contact with parents or siblings. Further, when women earn they simultaneously gain greater economic power, and need greater authority within the family — unless they are to carry a wholly inequitable load of domestic labour, a not uncommon occurrence with social costs that no society can afford.[290] Consequently, Cass's changes accrete, usually in a disconnected and piecemeal way, into a challenge to the father's ultimate economic control, into a challenge to any legitimacy that might have attached to expectations of domestic service performed for a breadwinner by his subordinate dependents, and thence into a challenge to his authority.

Such a challenge must create strain within the relationships of nuclear families. But when, as a present, the challenge is accompanied by the gap between the prevalent image of the ideal nuclear family, and reality — a gap which the challenge to patriarchal authority inevitably widens — then there is even greater strain. It occurs not only between members of a family, but also within individuals suffering various combinations of guilt, resentment, frustration, disillusionment, and bewilderment. Why does this gap survive, apparently unscathed, even after a decade of work by social scientists and community service workers, pointing to the casualties of its existence? Is its continuance simply an instance of ideology lagging behind social change? Or is it maintained as a mystified and mystifying refusal to concede any reduction in the authority of the father, any lessening of the supremacy of the patriarch? At least some feminists would argue that the behaviour of the man in the story that I began with symbolises a last-ditch stand by the patriarchy to maintain its dominance against the challenges brought into being by the present stage in the development of capitalism and capitalist technology.

---

[289] ibid.

[290] It may not be irrelevant to note, here, that there was a striking rise in suicide rates in Australia after 1960, and that the rate among women increased most — indeed doubled. See Basil S. Hetzel, *Health and Australian society*, Penguin, Ringwood, 1974, pp. 141-2.

Whatever the answers to such questions, we can be sure that stress within nuclear family groups will continue, and may even grow, unless something is done to make the idealised image of the family conform more closely to reality. But to call for that might also be a challenge to the supremacy of men.

7

Women and technological change

Invited lecture in a series of Foundation Lectures at the University of Adelaide in 1984 and published in Australian Feminist Studies, *vol. 1, no. 1, Summer 1985. Everything that I wrote that was published in* Australian Feminist Studies — *of which I was the founding editor 1985-2005 — was peer-reviewed. Taylor & Francis, publishers of* Australian Feminist Studies *since 1996, have granted permission for some of that material to appear here.*

I would like to begin with two quotations. The speaker in each is the same: a young man who had gained esteem at his university by making improvements to some chemical instruments. In the first quotation he is speaking about his discoveries in a subsequent piece of research; in the second quotation he is speaking about the object that he made as a result of those discoveries. Here is the first.

> From the midst of this darkness a sudden light broke in upon me — a light so brilliant and wondrous, yet so simple, that while I became dizzy with the immensity of the prospect which it illustrated, I was surprised that among so many men of genius who had directed their enquiries towards that same science, that I alone should be reserved to discover so astonishing a secret … Some miracle may have produced it, yet the stages of the discovery were distinct and probable. After days and nights of incredible labour and fatigue, I succeeded in discovering the cause of generation and life; nay, more, I became myself capable of bestowing animation upon lifeless matter.

> The astonishment which I had first experienced on this discovery soon gave place to delight and rapture ... What had been the study and desire of the wisest men since the creation of the world was now within my grasp.

Here is the second quotation, from two years later in the narrative.

> With an anxiety that almost amounted to agony, I collected the instruments of life around me, that I might infuse a spark of being into the lifeless thing that lay at my feet ... [T]he rain pattered dismally against the panes, and my candle was nearly burnt out, when, by the glimmer of the half-extinguished light, I saw the dull yellow eye of the creature open; it breathed hard, and a convulsive motion agitated its limbs ... I had worked hard for nearly two years, for the sole purpose of infusing life into an inanimate body. For this I had deprived myself of rest and health. I had desired it with an ardour that far exceeded moderation; but now I had finished, the beauty of the dream vanished, breathless horror and disgust filled my heart ... [W]hen those muscles and joints were rendered capable of motion, it became a thing such as even Dante could not have conceived.

Those familiar with this story will have had no difficulty in identifying the speaker as Frankenstein, in the novel of the same name.[291] After constructing and giving life to the creature, which he does not name and from then on refers to only as 'the monster', Frankenstein flees in revulsion, leaving his creation to look after itself. Most of the remainder of the novel, roughly two of its three volumes, recounts the retribution which the creature visits upon him.

This novel raises a cluster of issues relevant to my theme. It was published in 1818, in a period which saw radically new departures in mathematics, chemistry, geology, and the biological and social sciences.[292] There were two conflicting attitudes to scientific and technological progress current at the time. One was the classical rationality which the nineteenth century had inherited from Descartes, from Newton's mechanistic universe, and from the discovery of logically compulsory laws governing the physical world. The other was the far more recent growth of romanticism and its association with the speculative and intuitive researches of natural philosophy, natural

---

[291] Mary Shelley, *Frankenstein; or the modern Prometheus*, first published in three volumes, 1818; republished in Peter Fairclough (ed.), *Three gothic novels*, Penguin, Harmondsworth, 1968, pp. 311-18.

[292] E.J. Hobsbawm, *The age of revolution: Europe 1789-1848*, Cardinal, London, 1973, pp. 340-2, 347-52.

history's concern with the organic unity of all things with each other, and its resistance to precise quantitative measurement and Cartesian clarity.[293] The novel *Frankenstein* can be read as embodying both attitudes, encapsulated in the two passages that I quoted. But the emotional weight of the story all lies with romanticism, expressed in the hero's revulsion when faced with the product of his presumption in usurping the powers of nature, a revulsion which determines the remainder of the story.

Such an emphasis could be considered surprising. The story's author was familiar with current developments in biology, in chemistry, in electricity and in what was called galvanism, and knew that Erasmus Darwin believed an achievement like Frankenstein's to be within the reach of science and technology.[294]

But the author was also Mary Wollstonecraft Shelley, a young woman who could hardly have avoided knowing the effects that technological change was having, at the time she was writing, upon large numbers of women in Britain. In the textile industry, one of the two largest kinds of production in Britain in the eighteenth century, capitalist imperatives had early introduced divisions in the labour process. Similarly, patriarchal imperatives had ensured (on the grounds that women should not compete with men) that those divisions also clearly demarcated women's work from men's work. Women were spinners of wool, cotton, linen, flax and silk; men were weavers. Industrialisation was introduced into spinning in the 1780s in Britain, and while women continued to be the majority of workers in the new water-powered spinning mills, and later in those powered by steam, the mechanisation of spinning greatly reduced the total number of workers that the industry needed to employ. In the early years of the nineteenth century, as Mary Shelley was growing up, technological change meant, for very large numbers of women in many regions of England, destitution.[295]

Besides having good reasons for regarding technological change as menacing, Mary Shelley had considerable personal experience of the perils of generating life. Her mother, the brilliant English feminist, Mary Wollstonecraft, had died giving birth to her. She was pregnant herself in July 1814, when she ran off with the poet Shelley at

[293]   ibid., pp. 352-7.

[294]   Fairclough (ed.), op. cit., p. 267; Ellen Moers, *Literary women*, Doubleday, New York, 1977, p. 144.

[295]   Ivy Pinchbeck, *Women workers and the Industrial Revolution 1750-1850*, Frank Cass, London, 1977 (1930), *passim*; E.J. Hobsbawm, *Industry and empire*, Penguin, Harmondsworth, 1970 (1969), pp. 34-96.

the age of sixteen, and that baby died a month after it was born. She had given birth to another child, one who lived, by the time she began writing *Frankenstein* in June 1816.[296]

One critic has drawn attention to the similarity between Frankenstein's description of the creature that he gave life to, and Dr Spock's description of a newborn baby.[297] But no critic that I know of has yet suggested that *Frankenstein* is the story of a hero who — armed with the instruments of science and technology — usurped not the powers of nature, but rather the single greatest power of the female sex, that of bringing forth new life. The hero's horror at his own creation, his helplessness before the creature's attacks on everyone he loves, his obsession with it and his terror of it — all can be read as the vengeance taken by the feminine upon his overweening, masculine appropriation of the painfully held power of women. It is not the unnamed, un-mothered, abandoned creature that Frankenstein made who is the monster in Mary Shelley's story. It is Frankenstein himself.

Such a reading places Mary Shelley early in, perhaps at the beginning of, a slender, though not inconsiderable, tradition of women's writing which has protested at masculine control of technology and technological change, and its capacity to damage and disadvantage women. That tradition includes Charlotte Brontë: her novel *Shirley* conveys a direct, though implicit, parallel between unemployed men driven to Luddism (attempting to smash the new machines in the mill) and the struggle against the constraints of economic dependence of single, middle-class women.[298] Virginia Woolf, too, nearly a century later, on the eve of the Second World War, explicitly linked that great impetus to scientific and technological advance — war-making — with manliness; militarism with masculinity.[299] And a generation or two later, in May 1984 in Canberra in Australia, Petra Kelly, member of the German Bundestag and co-founder of the German Green Party, made the same point, far less circumspectly than Woolf had. 'Often in the women's movement and in the peace movement', she said,

> there has been the debate, that if women are struggling against the bomb, against deterrence, against nuclearism, they will begin to forget their own

---

[296] Moers, op. cit., pp. 140, 145-7, 148.

[297] ibid., pp. 137, 142.

[298] Charlotte Brontë, *Shirley*, Penguin, Harmondsworth, 1974 (1849), Chapters 10, 19, 20.

[299] Virginia Woolf, *Three guineas*, Harbinger, New York, 1966 (1938), pp. 52-3.

struggle for their own rights. But in fact these are all interconnected. Violence, oppression, domination, are all related ways to keep the powerless in their place. The same respect for machismo that breeds wars also encourages rape, pornography and the battery of women. There can be no peace while one race dominates an other, or one people, one nation, one sex despises an other.[300]

There are several ways of answering this tradition of protest. One would be to dismiss it as uninformed about present developments, to say nothing of being ungrateful. Women, quite as much as men, and children, have derived enormous benefits from advances in science and technology. In societies like our own, they have given us sanitation, clean water supplies, basic hygiene, the vaccines and antibiotics which have eliminated most of the epidemic diseases which once decimated populations across the globe. Our expectation of life and our standards of living have been revolutionised by scientific advances and technological innovation. Who would protest at technologies which have given us electric light, the wireless, the telephone, motor cars, air travel, television and computer games? Who could object to technologies designed to render domestic animals resistant to disease, to improve the hardiness and productivity of a grain crop used widely in the so-called Third World, to further research into the prevention of cancer, or diabetes?[301]

Women, in particular, have benefited from developments in science and technology, in ways that are specific to our sex. Such developments have given us the means of controlling our human reproductive capacity. In the last decade, they have opened up greatly increased opportunities for us to find paid work. In the last few years, they have offered us the possibility of bearing children, even if we, or the men we choose to father those children, should be sterile. Indeed, discussion only recently has suggested that advances in human reproductive technology may soon relieve us of our responsibility in the perpetuation of the species altogether.

But it is precisely those last two so-called benefits of technological change that are at present causing widespread anxiety and anguish among women. It is in relation to precisely those two areas of technological advance that we can already hear new voices raised in the tradition of protest against masculine control of technological change that we encountered in *Frankenstein*.

---

[300] Petra Karin Kelly, 'Women must link arms and have a planetary vision', address to Section 44, Women's Studies, 54th Congress of Australian & New Zealand Association for the Advancement of Science (ANZAAS), 15 May 1984, p. 8.

[301] E.g. *The Bulletin*, 17 September, 1977.

The first arises, partly, because we still live with a dual labour market, a division between women's work and men's work of the kind that developed between spinning and weaving in Britain two centuries ago. Today, 64 per cent of the female paid workforce is employed in only three occupations; clerical, sales and service jobs.[302] The dual labour market has other dimensions as well. The International Labour Organisation has concluded that it is no longer adequate to talk about the labour market in a general sense. It is more accurate to speak of a primary and secondary market. The former, says the ILO, is characterised by high status, stable employment, high skill requirements, high earnings, and good prospects for advancement. The latter displays the opposite traits — low status, high turnover and employment instability, low skill requirements, low earnings and few advancement opportunities. The overwhelming majority of people employed in the secondary labour market are women.[303] In his speech at the opening of the National Technology Conference, September 1983, Australian Prime Minister R.J. Hawke referred to the dual labour market and the seclusion of women in the secondary labour market, and went on to observe, 'In all probability [women] will be among the most seriously disadvantaged if technological improvements are effected in the absence of an appropriate policy framework'.[304]

The reason for this gloomy prognostication begins with a development which is, to industrial production in Australia now, what the application of steam power was to industrial production in Britain in the time of Mary Shelley. This development is labelled, variously, the 'technological revolution', the 'electronic revolution' or the 'cybernetic revolution'. The micro-computer, and its offspring, the super-chip or wafer, have made possible a shift from electro-mechanical to electronic components, and hence the installation of industrial robots in the motor car industry, of computerised exchanges in telecommunications, of computerised cash registers in department stores, supermarkets and petrol stations, and of word-processors and micro-computers in offices.[305] These devices have made possible a restructuring of the

---

[302] Susan Ryan and Gareth Evans, *Affirmative action for women: a policy discussion paper*, Australian Government Publishing Service, Canberra, 1984, pp. 18-19.

[303] Hon. R.J. Hawke, 'Official opening speech', National Technology Conference, *Proceedings and report*, Canberra, 26-28 September 1983, p. 5.

[304] ibid.

[305] Ted Wheelwright, 'Transnational corporations and the new international development of labour: some implications for Australia', in Gareth Evans and John Reeves (eds),

work process in the places where they have been introduced, and such restructuring has created new divisions, not merely between management and labour, but also and predominantly between the skilled jobs associated with design, analysis and assessment, and the less skilled, or de-skilled, jobs which have been fragmented and rendered almost entirely mechanical. Those de-skilled and fragmented jobs have, then, been offered as part-time, rather than full-time, work.[306] Developments of this kind have been taking place in the three sectors of the labour market which have been the major employers of women for more than a decade. And that has brought an enormous increase in the employment of women.

> Between August 1974 and August 1982, part-time job growth accounted for about four-fifths of the overall rise in the employment of women. At August 1983, 36.4% of all employed females compared with only 6.1% of males were in part-time employment. Of all part-time workers, 77.9% were women.[307]

This is in spite of the fact that as many as 21 per cent of those women would prefer to work longer hours than those in the jobs available to them.[308] Clearly, the brunt of the process of de-skilling and fragmenting jobs, which the super-chip has made possible, is being borne by the people in the secondary labour market, a labour market consisting almost entirely of women.

This development has three consequences which are already with us, and the potential for a fourth which the Prime Minister hinted at. The first is one which has not been widely recognised yet, even by the unions. The process of de-skilling and fragmenting sections of the work process has meant that the worker at the keyboard end of the process is given no understanding of where her module fits in the whole process, nor is she consulted about advisable ways of dividing that process up.[309] Her contribution to the whole process has become so mechanical that she might as well be a robot herself. This has been causing stress among those workers in ways which are

---

Labour essays 1980, Drummond, Richmond, 1980, p. 98; Allen McArdle, 'Unemployment — a question without an answer?', unpublished address to the Industrial Relations Society of New South Wales at Bathurst, 22 April 1979, pp. 4-6.

[306] See, e.g., Sandra Prerost, 'Technological change and women's employment in Australia', and Red Fems, 'The implications of technological change for women workers in the public sector', both in Margaret Bevege, Margaret James and Carmel Shute (eds), *Worth her salt: women at work in Australia*, Hale & Iremonger, Sydney, 1982.

[307] Ryan and Evans, op. cit., p. 22.

[308] ibid.

[309] See, e.g., Red Fems, op. cit., pp. 152-4.

only now beginning to be acknowledged. The Senior Occupational Therapist of the Capital Territory Health Commission presented a paper on 'The Health Implications of Screen Based Equipment for Women Workers' to the Women's Studies section of the ANZAAS Congress in May 1984. In it, she identified 'lack of control over job situation' as one of four factors generating the job stress that is bringing workers to her for help.[310] Her point was elaborated in another paper presented in the same session by the Senior Industrial Officer of the Tasmanian Public Service Association. Union guidelines, she observed, focus on individual workstations and the design of individual jobs, rather than on job design and work organisation.[311] Both speakers agreed that what they politely called 'specialisation' is already an important work hazard for those workers, and that it must soon enter employer or management considerations since it is reducing productivity.

The second consequence of such 'specialisation' is a range of phenomena that we have all heard referred to as 'repetition strain injury'. They are 'musculotendinous injuries of the upper limbs, shoulder girdle and neck, caused by over-load of particular muscle groups from repeated use, or by the maintenance of constrained postures'.[312] Such injuries are often associated with jobs where workers have to match the pace of their work to a machine, and where there is frequent pressure to meet deadlines. These injuries may, at worst, render a worker incapable of work altogether. At best, they keep her out of work for a protracted period of time, since the only cure available seems to be rest. But work is not the whole of any worker's life, particularly if it is only a part-time job. A newsletter produced by a firm of Melbourne solicitors has recently drawn attention to the broader implications of the repetition strain injury. It 'involves every aspect of a person's life', they observed.

> It is common for everyday tasks such as twisting a door knob or tap or
> performing simple domestic chores to present considerable pain … In many

---

[310] Kerry Liddicoat, 'The health implications of screen based equipment for women workers', Section 4, Women's Studies, 54th Congress of ANZAAS, Australian National University, 17 May 1984, p. 2.

[311] Margaret Thurstans, 'Restructuring the workplace for keyboard workers', Section 44, Women's Studies, 54th Congress of ANZAAS, Australian National University, 17 May 1984, pp. 6-7.

[312] Liddicoat, op. cit., p. 2; see also Mary McLeod (Manpower Forecasting Unit, South Australian Department of Labour), 'Repetition injury — recognition and prevention', unpublished paper, 12 July 1983. I am grateful to Mary for lending me a copy of this paper.

cases [they continued], and especially in the case of married women, the family must take over a large share of the injured worker's domestic duties. As often no external signs of the injury are present, this is often a source of conflict [particularly] as this injury may continue for many months or years ... The general dilapidation of the social relationships of the worker is often interpreted by [a] medical practitioner as supporting the view that the condition is psychiatric or psychological in origin ... Given the stresses already placed on the worker the severity of such an insult can cause greater stress. There have been several cases of suicide as a direct result of reaction to a repetitive strain injury.[313]

This result of technological advance is being felt by workers in large Japanese firms like Mitsumi Electrical[314], quite as much as by keyboard workers in Adelaide. And their employers face the prospect of paying large awards for damages, if courts in other places follow precedents set in New South Wales.[315]

The third consequence of the impact of the super-chip has not, as far as I know, appeared in Australia yet, but it is already established in Britain, though to only a small extent. This is the appearance of the new 'home worker' data processors working in their own households. 'Cheap computing power, allied to the telephone grid (and, in the near future, to cable and satellite networks), can make it less expensive and more efficient to take work to and from the worker rather than to transport the worker to the workplace.'[316] So far, these workers are highly skilled professionals with about ten years' experience, but it is predicted that, once cable networks are widely operative, high-tech homeworking will spread rapidly downmarket. These workers, overwhelmingly married women in their thirties with young children to care for, have quite enough interruptions to their work to prevent them incurring repetition strain injuries, or stress and depression resulting from 'specialisation'. But nearly two-thirds of them suffer a sense of isolation, and for some, this is very acute.

One programmer sometimes found the need for like-minded companionship so great that she would get into her car and drive fourteen miles to see another

313   Maurice Blackburn and Co., *Newsletter*, no. 8, November/December 1983.

314   Nakajima Keiko, 'Women organize to tackle the world of new technology', *Japan-Asia Quarterly Review*, vol. 15, no. 2, 1983. I am grateful to Sandra Buckley, Asian Studies, University of Adelaide, for providing me with a copy of this article.

315   Blackburn and Co., op. cit.

316   Ursula Huws, 'The new home workers', *New Society*, 22 March 1984, pp. 454-5.

homeworker employed by the same company, 'just for a bit of human contact and understanding'. Another admitted that she sometimes cried from sheer loneliness.[317]

The fourth, potential, consequence of the spread of the super-chip, the one which Prime Minister Hawke alluded to, may well remedy the other three that I've outlined. In 1980, the economist Joy Selby-Smith observed that

> because women are disproportionately concentrated in those occupations where the spread of micro-electronics is likely to be comparatively rapid, women will disproportionately bear the burden of job displacement imposed by the widespread adoption of this technology.[318]

The secondary labour market, at least as it is composed at present, could disappear altogether, women being replaced by machines. There would seem to be good reason for women to regard technological change with some apprehension.

Of course, one of the major factors contributing to such an alarming prospect, and to the existence of the dual labour market, is the sexual division in labour in the domestic sphere. Women are the bearers, and in most societies, the primary nurturers, of children. At least they have been so far in human history. However, advances in reproductive technology now make it possible to ask if women will continue to fulfil this function.

Human reproductive technology is developing with lightning speed, said John Leeton, Professor of Gynaecology at Monash University and the Queen Victoria Medical Centre, in May 1984.[319] The pioneering work that Patrick Steptoe and Robert Edwards began in Britain in the late 1960s resulted in the birth, in 1978, of Louise Brown, the world's first test-tube baby.[320] By 1984 in May, 450 more test-tube babies had been born, 200 of them in Australia.[321] Such information represents a

---

[317]   ibid.

[318]   Joy Selby-Smith, 'Developments in microelectronic technology and their impact on women in paid employment', *Australian Quarterly Review*, Summer 1980, quoted in Ryan and Evans, op. cit., pp. 22-3.

[319]   My own notes taken while listening to Professor Leeton speaking to his paper, 'Present and future aspects of infertility treatment: *in vitro* fertilisation, frozen embryos, donor eggs, surrogacy', Section 44, ANZAAS, op. cit.

[320]   Helga Kuhse, 'Ethical issues in *in vitro* fertilisation and related technologies', Section 44, ANZAAS, op. cit.

[321]   Notes, Leeton, op. cit.

remarkable achievement in overcoming human infertility. But the *in vitro* fertilisation techniques developed for this purpose offer possibilities with very much more far-reaching implications, for this technological advance has made human genetic material available for manipulation and use.

People who are not engaged in such research might well find it difficult to imagine what kind of manipulation or use could be made of such material. I did, before I began reading about it. Here are some of the possibilities I gleaned from my reading. Dr Helga Kuhse, of the Centre for Human Bioethics at Monash University, has suggested two kinds of possible use of human genetic material: to create embryos which are not intended to result in mature living human beings, and to create embryos which are intended to become mature human beings. In the first case, she observes:

> Human embryos could be used to examine a myriad of as yet unanswered
> questions regarding early human development, including the causes of various
> birth defects and their prevention ... They could also be used for the production
> of embryonic or foetal tissue ... [which] could be used to treat diabetes in
> children and adults, and it might even be possible to repair spinal injuries,
> giving back to paraplegics the mobility they have lost.[322]

These possibilities hinge on the claim that immunological rejection is less with foetal tissue than with adult tissue. Kuhse does not say how soundly, or weakly, that claim has been established. But since she does say that embryonic or foetal tissue has, so far, been available only from spontaneous or therapeutic abortions, she implies that there is at least some evidence to support the claim.[323] Such uses of the capacity that the reproductive technologists have developed, to grow human embryos artificially, would seem to be indisputably benign. In the second case, however, the creation of human embryos which are intended to become mature human beings, Kuhse retreats into a question: 'What sort of people should there be?'

Dr Robyn Rowland, a social psychologist at Deakin University, avoids the huge moral absolutes raised by that question, to ask a different one: what has reproductive technology on other animals developed so far? Her answer focuses on the variety of techniques available. Parthenogenesis, the production of an embryo from an egg without fertilisation by sperm, has been used to induce birth in mice, rats and ferrets. Cloning, by any one of a number of methods, has been carried out successfully with

---

[322]   Kuhse, op. cit., p. 7.

[323]   ibid.

frogs.[324] Genetic engineering can produce an almost new species: in one experiment, a growth hormone gene was taken from a rat and introduced into the embryo of a mouse; the result was a mouse twice the normal size, which its human parents designated the 'super mouse'. Genetic engineering can also produce hybrid species: people at the Institute of Animal Physiology at Cambridge in England took two cells from a four-cell sheep embryo and replaced them with two cells taken from the embryo of a goat. The resulting offspring was a mixture of the two animals. Behind Rowland's question lies another one which is only implied: what does the work that the reproductive technologists have done already suggest about what they might be inclined to do with human genetic material? She does not answer that question, though she does point out that human/animal hybrids are already possible.[325] That is a prospect that would have been unthinkable in Mary Shelley's time; the appearance of English writer Maureen Duffy's novel, *Gor Saga*, in 1983, can be seen as an indication of how easy it is, now, to imagine a version of Mary Shelley's hero using the techniques of *in vitro* fertilisation to see what would happen if he combined his own sperm with the egg of a gorilla.[326]

Of course, women have no monopoly of anxieties about the outcome of technological change in this field of human endeavour. Some men as well as some women have deemed any tampering with human embryonic material morally repugnant. Governments have instituted inquiries into the ethical, legal and moral questions that surround all aspects of human reproductive technology. General public controversy will continue, at least as long as the considerations which led to so much secrecy blanketing this research continue to hold sway. But women have a relationship to this kind of technological change which, even more than their relationship to the developments introduced by the technology of the super-chip, is distinct from that of men. And that prompts questions about reproductive technology that are often also different from the questions that men ask. Would the possibility of producing hybrid species lead to the development of an animal/human species to replace the women who at present constitute the secondary labour market? Would not the introduction

[324] Robyn Rowland, 'Of woman born? The relationship of women to reproductive technology', draft course-book for Women's Studies, Deakin University. I am grateful to Robyn for the opportunity to discuss her ideas with her, and to Susan Sheridan for lending me a copy of the course-book.

[325] Rowland, op. cit., p. 22.

[326] Maureen Duffy, *Gor saga*, Methuen, London, 1983.

of general sex preselection in a society that advantages men lead to a whole generation of male babies? Would not the development of ectogenesis, with artificial wombs and placentas, not render women superfluous in human reproduction? There is a hideous logic which, by bringing together the two kinds of technological change that I've been considering, would present the solutions to problems raised by both in a proposal for a technologically controlled breeding program that eliminated women altogether.

For anyone to argue against technological change, *per se*, in Australia in the mid-1980s, would be about as useful, productive and satisfying as whispering into the teeth of a howling gale. The Australian Government has placed technological change at the centre of its strategies for the recovery of the Australia economy.[327] Against this, we — women — will continue to protest, just as the forerunners in the tradition I've outlined protested, against the domination of technological change by the masculine. And anyone who paid close attention to the examples that I gave earlier will recall not only the progressive directness and stridency that such protests have developed through time, but also the increased politico-cultural power accorded, even in patriarchal societies, to those voicing such protests. Governments that are serious about objectives such as the second in South Australia's strategy for technological change — that 'the political, civil and human rights of both individuals and groups should not be adversely affected by the application of technology'[328] — will not be able to avoid hearing us. Moreover, they know that we contribute more to the welfare of society than the work for which we gain wages and our capacity to bear children. They, like other governments, and non-governmental bodies, know that they cannot afford, economically, to lose the resources that women contribute to our society.

Hearing these protests, and making a genuine response to them, could require a lot of hard rethinking among the present agents of technological change. It may even involve them in active participation in the Australian Government's policy of affirmative action in the employment of women. Consider how programs for reproductive technology might alter if the people making decisions about what should happen to frozen embryos were the feminist collective running a Women's

---

[327]   Department of Science and Technology, 'National technology strategy: discussion draft', April 1984.

[328]   *A technology strategy for South Australia*, draft for Parliamentary Debate, 12 April 1984, p. 1.

Health Centre, instead of the men at the head of the research teams in the hospitals and universities. Taking account of the perspective from which these protests are expressed requires more than simply adding it to an already established list. You don't simply add the idea that the world is round to the idea that the world is flat. The directions of movement in the two kinds of technological change that I've considered could result in monumental social dislocation, unless the architects of technological change ensure that their policies acknowledge that the world is round.

8

Dreams and desires: four 1970s feminist visions of utopia

First published in Australian Feminist Studies, *vol. 22, no. 53, July 2007, pp. 325-41.*

'The challenge', wrote Marilyn Lake — describing Women's Liberation as 'The Great Awakening' — 'was to invent new frames of reference, new forms of knowledge, new modes of living'.[329] Late twentieth-century feminists could, and did, readily produce critiques of the current positioning of women, of ways of thinking about women, of relations between women and men. But at least some of the most compelling emotional potency of such critiques emerged when they were positioned in contrast with a vision of an entirely different cultural, political and social order, an imagined ideal, a utopia.

Activist feminists from a century earlier in Australia understood this well. Henrietta Dugdale, for instance, elected president of the Victorian Women's Suffrage Society in 1885, was also the author of a short novel titled *A Few Hours in a Far-Off Age*.[330] It depicts a society called Alethia, several centuries in the future, that vantage point providing a position for perception and analysis of the evils of the late nineteenth-century present. Most of the action takes place in a city of clusters of

---

[329] Marilyn Lake, op. cit, p. 230.

[330] Mrs. H.A. Dugdale, *A few hours in a far-off age*, McCarron, Bird & Co., Melbourne, 1883.

huge buildings that are 'truly works of art'.[331] Dugdale held that the key to women's emancipation was education, so, not surprisingly, these buildings are Instruction Galleries, each alcove equipped with a display cabinet and books demonstrating some aspect of past life among humans. There, young people of both sexes from the age of seven to early adulthood are taught by their parents for two mornings a week. The substance of that education, which occupies most of the novel, involves a thorough-going critique of 'what was once called the "Christian Era," subsequently designated by historians as "The Age of Blood and Malevolence"'[332], lasting — presciently if over-optimistically — *until* the twenty-first century.

The principal target in the present that Alethia's future perspective identifies was, Mrs Dugdale declared, 'what has been, during all the ages, the greatest obstacle to human advancement; the most irrational, fiercest and most powerful of our world's monsters — the only devil — MALE IGNORANCE'.[333] The work illustrates this dictum, encapsulating Dugdale's conviction that women were more morally and emotionally intelligent than men, as well as more technologically competent, in its account of a kind of technological innovation that would come to be considered characteristic of twentieth-century science fiction. Transport in Aletha is provided by vehicles that can fly.[334] One is 'a handsome, comfortably constructed carriage' which starts when one of its passengers moves a small handle: it rises over the throngs of people, clear of the buildings into the air[335], apparently soundlessly, and can travel at about eighty miles an hour.[336] Another, called 'Scud', is a new invention which can fly much faster, 140 miles an hour.[337] When men first devised flying machines, even with the most skilled guiding them, 'they frequently collided several hundred feet above the ground, and went crashing through the air — a burning tangled mass! Corpses sometimes fell upon living persons in the streets', elaborated Dugdale, with relish, 'adding to the dread scene of cruel deaths'.[338] What has subsequently made these vehicles safe is a device called a 'Repellor' which activates a 'Repelling Current'

[331] ibid., p. 5.
[332] ibid., p. 7.
[333] ibid., 'Dedication', emphasis in the original.
[334] ibid., p. 7.
[335] ibid., p. 73.
[336] ibid., p. 83.
[337] ibid., p. 100.
[338] ibid., p. 40.

ensuring that no vehicles can bang into each other. The crucial invention was, of course, the work of a woman.[339]

This largely neglected novella belongs with Catherine Spence's reworking of the ideas of Scotswoman Jane Hume Clapperton in *A Week in the Future*.[340] Both Dugdale's and Spence's works were Australian forerunners of the North American novel held to be the foundation text of modern future-vision — utopian-feminist fiction: Charlotte Perkins Gilman's *Herland*.[341] All three connect with an older non-feminist tradition which includes Plato's *Republic*, Thomas More's *Utopia* (1516), Francis Bacon's *New Atlantis* (1627), Edward Bellamy's *Looking Backward* (1888), William Morris's *News From Nowhere* (1890) and H.G. Wells's *A Modern Utopia* (1905). The term 'utopia', once a term meaning good *place* — or 'no place', the implication being that nowhere could match the virtues being depicted — has undergone translation in the post-Enlightenment centuries so that it is now more often a term referring to a better, future *time*.[342] The impulse to create a utopian vision is integrally optimistic; late twentieth-century theorist Ruth Levitas considers that the word 'utopia' refers to the expression of a *desire* for different, better, ways of being, a view owing something to Ernst Bloch's study, *The Principle of Hope*, and his view that such an impulse 'is grounded in our capacity to fantasize beyond our experience, and in our ability to rearrange the world around us (he calls this "forward dawning" ...)'.[343] Feminist utopian thinking has, as feminist critic Anne K. Mellor noticed, forged a close link with the literary genre of science fiction, 'a genre which provides the opportunity to test various hypotheses concerning societal organization

[339] ibid., p. 40-1.

[340] Catherine Helen Spence, *A week in the future*, serialised in the *Centennial Magazine: An Australian Monthly*, December 1888-July 1889. Republished with Introduction and Notes by Lesley Ljungdahl, Hale & Iremonger, Sydney, 1987.

[341] Charlotte Perkins Gilman, *Herland*, 1915, republished with Introduction and Notes by Ann J. Lane, Pantheon Books, New York, 1979. Lucy M. Freibert, 'World views in utopian novels by women', *Journal of Popular Culture*, vol. 17, Summer 1983, p. 49; Lucy Sussex, 'Introduction', in Lucy Sussex and Judith Raphael Buckridge (eds), *She's fantastical*, Sybylla Co-operative Press and Publications Limited, Melbourne, 1995, p. 14.

[342] Andrew Milner, Matthew Ryan and Robert Savage, 'Introduction', in Andrew Milner, Matthew Ryan and Robert Savage (eds), *Imagining the future: utopia and dystopia*, Arena Publications Association, North Carlton, Vic., 2006, pp. 7-8.

[343] See Ruth Levitas, *The concept of utopia* 2010 (1990), Chapters 4 and 5, and Ernst Bloch, *The principle of hope*, trans. N. and S. Plaice and P. Knight, 1986 (1955-9), cited in Lucy Sargisson, *Contemporary feminist utopianism*, Routledge, London, 1996, p. 1.

and ethical codes'.[344] Feminist utopian fiction, accordingly, also connects with a second non-feminist tradition of writing. This one, loosely termed science fiction, is said to have begun with Mary Shelley's *Frankenstein* (1818), includes H.G. Wells's *The Time Machine* (1895), Jules Verne's *Twenty Thousand Leagues Under the Sea* (1917), the works of Isaac Asimov (fl. 1950-68), and William Gibson's *Neuromancer* (1984). All expressions of cultural and political disruption in their times, the specifically feminist utopias/science fictions emerged from an activist Women's Movement. Dugdale, Spence, Clapperton and Gilman offered visions of wholly new modes of living in which one of the central and crucial changes from the present was the character of difference between women and men.

The Women's Liberation Movement of the 1970s was no less inclined to what Lyman Tower Sargent defined as 'social dreaming'[345], social dreaming that added the emotional intensity of hope to the critiques of the position and condition of womanhood. Indeed, in the United States the number of published works of feminist utopian fiction leapt from about 8 per cent of all utopias in 1960 to 32 per cent in 1970[346], its peak coinciding with the period of the greatest optimism and inventiveness in the Women's Movement of the late twentieth century. Consider — beside the demonstrations, the meetings, the avid reading and discussion, the writing, printing and proselytising, the singing and celebrating — the electrifying quality of the ideas being developed. A standard account[347] lists North American Kate Millett linking power, the core concept in any kind of politics, to sex[348]; expatriate Australian Germaine Greer making the same connection, declaring women to be sexual eunuchs, and urging an assertion of 'cunt power'[349]; another North American, Shulamith Firestone, urging the abolition of sex differentiation altogether, arguing that reproduction and child-rearing should be disengaged from biology, rendering

---

[344] Anne K. Mellor, 'On feminist utopias', *Women's Studies*, vol. 9, no. 3, 1982, p. 244.

[345] Quoted in Sargisson, op. cit., p. 1.

[346] Carol Farley Kessler, 'Distribution of utopias by United States women 1830-1980', in Carol Farley Kessler, *Daring to dream: utopian stories by United States women, 1836-1919*, Pandora Press, Boston, 1984, p. 236.

[347] See, for example, Ann Curthoys, 'Cosmopolitan radicals', in Barbara Caine, Moira Gatens, Emma Grahame, Jan Larbalestier, Sophie Watson and Elizabeth Webby (eds), *Australian feminism: a companion*, Oxford University Press, Melbourne, 1998, pp. 44-5.

[348] Millett, *Sexual politics*.

[349] Greer, op. cit.

the biological family unnecessary and making possible sexual freedom, economic independence and self-determination for everyone, women as well as men, and children, too[350]; and English Juliet Mitchell deploying an Althusserian identification of the 'key structures' of women's situation in an analysis which heralded 'the eventual dissolution of the "family"'.[351]

Alongside these head-spinningly new frames of reference, more scholarly new forms of knowledge developed. In the United States, Joan Kelly announced, startlingly, that in

> seeking to add women to the fund of historical knowledge, women's history has made problematical three of the basic concerns of historical thought: (1) periodization, (2) the categories of social analysis, and (3) theories of social change.[352]

Eleanor Maccoby and Carol Jacklin demonstrated with exemplary thoroughness that time-honoured assumptions about the psychology of sex-differences were entirely without empirical basis.[353] Michelle Rosaldo and Louise Lamphere explored and exploded the analogies drawn so often among anthropologists between men and 'culture', women and 'nature'; Margaret Mead regained her crown.[354] Sociologist Nancy Chodorow argued that the Oedipus complex in men, and all manner of destructive consequences of that formation, followed from responsibility for child care being allocated so exclusively to women.[355] At the end of the seventies, that wonderful poet Adrienne Rich challenged a host of unquestioned assumptions about love and sexuality by coupling the terms 'heterosexuality' and 'compulsory'.[356]

---

[350]   Shulamith Firestone, op. cit.

[351]   Juliet Mitchell, *Woman's estate*.

[352]   Joan Kelly-Gadol, 'The social relation of the sexes: methodological implications of women's history', in *Signs: Journal of Women in Culture and Society*, vol. 1, no. 4, Summer 1976, pp. 809-23.

[353]   Eleanor Maccoby and Carol Jacklin, *The psychology of sex differences*, Oxford University Press, Oxford, 1974.

[354]   Michelle Rosaldo and Louise Lamphere (eds), *Woman, culture and society*, Stanford University Press, Stanford, 1974, pp. 17-42, 67-87.

[355]   Nancy Chodorow, *The reproduction of mothering: psychoanalysis and the sociology of gender*, University of California Press, Berkeley, 1978.

[356]   Adrienne Rich, 'Compulsory heterosexuality and lesbian existence', in *Signs: Journal of Women in Culture and Society*, vol. 5, no. 4, Summer 1980, pp. 631-60.

Central to all of these path-breaking analyses was the issue of sexual dimorphism. It demanded explanation. As English feminist Juliet Mitchell exclaimed:

> The longevity of the oppression of women must be based on something more than conspiracy, something more complicated than biological handicap and more durable than economic exploitation.[357]

Why, asked seventies feminists, did sexual difference mean oppressive differences in power between women and men? How did such differences come about? And how could they be overcome? What would life be like without them?

Seeking answers to that last question, many of us read feminist utopian fiction. It rendered our dreams of new modes of living imaginatively concrete and detailed. These are my subject here. I will consider only four such works, probably the most famous, by three writers. I have chosen these works because each endeavours to depict a society without the power imbalances consequent upon sexual dimorphism. All three writers are citizens of the United States of America: Joanna Russ, Ursula Kroeber Le Guin and Marge Piercy.

Russ was born in 1937, grew up in the Bronx, graduated from Cornell and Yale Universities, and has held posts at several universities in the United States. An important contributor to the feminist wave that broke upon science fiction in the 1960s and 1970s, she wrote around a dozen books and collections of stories, and has stories and essays in another dozen collections. She is most famous for *The Female Man* (1975, 1986). The short story 'When it Changed' provides the germ of the utopian vision in *The Female Man*, which, although it is a very different work[358], also depicts an all-female society on a planet called Whileaway. In the story, this society is caught at the moment just before its dissolution. There are few events: a fast car journey, two conversations and a gunshot, the narrative serving chiefly to provide location and rationale for an exposition of the social, technological, sexual and reproductive organisation of people on Whileaway. The narrator is Janet. A reader is positioned to identify with her: a mixture of softness and protectiveness (fearing for the safety of her wife and daughter on hiking and hunting trips) with technical competence and toughness (familiar with farm machinery and guns; she has fought three duels). She is a product of socialisation in a society where there is no sexual difference and no

---

[357] Mitchell, *Psychoanalysis and feminism*, p. 362.

[358] Sarah Lefanu, *In the chinks of the world machine: feminism and science fiction*, The Women's Press, London, 1988, p. 175.

sexual division of labour. A central passage dramatises the moment signalled by the title, when Janet, wife of Katy, mother of Yuriko and one other daughter — Katy also describes herself as a wife, of Janet, and mother of their third daughter — meet some men: '"Real Earth men!"'

> They are bigger than we are. They are bigger and broader. Two were taller than me, and I am extremely tall, one meter eighty centimeters in my bare feet. They are obviously of our species but *off*, indescribably off, and as my eyes could not and still cannot quite comprehend the lines of those alien bodies, I could not, then, bring myself to touch them, though the one who spoke Russian — what voices they have! wanted to 'shake hands,' a custom from the past, I imagine. I can only say they were apes with human faces. He seemed to mean well, but I found myself shuddering back almost the length of the kitchen — and then I laughed apologetically — and then to set a good example (interstellar amity, I thought) did 'shake hands' finally. A hard, hard hand. They are as heavy as draft horses. Blurred deep voices …
>
> 'Where are all your people?' he said conversationally.
>
> I translated again …
>
> 'This is Whileaway,' I said.
>
> He continued to look unenlightened.
>
> 'Whileaway,' I said. 'Do you remember? Do you have records? There was a plague on Whileaway.'
>
> He looked moderately interested …
>
> 'Plague?' he said. 'That's most unfortunate.'
>
> 'Yes,' I said. 'Most unfortunate. We lost half our population in one generation.'
>
> He looked properly impressed.
>
> 'Whileaway was lucky,' I said. 'We had a big initial gene pool, we had been chosen for extreme intelligence, we had a high technology and a large remaining population … '

Janet explains, with pride and hope, how much they have achieved. Give them another generation or two, and they will have more than one real city, more industrial centres, people will be able to work full-time as professionals, radio-operators, even eventually artists, rather than everyone still having to spend three-quarters of a lifetime working on a farm. She tries, too, to tell him about their system of government. But he is not following her.

> 'Where are all the people?' said that monomaniac.
>
> I realized then that he did not mean people; he meant men …

'They died,' I said. 'Thirty generations ago.'

I thought we had poleaxed him. He caught his breath. He made as if to get out of the chair he was sitting in; he put his hand to his chest; he looked around at us with the strangest blend of awe and sentimental tenderness. Then he said, solemnly and earnestly:

'A great tragedy.'

I waited, not quite understanding.

'Yes,' he said, catching his breath again with that queer smile, that adult-to-child smile that tells you something is being hidden and will be presently produced with cries of encouragement and joy, 'a great tragedy. But it's over.' And again he looked around at all of us with the strangest deference. As if we were invalids ...

With an odd exhilaration — as if we were something childish and something wonderful, as if he were doing us an enormous favor — he took one shaky breath and said, 'Well, we're here.'[359]

On Whileaway, as in Gilman's *Herland*, women necessarily control reproduction. Russ has another character explain that on Whileaway this is not parthenogenesis 'which is so easy that anyone can practice it', but instead 'the merging of ova'.[360] Nevertheless, reproductive control is a central political issue in this story, for the men have come to Whileaway because on their planet, Earth, there has been extensive genetic damage, and they want access to Whileaway's genes. This will not be any egalitarian trade or exchange, it becomes clear. Another of the men tells Janet, that the kind of society the women have formed is 'unnatural'[361], and goes on to tell both Janet and her wife Katy that he believes in instincts. '"I can't think that the two of you ... don't feel somehow what even you must miss ... There is only half a species here"'. Then, at the end of a paragraph of Janet's rising rage and grief, as if to ram his point home, he announces: 'Men must come back to Whileaway'.[362]

Russ's story, like Dugdale's novella, is an ironic narrative device for exposing sexism. In depicting the men's attitudes to the women, attitudes which offer — in an exotic setting — a mirror image of those to be encountered daily here and now (still, or again, in the twenty-first century), the story makes its critique of gender relations

---

[359] Joanna Russ, 'When it changed', in *The Zanzibar cat*, Arkham House Publishers, Inc., USA, 1983, pp. 5-7, emphasis in the original.

[360] ibid.,p. 8.

[361] ibid., p. 9.

[362] Ibid.

in our society, here and now. The distance from the present, both in time and place, makes the present social organisation appear strange: on Whileaway, it is the oh-so-recognisable men who are not merely strange, but '*off*, indescribably off', and — as if always — predatory. The critique gains force from the contrast between the hope and pride of Janet's exposition of Whileaway's development and the rage and grief with which the story ends. But there is also a glimpse of the utopian possibility, a society entirely without sexual difference. Russ described the story's origin:

> This story won the Nebula Award, given by the Science Fiction Writers of America, for 1972. Three years before, feminism had hit the university at which I was then teaching and in the crash of failing marriages and the sturm-und-drang of fights at parties, this story wrote itself.[363]

Far more carefully crafted than such an account would allow, this feminist utopia eliminates sexual dimorphism quite simply by eliminating one sex altogether.

Men are absent from the second work of feminist science fiction with which I am concerned, too. Or rather, men are absent, except for one, the central narrator, Genly Ai, a sexed male from Earth, visiting Gethen, a planet he calls Winter.[364] But Gethen is a very different society from Whileaway, for there are no women on Winter, either. There certainly are people, though. They are androgynous. Genly Ai describes his difficulty in seeing these people 'through their own eyes'.

> I tried to, but my efforts took the form of self-consciously seeing a Gethenian first as a man, then as a woman, forcing him into those categories so irrelevant to his nature and so essential to my own. Thus … I thought that at table Estraven's performance had been all womanly, all charm and tact and lack of substance, specious and adroit. Was it in fact perhaps this soft supple femininity that I disliked and distrusted in him? For it was impossible to think of him as a woman, that dark, ironic, powerful presence near me in the firelit darkness, and yet whenever I thought of him as a man I felt a sense of falseness, an imposture: in him, or in my own attitude towards him?[365]

The Gethenians, in turn, see Genly Ai (who is also taller, and blacker, than they are) as 'a sexual freak or an artificial monster', one in 'a society of perverts'.[366] Instead of a continuous sexuality, like Ai's — and our own — Gethenians have periods of oestrus

---

[363]   Russ, quoted in Lefanu, op. cit., p. 183.

[364]   Ursula K. Le Guin, *The left hand of darkness*, Orbit, London, 1997 (1969).

[365]   ibid., p. 18.

[366]   ibid.

during which they are sexually active, and may conceive, but between those periods they are sexually inactive and impotent. They call oestrus 'kemmer'. An earlier visitor to their planet describes how it works.

> In the first phase of kemmer [the individual] remains completely androgynous. Gender, and potency, are not attained in isolation … Yet the sexual impulse is tremendously strong in this phase, controlling the entire personality … When the individual finds a partner in kemmer, hormonal secretion is further stimulated (most importantly by touch — secretion? Scent?) until in one partner either a male or female hormonal dominance is established. The genitals engorge or shrink accordingly, foreplay intensifies, and the partner, triggered by the change, takes on the other sexual role (apparently without exception) … Normal individuals have no predisposition to either sexual role in kemmer; they do not know whether they will be the male or the female, and have no choice in the matter … The culminant phase of kemmer lasts from two to five days, during which sexual drive and capacity are at a maximum. It ends fairly abruptly, and if conception has not taken place, the individual returns to the latent phase and the cycle begins anew. If the individual was in the female role and was impregnated, hormonal activity of course continues, and for the gestation and lactation periods this individual remains female … With the cessation of lactation the female becomes once more a perfect androgyne. No physiological habit is established, and the mother of several children may be the father of several more.[367]

The consequences for every other aspect of life constitute immense differences from the society on Earth from which Genly Ai and the other visitors come — implicitly, our society in the late twentieth century. Everyone has a holiday once a month. No-one has to work when in oestrus. 'Everything gives way before the recurring torment and festivity of passion'.[368] Equally, though, for 'four-fifths of the time, these people are not sexually motivated at all':

> [r]oom is made for sex, plenty of room; but a room, as it were, apart. The society of Gethen, in its daily functioning and in its continuity is without sex.[369]

From this one central phenomenon, it follows that 'everyone between seventeen and thirty-five or so is liable to be … "tied down to childbearing"'. This means that no-

---

[367] ibid., pp. 82-3.

[368] ibid., p. 84.

[369] ibid.

one is quite so thoroughly 'tied down' on Winter as women are — psychologically or physically — everywhere else. Concomitantly, 'nobody here is quite so free as a free male anywhere else'. It follows that a child does not form a psychosexual relationship with either mother or father: '[t]here is no myth of Oedipus on Winter'. It follows that there is 'no unconsenting sex, no rape'. There is no question of who controls reproduction. It follows, too, that there is no war. The very dualism that forms sexual differentiation is absent: '[t]here is no division of humanity into strong and weak halves, protective/protected, dominant/submissive, owner/chattel, active/passive'.[370]

The whole narrative balances opposites: images of light against those of darkness, unfolding through the long journey that sexed male Genly Ai and the androgyne Therem Estraven make together through the Antarctic void of the white darkness. Estraven spells it out:

> Light is the left hand of darkness
> and darkness the right hand of light.
> Two are one, life and death, lying
> together like lovers in kemmer,
> like hands joined together,
> like the end and the way.

It was from this Taoist epiphany that its author, Ursula Kroeber Le Guin, fashioned her strikingly original and innovative novel titled *The Left Hand of Darkness*, published in 1969.

Le Guin was forty, that year. The daughter of anthropologist Alfred L. Kroeber and writer Theodora Kroeber, raised in Berkeley, California, a graduate of Radcliffe College and Columbia University, she had studied in France where she met and married historian Charles Le Guin. They had three children and have lived in Portland, Oregon since 1958.[371] *The Left Hand of Darkness* won her both the Hugo and Nebula awards and made her famous. In an essay first published in 1976, revised in 1987, she described how she began this work.

> In the mid-1960s the women's movement was just beginning to move again, after a fifty-year halt. There was a groundswell gathering. I felt it, but I didn't know it was a groundswell; I just thought it was something wrong with me. I

---

[370] ibid., pp. 84-5, 87.

[371] Susan Bassnett, 'Remaking the old world: Ursula Le Guin and the American tradition', in Lucie Armitt (ed.), *Where no man has gone before: women and science fiction*, Routledge, London, 1991, p. 52.

considered myself a feminist; I didn't see how you could be a thinking woman and not be a feminist; but I had never taken a step beyond the ground gained for us by Emmeline Pankhurst and Virginia Woolf ...

Along about 1967, I began to feel a certain unease, a need to step on a little farther, perhaps, on my own. I began to want to define and understand the meaning of sexuality and the meaning of gender, in my life and in our society ... It was the same need, I think, that had led Beauvoir to write *The Second Sex*, and Friedan to write *The Feminine Mystique*, and that was, at the same time, leading Kate Millett and others to write their books, and to create the new feminism. But I was not a theoretician, a political thinker or activist, or a sociologist. I was and am a fiction writer. The way I did my thinking was to write a novel. That novel, *The Left Hand of Darkness*, is the record of my consciousness, the process of my thinking.[372]

It is a beautifully written and absorbing work. It combines an engaging, even heartbreaking, story about betrayal, fidelity, love and a growing understanding between two people, with all the compulsions of an odyssean journey. To these it adds the conceptual challenges and intrigues of the balanced dualisms — most compellingly, the sexual androgyny of the people. There are, too, the mesmerically related myths and stories of this extraordinary society.

Asked why she invented such people, Le Guin first prevaricated: 'Not just so that the book could contain, halfway through it, the sentence "The king is pregnant" — though I admit that I am fond of that sentence'. Nor was she proposing the socio-sexual society on Winter as a model for humanity: 'I am not in favor of genetic alteration of the human organism — not at our present level of understanding'. Then she explained. Rather than *recommending* androgyny, she was *exploring* it as a 'thought experiment'. This book is not a utopia, she observed: '[I]t poses no practicable alternative to contemporary society, since it is based on an imaginary, radical change in human anatomy'.[373] Utopias do not have to be practical, though, and this work performs the same function as many feminist works of utopian fiction in depicting a society without sexual dimorphism, and thence without dominance, exploitation, rape or war — feminist 'social dreaming'.

---

[372] Ursula K. Le Guin, 'Is gender necessary? Redux', 1987 (1976), in Ursula K. Le Guin, *Dancing at the edge of the world: thoughts on words, women, places*, Grove Press, New York, 1989, pp. 7-8.

[373] ibid., pp. 9, 16.

It prompted criticism from other feminists. When I taught it in a Women's Studies course at the Australian National University in the late 1970s, I criticised the dependence of the social and cultural androgyny on biological androgyny. The distinction that we learned from English feminist sociologist Ann Oakley between sex and gender — sex belonging with biology and nature and essentially fixed; gender, by contrast, belonging with nurture and culture and essentially malleable — should, I thought, have enabled Le Guin to imagine a society without male dominance, rape and war without that having to be a consequence of something as fixed and immutable as biology. I have since learned, from philosophers like Moira Gatens[374] and historians like Thomas Laqueur[375], to consider biology as far less immune to cultural and social shaping, to say nothing of historical interpretation. That has meant that I can reread *The Left Hand of Darkness* with even greater admiration for its inventiveness and originality.

Other feminists objected that Le Guin used the masculine pronoun to refer to her biological androgyne throughout the novel.[376] At first, Le Guin responded very sharply: 'I call Gethenians "he" because I utterly refuse to mangle English by inventing a pronoun for "he/she"'. Later, though, she confessed that this utter refusal had collapsed. 'I still dislike invented pronouns', she observed,

> but I now dislike them less than the so-called generic pronoun he/him/ his, which does in fact exclude women from discourse; and which was the invention of male grammarians, for until the sixteenth century the English generic singular pronoun was they/them/their, as it still is in English and American colloquial speech. It should be restored to the written language, and let the pedants and pundits squeak and gibber in the streets.[377]

She changed all of the pronouns from masculine to feminine in a reprint of the short story that was the kernel of the *Left Hand of Darkness*, so that 'Winter's King' is female. This, she commented, 'may drive some nonfeminists mad, but that's only

---

[374] Moira Gatens, 'A critique of the sex/gender distinction', in Judith Allen and Paul Patton (eds), *Beyond Marxism? Interventions after Marx*, Intervention Publications, Sydney, 1983.

[375] Thomas Laqueur, *Making sex: body and gender from the Greeks to Freud*, Harvard University Press, Cambridge, MA, 1990.

[376] Mellor, 'On feminist utopias', p. 253; Carolyn Wendell, 'The alien species: a study of women characters in the Nebula Award winners, 1965-1973', in *Extrapolation*, vol. 20, no. 4, 1979, p. 351.

[377] Le Guin, 'Is gender necessary? Redux', pp. 14-15.

fair'.[378] Even so, there were some feminist readers who considered that her attempt at depicting androgyny had simply failed: Joanna Russ objected that there were no women in this novel at all.[379] Le Guin never conceded that, but when Anne Mellor asked her what she would change, were she to rewrite the novel, to make readers see Estraven as anything but male, she said that 'a genuinely androgynous Estraven would have appeared as often with his children as with his king'.[380]

None of these objections could be made to the third work I want to consider, Marge Piercy's *Women on the Edge of Time* (1976), a work which English feminist critic Lucy Armitt pronounced to be 'one of the landmarks of the genre for decades to come'.[381] The feminist utopia, here, is called Mattapoisett. It makes concrete Firestone's list of what a feminist revolution would achieve. It is a two-sexed, gender-free utopia, a Wamponaug Indian village in the year 2137, 'a conglomeration of the various utopian aspirations of the '60s and '70s: it strives to bring together the concepts of racial, cultural and sexual liberation'. This writer, Bülent Somay, considers it a vision predicated on economic transformation.[382] Anne Mellor sees it as a vision requiring 'a radical population decrease'; a new child is begun only when someone has died.[383] Sarah Lefanu observes that the utopia 'depends upon a conscious choice made by people in the present' of the novel's time, and comments sceptically: 'This ... reflects a kind of revolutionary idealism and faith in the efficacy of agency, or indeed of cause and effect'.[384] My own reading suggests that Mattapoisett has to be the accumulated result of a multitude of individual acts against oppression and exploitation.

This surprised me. After all, Marge Piercy was born into working-class Detroit in the late 1930s, grand-daughter of a union organiser who had been murdered while organising bakery workers. She had been involved with the civil rights movement in Chicago during the 1950s, and subsequently with Students for a Democratic Society

---

[378]   Le Guin, 'Winter's king', in *The wind's twelve quarters*, Granada, London, 1978, p. 94.

[379]   Joanna Russ, quoted in Lefanu, op. cit., p. 132.

[380]   Mellor, 'On feminist utopias', pp. 253-4.

[381]   Lucy Armitt (ed.), *Where no man has gone before: women and science fiction*, Routledge, London, 1991, p. 3.

[382]   Bülent Somay, 'Towards an open-ended utopia', *Science-Fiction Studies*, vol. 11, no. 1, 1984, p. 30; Mellor, 'On feminist utopias', pp. 256-7; Freibert, op. cit., p. 55.

[383]   Mellor, 'On feminist utopias', pp. 256-7.

[384]   Lefanu, op. cit., p. 190.

during the 1960s in New York.[385] These were all engagements which emphasised the importance of collective — not individual — action. Moreover, Piercy is also the author of *The High Cost of Living* (1978) and *Vida* (1980), novels which convey all too acute an understanding of the mutual dependences and collectivist loyalties necessary in groups committed to revolutionary change. How had I read such importance for individual action in *Woman on the Edge of Time*, then?

Like this.

Mattapoisett is framed by two dystopias. One, which occupies a large portion of the novel, is set in the present in the United States. Its central character, Connie Ramos, has been committed for the second time to a mental hospital for reasons which illustrate all too vividly the intransigent structural barriers to opportunity — even to an adequate existence — in the way of the poor, the non-white, the female. In the hospital, she is selected for an experiment in controlling human behaviour by implanting electrodes in the brain. This only too realistic nightmare establishes the present — 1970s United States — as inhumane and inhuman.

Connie learns, under tutelage from a telepath in Mattapoisett, to visit this future society telepathically. She also learns, gradually, to regard Mattapoisett as a utopian future. But then the people of Mattapoisett explain to her that they are only one possible future for Connie's society, and the immense contrast between the hospital and Mattapoisett emphasises how very much would have to change for that future to be realised.

The second dystopia, which Connie visits telepathically, briefly and by mistake, after one of the operations on her brain, presents an alternative future which is just as much of a nightmare, though of a very different kind, as the present. That dystopia shows women as caged playthings for men, living in isolation from each other, in tower-blocks above the polluted atmosphere of the earth, each visited only by the man who owns her, when he takes time off from being a human fighting-machine in a war.

This now-you-see-me, now-you-don't device leads Connie, and the reader, to see Mattapoisett as a utopian future that can be won only by struggle in the present. So Connie does struggle. The novel ends when she has poisoned the leading brain surgeon in the team conducting the experiment with the electrodes. But this cannot

---

[385] http://margepiercy.com/about-marge/biography, accessed 23 July 2012.

be a blueprint for struggle. For Connie is then sent back to the worst of the mental hospitals and a personal future of drugged imprisonment; and no-one has benefited from her individual act of refusal and protest. Yet such a critique may be gratuitous: who but pragmatic North American readers would ask a work of fiction to provide them with a recipe for revolution.[386] Poets may be, as Shelley so memorably pronounced, 'the unacknowledged legislators of the world', but they do not necessarily provide imagined road maps to the utopian futures they depict. And there is no question but that Mattapoisett is a feminist utopia.

Technological sophistication has enabled its inhabitants to break completely the nexus between sex and reproduction and that between gender and mothering. This is Shulamith Firestone's key to the liberation of women translated into a vividly imagined and detailed social formation. Piercy's novel even manages to overcome Le Guin's initial difficulty with pronouns by inventing the gender-neutral 'per' and 'pers', a device which proves far less disruptive to the elegance of the English language than Le Guin had anticipated. Human foetuses are created and nurtured until birth in something called a 'brooder'. Their genetic mix is determined by computer which, following a collective decision, has been programmed to ensure racial and psychological diversity. This also breaks the nexus between genetics and culture which the novel presents as the foundation of racism. Once born, children are assigned to three mothers, though the novel uses an invented gender-free term 'mems' for all of them regardless of their sex. Indeed, their sex is irrelevant, since men have been rendered capable of suckling. Piercy dramatises this crucial feature of Mattapoisett when Connie visits the nursery. (The 'kenner' referred to is an instrument that looks like a wristwatch but serves as a personal computer, encyclopedia and communicator.)

> The infants lay in low cradles with slatted sides that moved on runners to and fro. Connie counted five babies, including one yelling its lungs out …
>
> Barbarossa burst in, out of breath. 'I hear you, I hear you. You almost blew the kenner off my wrist, you rascal! What a pair of lungs.' He picked up the crying baby. 'They can hear you ten miles out on the shelf farm, you hairy little beast!' He sat down with the baby on a soft padded bench by the windows and unbuttoned his shirt. Then she felt sick.
>
> He had breasts. Not large ones. Small breasts, like a flat-chested woman temporarily swollen with milk. Then with his red beard, his face of a sunburnt

---

[386] For example, see Nan Bowman Albinski, *Women's utopias in British and American fiction*, Routledge, London, 1988, p. 5.

forty-five-year-old man, stern-visaged, long-nosed, thin-lipped, he began to nurse. The baby stopped wailing and began to suck greedily. An expression of serene enjoyment spread over Barbarossa's intellectual schoolmaster's face. He let go of the room, of everything, and floated ...

> She felt angry. Yes, how dare any man share that pleasure. These women thought they had won, but they had abandoned to men the last refuge of women. What was special about being a woman here? They had given it all up, they had let men steal from them the last remnants of ancient power, those sealed in blood and in milk.[387]

Connie's guide explains to her:

> 'It was part of women's long revolution. When we were breaking all the old hierarchies. Finally there was that one thing we had to give up too, the only power we ever had, in return for no more power for anyone. The original production: the power to give birth. Cause as long as we were biologically enchained, we'd never be equal. And males never would be humanized to be loving and tender. So we all became mothers. Every child has three. To break the nuclear bonding.'[388]

So sexual dimorphism is retained in this utopia, but free of all of the power differences between women and men to be found in the present. This is, Dorothy Berkson observes, a 'truly androgynous society'.[389] Other utopian characteristics of Mattapoisett include its flexible division of labour, allowing everyone who parents to combine work and child care. Technology is deployed not for profit but rather to eliminate monotonous repetitive labour, to ensure a just and rational distribution of resources, and to maximise communication. Industrial and agricultural production is automated, allowing everyone to engage predominantly in work which is rewarding: farming, which means helping things to grow; arts, crafts, design and performance; and research designed to improve the quality of life. Work is allocated according to inclination and aptitude. There is unpleasant work — military service (for this utopia is still fending off enemies) and waste disposal — and it is shared equally by everyone.

---

[387] Marge Piercy, *Woman on the edge of time*, The Women's Press, London, 1979, p. 134.

[388] ibid., p. 105.

[389] Dorothy Berkson, '"So we all become mothers": Harriet Beecher Stowe, Charlotte Perkins Gilman, and the new world of women's culture', in Libby Falk Jones and Sarah Webster Goodwin (eds), *Feminism, utopia and narrative*, University of Tennessee Press, Knoxville, 1990, p. 111.

Consultation and discussion lie at the heart of processes of decision-making. Self-knowledge and strongly supportive relationships form the basis of social cohesion. Sexual connection occurs heterosexually and homosexually, frequently, occasionally, or not at all, according entirely to individual interaction. And so on.

If I am making Mattapoisett sound slightly flat, in spite of its manifold virtues and pleasures, it is at least partly because a reader encounters this society in a fashion not unlike that in which a 1970s Australian tourist used to be introduced to the People's Republic of China — with a great deal of exposition and explanation. It is also because, while the direction of desire — and struggle — in the novel is all towards Mattapoisett, Mattapoisett itself has no direction of vision, no sense of, itself, moving towards a future. The feminism of the 1970s, overwhelmingly, expressed a belief in possibility, in becoming; an aspect of its optimism. The multiple feminisms of the 1980s and 1990s have included, often, as English political theorist Lucy Sargisson labours to demonstrate through an engagement with various theoretical works under the umbrella term 'post-modernism', a refusal of closure, a refusal of perfection achieved, as a kind of death.[390] Mattapoisett is certainly a utopian vision, but it lacks that sense of continuing possibility, of open-endedness and that, I think, detracts from its persuasiveness.

The last feminist science-fiction/utopian novel that I will consider here, by contrast, is all movement, all possibility. This is Le Guin's work *The Dispossessed: An Ambiguous Utopia* (1975), a book which Anne Mellor describes as the 'most complex and politically sophisticated of contemporary feminist utopian fictions ... a major text both in the genre of utopian literature ... and of science fiction (where it has received both the Hugo and Nebula awards)'.[391] At first sight, it could appear an odd inclusion in a consideration of feminist fiction, utopian or otherwise: its central character is a man, Shevek, a theoretical physicist, and the central narrative focuses on his life and work. Ironically, given that the name of his inspiration is most often associated with the atom bomb, the reader is positioned to fall in love with him. Le Guin described how this character came to her:

> I saw the face more clearly than usual, a thin face, large clear eyes, and large
> ears — these, I think, may have come from a childhood memory of Robert

---

[390] Sargisson, op. cit., pp. 2-3, *passim.*

[391] Mellor, 'On feminist utopias', p. 257.

Oppenheimer as a young man. But more vivid than any visual detail was the personality, which was most attractive — attractive, I mean, as a flame to a moth.[392]

However, it is when he goes on to tell her who he is — 'a citizen of Utopia' — that emerges the reason for including this novel here. For Le Guin's reading about utopia included Godwin and Shelley, Peter Kropotkin, Emma Goldman and Paul Goodman, the major theorists invoked by the pacifist anarchism of the pre-feminist counter-culture of the 1960s.[393] Indeed, 'The Day Before the Revolution', Le Guin's story about the theorist whose ideas provided the basis for her utopian — anarchist — society, is dedicated to Paul Goodman (1911-72).[394] She noted, too, that she thought it 'a perfectly natural step to go from Taoism to anarchism'.[395] Moreover, as she pointed out in her discussion of *The Left Hand of Darkness*:

> The 'female principal' has historically been anarchic; that is, anarchy has historically been identified as female. The domain allotted to women — 'the family', for example — is the area of order without coercion, rule by custom not by force. Men have reserved the structures of social power to themselves (and those few women whom they admit to it on male terms, such as queens, prime ministers); men make the wars and peaces, men make, enforce, and break the laws.[396]

So her anarchist planet, Anarres, is not only the planet of an ideal future but a planet whose society is shaped around the 'female principle'; her male hero, Shevek, is balanced by Odo, the theorist on whose teachings all of Anarres society is based, who was — we learn slowly — a woman.

---

[392] Ursula K. Le Guin, 'Science fiction and Mrs. Brown', in Ursula K. Le Guin (ed.), *The language of the night: essays on fantasy and science fiction*, with introductions by Susan Wood, Berkley Books, New York, 1979, p. 101.

[393] Le Guin, 'Is gender necessary? Redux', pp. 11-12; Freibert, op. cit., p. 257. It has to be noted, sadly for political descendants of Emma Goldman, that North American feminists sometimes seem unaware of the need to distinguish between anarch*ism*, a political philosophy, and anarchy, a synonym for chaos. See, for example, Freibert, ibid., p. 50 and Mellor, 'On feminist utopias', p. 257.

[394] Ursula K. Le Guin, 'The day before the revolution', in Pamela Sargent (ed.), *More women of wonder: science fiction novelettes by women about women*, Vintage Books, New York, 1976, p. 279.

[395] Quoted in Charlotte Spivack, *Ursula K. Le Guin*, Twayne Publishers, Boston, 1984, p. 74.

[396] Le Guin, 'Is gender necessary? Redux', pp. 11-12.

This is, then, a book that all Australian feminists wanted to read — at least, during the 1970s. It cannot be entirely coincidental that in 1975, feminists in Canberra organised a conference on Feminism and Anarchism, and in the same year the Thirty-Third World Science Fiction Convention in Melbourne invited Le Guin to be their Guest of Honour and presented her with a fourth Hugo, for *The Dispossessed*.[397] Other feminists since then, notably Sarah Lefanu, have criticised this work as less feminist than many, since it has a male hero, and three unsympathetic female characters. Lefanu also argues that the synthesis of 'the ideational oppositions of the narrative' within the male heroes of both *The Left Hand of Darkness* and *The Dispossessed* pushes these works 'into the tradition of the bourgeois novel with its construction rather than deconstruction of the subject as hero'. She condemns *The Dispossessed* as well on the grounds that it does not depict interaction or movement.[398] My reading does not so much disagree with Lefanu's as approach the novel from an entirely different perspective, one concerned with its politics rather than its place in traditions of literature. Three unsympathetic female characters fade in importance, in my view, before a whole society organised on anarchist — 'female' — principles; besides, I find only one of these female characters entirely unsympathetic. I find the depiction of an anarchist society of far greater interest and importance than the novel's proximity to traditions of 'the bourgeois novel'. And I simply do not understand how Lefanu could fail to see the movement in both the structure of this novel and its narrative.

The story begins with the adult Shevek leaving the anarchist society on Anarres, which is the moon of Urras, a larger planet to which he travels on a space freighter usually employed only in transporting petroleum and mercury from the bare and barren planet of Anarres. These are the price exacted for the anarchist colony's very existence, for Anarres was founded by the million or so Odonians on Urras who rose in revolutionary struggle against the Urrastian regime 170 years ago. The first chapter takes theoretical physicist Shevek from Anarres to Urras, where he is made enthusiastically welcome by their scientists, who want to know more about his pioneering work towards a Theory of Simultaneity which could be the key to interplanetary communication.

---

[397] See above, Chapter Four; Susan Wood, 'Discovering worlds: the fiction of Ursula K. Le Guin', in *Ursula K. Le Guin*, edited with an introduction by Harold Bloom, Chelsea House Publishers, New York, 1986, p. 187.

[398] Lefanu, op. cit., p. 142.

The second chapter, set on Anarres, jumps back to a time when Shevek is a baby being installed in the collective nursery. His mother has been posted to a workstation a great distance away; his father will move from the room that they shared into a dormitory. Shevek is having to learn that the sunlight he claims is not his: 'Mine sun!' he shouts. 'Nothing is yours', the matron tells him. 'It is to use. It is to share. If you will not share it you cannot use it'[399], and so his — and our — education in the basic principles of anarchism begins. At the age of eight, he has thought of Zeno's paradox, all by himself, and tells his Speaking-and-Listening group about it, but is stopped: 'Speech is sharing — a co-operative art. You're not sharing, merely egoizing'.[400] The children learn about Urras in history, lessons which introduce them to the idea of prisons; famine in which only those who are poor die; women with jewels in their navels are 'kept for the sexual use of male members of the propertied class'; servants.[401] They learn words of abuse: 'excremental', 'profiteering'. 'Forbidden' is a 'non-organic word': 'Who forbids?' 'Order is not "orders"'.[402] Girls and boys grow up together, work together, play together.

The even-number chapters follow Shevek growing up on Anarres, forming a life-partnership with Takver, a fish geneticist[403], having children, developing his pioneering General Temporal Theory. The odd-number chapters follow him in his pioneering visit to Urras, where he learns to distrust the Urrastians' propertarian desire for his theory, since they will use it for their own exclusive profit. His journey is, as Raymond Williams observed, 'the way back and the way forward: a dissatisfaction with what has happened in the alternative society, but then a strengthened renewal of the original impulse to build it'.[404]

He also learns, from as early as his journey to Urras, how very peculiar is Urrastian society's attitude to sexual difference.

> He had asked why there were no women on the ship, and Kimoe had replied that running a space freighter was not women's work. History courses and his knowledge of Odo's writings gave Shevek a context in which to understand

---

[399] Ursula Le Guin, *The dispossessed*, p. 30.

[400] ibid., p. 32 .

[401] ibid., pp. 35-41, 42.

[402] ibid., p. 44.

[403] ibid., p. 158.

[404] Raymond Williams, 'Utopia and science fiction', in *Problems in materialism and culture*, New Left Books, London, 1980, p. 210.

this tautological answer, and he said no more. But the doctor asked a question in return, a question about Anarres. 'Is it true, Dr Shevek, that women in your society are treated exactly like men?'

'That would be a waste of good equipment,' said Shevek with a laugh, and then a second laugh as the full ridiculousness of the idea grew upon him.[405]

The Urrasti, Kimoe, endeavours to justify difference by referring to men's greater physical strength. Shevek points out that such strength doesn't matter when there are machines to do the work, and adds that strong men may work faster but the women work longer: '"Often I have wished I was as tough as a woman"'. Kimoe is profoundly shocked. '"But the loss of everything feminine — of delicacy — and the loss of masculine self-respect — You can't pretend, surely, in your work, that women are your equals? In physics, in mathematics, in the intellect?"'[406]

These lessons are not confined to such exchanges. Shevek has found himself distracted by the softness of his bunk on the space freighter; its mattress '[gives] under his weight with caressing suppleness', the 'hot-air-nozzle-towel device' tickles, and the furniture has smooth plastic curves — he finds all of them 'decidedly erotic'.[407] Le Guin goes so far as to suggest that the emotional ferocity of the Urrastian scientists' misogyny was because they themselves 'contained a woman, a suppressed, silenced, bestialised woman, a fury in a cage'; '[t]hey knew no relation but possession. They were possessed'.[408]

Ultimately, in each society Shevek gets into trouble. On Anarres, he finds himself up against a bureaucracy that has gradually developed at the centre of the administration, a bureaucracy that would block the development of his theory and the communication with Urrastian scientists that has assisted him. The image is there from the beginning of the book: the wall[409] around the Port of Anarres, where the freighter ships land, an ambiguous, two-faced wall which keeps everyone else out, but also keeps all Annaresti in. So Shevek's decision to go to Urras is at once defiance of all of the principles in which he has been educated, but simultaneously a reassertion of

---

[405] Le Guin, *The dispossessed*, p. 21.

[406] ibid., p. 22.

[407] ibid., p. 23.

[408] ibid.

[409] An image derived from Kropotkin; see Donna R. White, *Dancing with dragons: Ursula Le Guin and the critics*, Camden House, Columbia, 1999, p. 87.

those principles: he wants to share.[410] On Urras, though, he finds himself up against charming profiteers who would steal his theory for their own exclusive benefit, the kind of society against which Odonians revolted in the first place. He finds himself also amid a society in which sexual dimorphism is highly marked and exploitative, occasioning a distressing failure of communication and embarrassing bad behaviour. He joins in another anarchist uprising, bloodily quelled, seeking refuge at the embassy of the — significantly named — Terrans, finally travelling back to Anarres with a person from an entirely other planet who wants to land with him, to become an anarchist, and then, as Shevek tells this new person, they will have to see what happens. After all, anarchism is about perpetual revolution.

> 'Once you are there, once you walk through the wall with me, then as I see
> it you are one of us. We are responsible to you and you to us; you become an
> Anarresti with the same options as all the others. But they are not safe options.
> Freedom is never very safe.'[411]

All of the future opens ahead of them on a note of intense optimism.

So 1970s feminism wrought four dreams of new modes of living in which sexual difference would not mean major differences of power. Russ's could be characterised as the lesbian solution: do away with sexual difference altogether. But even Russ, who declared herself a lesbian in 1969, did not consider this a desirable possibility. She would not want to live on Whileaway, she said, because there are no men there.[412] Her purpose in creating this planet was to satirise what she saw as the primary failings of a social order in which sexual difference *does* mean serious differences in power. Similarly, Le Guin was not, ever, considering biological androgyny desirable: she was, rather, engaged in a thought experiment.

Woman on the Edge of Time and *The Dispossessed* are rather different dreams, though, for there are elements — at least — both in Mattapoisett and on Anarres that are not only desirable but could also be achievable. Both are utopias in which sexual dimorphism still exists, but entirely without any differences in power between one sex and another. Writing as long as a quarter of a century ago, Anne Mellor observed that

> Piercy's utopian society is, by the standards of utopian fiction, remarkably
> realistic. Completely automated factories, computer memory-banks and

---

[410]   Le Guin, *The dispossessed*, p. 285.

[411]   ibid., p. 317.

[412]   Russ, quoted in Wendell, 'The alien species', p. 351.

transmitters, and the mechanized breeding of babies from fertilized eggs are well within the capacities of modern science.[413]

Indeed, reading towards the end of the first decade of the twenty-first century the ways in which *Woman on the Edge of Time* overcomes differences of race and age, as well as sex and sexuality, could engender despair. All the technology described is already with us. *In vitro* fertilisation may not have developed 'brooders' yet, but it is widely practised among those who can afford it. The World Wide Web, email, mobile phones and i-pads do everything that a kenner did, and the phones can be more fun than kenners seem to have been. Even Piercy's more recent *Body of Glass* (1992) offers nothing as scientifically or technologically innovative as, just for example, the continuing ramifications of the Human Genome Project, developments in Artificial Intelligence and the Visible Human Project, the subject of searching analyses in a special issue of *Australian Feminist Studies* edited by Elizabeth A. Wilson in 1999.[414] But the imperatives of patriarchal and global corporate capitalism ensure that the social and political uses of such science and technology are entirely different from the collectivist egalitarianism of Mattapoisett. And the last decade of the twentieth century and the first of the twenty-first have been marked by the publication of *dys*topian fiction, rather than the hopeful visions of the 1970s.

As for *The Dispossessed*, Mellor also suggested that Shevek's theoretical achievement

> depends on his androgynous ability to combine a 'masculine objectivity' with a 'feminine subjectivity,' with an empathetic capacity to understand and embrace opposites, to overcome the distances between the self and the other, between the present and the past and the future.[415]

Certainly, it is in recognising the necessity of such a combination, a balance of the static and the dynamic in his theoretical work[416], of the mutuality and reciprocity of society and individual in their social and political lives[417], of the necessary interdependence of the linear and the circular[418], that Shevek learns to make the crucial decisions

---

[413] Mellor, 'On feminist utopias', p. 256.

[414] Elizabeth A. Wilson, 'Feminist science studies', Elizabeth A. Wilson Guest Editor, *Australian Feminist Studies*, vol. 14, no. 29, April 1999.

[415] Mellor, op. cit., p. 259.

[416] ibid., p. 233.

[417] ibid., p. 276.

[418] ibid., p. 277.

determining the narrative's development. I would argue that Le Guin has achieved in *The Dispossessed* exactly what *The Left Hand of Darkness* aimed to depict: a society that has established an androgyny of gender, a complete and genuine equality between women and men.[419] Reading *The Dispossessed* in 2007 is still compelling for a feminist — this old feminist, anyway — even at a time when the possibilities of anarchism and androgynous gender seem utterly unthinkable. I think that this is because the open-endedness of this work of feminist utopian fiction conveys hope.

Hope, as Hannah Arendt insisted, is 'the human capacity that sustains *political being*'.[420] Feminism has always been a grouping forged from *shared political interests* rather than, despite claims to the contrary, from *common experiences*. Perhaps a reconsideration of some of these old dreams and desires could counter current political disillusion and despair, and give fresh impetus to a politically activist feminism, by reviving hope.

---

[419]   Le Guin, 'Is gender necessary? Redux', p. 16.

[420]   Jean Bethke Elshtain, 'Response', in Jones and Goodwin (eds), *Feminism, utopia and narrative*, p. 205, emphasis added.

9

The tampon

This article was first published as 'Tampon' in Alison Bartlett and Margaret Henderson (eds), Things that Liberate: An Australian Feminist Wunderkammer, *Cambridge Scholars Publishing, Newcastle upon Tyne, 2013. Now called 'The tampon', it is republished with the permission of Cambridge Scholars Publishing. I thank the editors for their encouragement.*

Introduction

'We have lived our lives as if there was something intrinsically inferior about us', wrote the Boston Women's Health Book Collective in the justly famous work, *Our Bodies, Ourselves*, first published in 1971.[421] The problem was — as it continues to be — differences in power between women and men: 'power is unequally distributed in our society; men, having the power, are considered superior and we, having less power, are considered inferior'. 'What we have to change', they continued, 'are the power relationships between the sexes'. That might not be easy, but 'at least the situation is changeable', they believed, 'since it is not based on biological facts'.[422]

---

[421] The Boston Women's Health Book Collective, *Our bodies, ourselves: a book by and for women*, Simon and Schuster, New York, 1971, p. 7. In Australia, feminists typed sections of this book onto stencils which they ran off on gestetners so that they could distribute hundreds of copies.

[422] ibid.

Feminism is always multiple and various, fluid and changing, defying efforts at definition, characterisation, periodisation. Nevertheless, there was a moment when, for some, late twentieth-century feminism's determination to alter differences in power between women and men depended on a rejection of biology. Feminist sociologist Ann Oakley encapsulated this moment when, in 1972, she asked, 'Does the source of the many differences between the sexes lie in biology or culture? If biology determines male and female roles, how does it determine them? How much influence does culture have?'[423] Technology had altered the relationships between biology and society, she noted, but there had been no corresponding shift in the relationships between society and culture. For that to occur, it would be necessary to draw a distinction between 'male and female roles' — a distinction between sex and gender.

> 'Sex' is a word that refers to the biological differences between male and female: the visible difference in genitalia, the related difference in procreative function. 'Gender' however is a matter of culture: it refers to the social classification into 'masculine' and 'feminine'.[424]

Her challenge followed directly:

> That people are male or female can usually be judged by referring to the biological evidence. That they are masculine or feminine cannot be judged in the same way: the criteria are cultural, differing with time and place. The constancy of sex must be admitted, but so also must the variability of gender. A failure to see this has led to overstated arguments and distorted conclusions. In fact prejudice has probably done more to determine the social roles of the sexes than biology ever could — and if 'prejudice' is what we mean by culture, our pretences to enlightenment are not worth a great deal.[425]

Forays into variabilities in biological sex and confusions about the part played in it by hormones[426] did not seriously modify her general statement.

At the time when I read Oakley, I was a young wife. I was on the Pill, so — while I might strive for various forms of domestic excellence — I could also pursue

---

[423]   Ann Oakley, *Sex, gender and society*, Temple Smith, London, 1972, p. 15.

[424]   ibid., p. 16.

[425]   ibid.

[426]   See, just for instance, Dee Ann Pappas, 'On being natural', first published in *Women: a journal of liberation*, Fall 1969, in Leslie B. Tanner (comp. and ed.), *Voices from Women's Liberation*, A Mentor Book, New York, 1970.

my academic research, safe, I believed, from procreative distraction. And since, in 1973, I was only the second female scholar admitted into the department which had given me a scholarship, it helped to feel that I was working in exactly the same manner as the other — male — postgraduates. I was fit and healthy, playing squash competitively. Oakley's exposition allowed me to reject the traditional limits of female biology — almost altogether.

But that rejection was always only 'almost' altogether. For in her reproductive years, even on the contraceptive pill, the female human menstruates. This reminder that I belonged to the female sex arrived monthly: the ultimate, irreduceable marker of sex — not gender, sex — and of my difference from the men among whom I worked.

Germaine Greer said it: 'The fact is that no woman would menstruate if she did not have to'.[427] I agree. 'I got the menstruation blues', sang Robyn Archer:

> I got a pain in my guts and my head is spinnin' around
> I feel like the lowest kind of animal crawlin' on the ground'.[428]

The menstrual cycle often involves pain or discomfort, fluid retention, weight-gain, pimples, sometimes headache, backache, stress, depression, sometimes acute embarrassment — and that is when you know what is going on.[429] Many young women don't. One study of early adolescent girls' knowledge about menstruation, published in 1979, reported that

> when Mary Jane Sherfey first menstruated she was told by a friend that the
> menstrual flow was the remains of a dead baby. On the basis of this knowledge
> she put all her stained napkins in a coffin made out of a shoebox, buried it in
> the garden and recited the 23rd Psalm and the Lord's Prayer over it.[430]

One girl said that menstrual blood was 'blood from the heart that is no good', and another that it was 'blood to clean out the sick in the ovary'. Many indicated that they thought menstrual blood to be bad and dirty.[431] No wonder when even

---

[427]   Greer, op. cit., p. 58.

[428]   *The Robyn Archer songbook*, McPhee Gribble Publishers, Melbourne, 1980, p. 21.

[429]   Lesley Barclay, 'Menstruation: a life span view', *Australian Family Physician*, vol. 11, no. 6, June 1982, pp. 456-8.

[430]   M.J. Sherfey, *The nature and evolution of female sexuality*, Vintage Books, New York, 1973, quoted in Mary Ann O'Loughlin, 'Wear blue line away from body: early adolescent girls' knowledge about menstruation', *Refractory Girl*, no. 17, March 1979, p. 2.

[431]   O'Loughlin, op. cit., p. 3.

the pamphlets published by Johnson & Johnson Pty. Ltd. — makers of Modess® Napkins, Modess® Belts and Feminine Garments, Modess® Beltless Adhesive Pads, Meds® Tampons, Carefree® Tampons, Stayfree® Beltless Pads, Stayfree® Mini-Pads — manage to indicate that menstrual blood stinks, is insanitary and so shameful that it must be kept hidden.[432] Moreover, as Greer also pointed out, menstruation had been used a great deal in arguments to restrict the kinds of work in which women can be employed.[433]

Not surprisingly, then, the best thing a girl could do was to endeavour to make sure that her menstruation was undetectable. This is the cue for a roll of drums. Enter the tampon.

The tampon

'The success of the tampon', observed Germaine Greer, 'is partly due to the fact that it is hidden'.[434] Johnson & Johnson describe tampons: '[T]hey are small cylinders of highly absorbent material, tightly compressed to the size and shape of a tiny lipstick'. They absorb menstrual fluid as it enters the vagina, expanding and thereby sealing off any chance of flow-pass. Because they are worn internally, they have several advantages. 'You can go swimming with complete freedom. Nothing can come out into the water.' 'You can wear anything you like — even a bikini. Tampons are quite invisible, inside you.' 'No worries about telltale smell — the flow has no contact with air. Odour is stopped before it has a chance to start.' With such descriptions, Johnson & Johnson had little difficulty in marketing a product named 'Carefree'. They made another called 'Meds', their advertisements showing a laughing young woman in a sleeveless summer dress getting out of a car, beneath an announcement that 'she enjoys *every* weekend'. Below the photograph, we read:

> For freedom unlimited on difficult days, she chooses Meds. Meds is the safe, absorbent, internal protection that ensures complete comfort, for even the most active girls. Enjoy company with confidence — with Meds.[435]

[432] Johnson & Johnson Pty Ltd Sydney, *Enjoy being a girl especially now you're growing up*, n.d. (my copy dates from the 1980s).
[433] Greer, op. cit., p. 59.
[434] ibid., p. 56.
[435] Johnson and Johnson, op. cit.; O'Loughlin, op. cit., p. 5, emphasis in the original.

Sydney's Powerhouse Museum displays a packet of Meds from 1970, noting that Johnson & Johnson first manufactured them in the 1930s and that they were available in Australia by 1941. But they were frowned upon in many circles, especially for unmarried girls, so it was not until the 1960s that

> women whose mothers might have forbidden the use of tampons when they were younger, had accepted tampons for all the reasons that manufacturers advertised, including their invisibility, their disposability (just flush down the toilet), and the greater freedom they offered for participation in active sports.[436]

It was even possible to purchase tampons with cardboard applicators, which meant that, apart from needing to locate her vaginal opening, a woman did not need to touch her genital area while inserting a tampon. Clumsy, I found these, myself. I had no problems with touching my genitals and I found the cardboard rough. I preferred Meds, each bullet-shaped tampon of compressed cotton individually wrapped in cellophane. So, too, did the 538 respondents to a questionnaire distributed by Lesley Barclay in 1982 when she was working at a Canberra hospital and was, at the same time, a student in Women's Studies at the Australian National University. Professor Barclay AO, as she is today, found that 57 per cent of her respondents used tampons, and a further 23 per cent used tampons in combination with pads.[437] But in 2002, journalist Bettina Arndt found that, while about 70 per cent of women in the USA, Australia and much of Western Europe used tampons, in such countries as Japan and Spain that percentage fell to single digits and was not even measurable in much of the world. In Sri Lanka, women were reluctant to touch their genitals, and only '2 percent of women use tampons in much of Latin America', she reported: '"Everywhere we go, women say, 'This is not for senoritas', says Silvaian Davali, marketing director for Tampax Latin America, quoted in a December 2000 edition of the Wall Street Journal'.[438]

Of course, the chief reason for tampons taking such a long run-up to take-off in countries like Australia was concern about preserving the hymen in unmarried

---

[436] http://www.powerhousemuseum.com/collection/database/?irn=12141&search=women, accessed 25 July 2012.

[437] Barclay, op. cit., p. 454.

[438] Bettina Arndt, 'Bodies without evidence', *Sydney Morning Herald*, 21 September 2002, on http://www.bettinaarndt.com.au/articles/bodies-without-evidence.htm, accessed 25 July 2012.

women. Probably the most famous hymen in recent Anglophone cultures was that of Lady Diana Spencer, required to undergo a gynaecological examination to confirm her virginity before her marriage to Britain's Prince Charles. But, as Arndt noted, there has been a seismic shift in the value of the hymen in such societies. Not only has sexual fulfilment replaced sexual innocence on the register of cultural value, but there is also widespread recognition that 'the membrane traditionally seen as prima facie evidence of a women's virginity has become increasingly unreliable, now failing to grace many a virgin body'. The reasons Arndt adduced included various kinds of sports, but predominantly 'the use by young women of tampons, or internal sanitary devices': 'The tampon is playing a major role in the deflowering of our nation and indeed of most Western countries', she pronounced.[439]

There was one pause in the rise and rise of tampon use. It occurred in 1978 in relation to a brand of tampon called 'Rely'. Dr Stephania Siedlecki donated one of these to the Powerhouse Museum together with a pamphlet for medical doctors issued in 1980 by Australian tampon manufacturers in consultation with the Commonwealth Department of Health. Dr Siedlecki was at that time Senior Advisor in Family Planning and Women's Health with the Commonwealth Department of Health. She was the author of this pamphlet, after consulting the manufacturers about its wording. It tells the story of Toxic Shock Syndrome [TSS].[440]

TSS was first described in 1978 as acute blood-poisoning associated with a subtype of the germ popularly known as 'Golden Staph'. In the USA in 1980 there was a sudden resurgence of cases of TSS, characterised by abrupt onset, fever, rash, vomiting, diarrhoea, faintness and shock; there were some deaths — thirty-eight, reported Sarah Kowalski in an article on 'Tampons in American History'.[441] Investigators identified 940 cases over the period 1970-80. Both men and women suffered, but by far the greater proportion was found to be young women who were menstruating and using 'Rely' tampons. 'Rely' had been advertised as having extra-high absorbency so that they could be left in place over a longer period of time. Its manufacturers, Proctor & Gamble, took it off the market in response to the adverse

[439]   ibid.

[440]   http://about.nsw.gov.au/collections/doc/rely-brand-sanitary-tampon-and-applicator, accessed 25 February 2011, and accessed again on 25 July 2012.

[441]   Sarah Kowalski, 'Welcome this new day for womanhood: tampons in American history', December 1999, on http://www.sccs.swarthmore.edu/users/01/sarahk/hers/school/tampon.html, accessed 25 July 2012.

publicity, even though, as Siedlecki's pamphlet argued, investigations had shown that the germ was probably carried on the young women's fingers, rather than being in the tampons themselves, and that TSS had also occurred with other brands of tampon. 'Rely' tampons were not sold in Australia, but other high-absorbency tampons were, and were implicated in producing TSS in a small number of cases, though they included some that were nothing to do with menstruation. After discussions between tampon manufacturers and government health departments, all tampon packages have carried leaflets warning about the possibility of TSS, advising women to use the lowest absorbency tampons possible, to change them frequently and to wash their hands before and after doing so.

Times change. Different feminists think differently about injustice and power differences. In 1973, when Robyn Archer first sang 'Menstruation Blues' on the stage in the Union Hall at Adelaide University, her audience was as appalled as it was delighted.[442] In 1981 a group of students in Women's Studies at the Australian National University, led by Dr Dorothy Darroch (now Professor Emerita Dorothy Broom AM), undertook as their research project the production of a booklet to substitute for the Johnson & Johnson pamphlets a view of menstruation that was — well, not celebratory, quite; no-one was about to disagree with Germaine Greer, but far less negative. It was titled *The Public Secret: a Story about Menstruation*.[443] Their subject was still a secret, but a public one. A decade later, the cultural context of feminist thought saw tampon advertisements that included boys as well as girls, images to invoke fond laughter, in prime-time television shows which attracted young audiences. In that same context, journalists reported Britain's Prince Charles on his mobile phone, telling his beloved Camilla Parker Bowles, now his consort, that he wished he was her tampon. But these reports encountered mirth — often derisory — rather than the kind of shock associated with an offence against a taboo. In April 2000, Marita Borton described protests across Australia against the conservative Australian Government's proposal to include tampons and sanitary napkins in its new Goods & Services Tax. One protest, at Nowra in New South Wales, she reported, 'saw the entire Federal Cabinet literally bombarded — with tampons and sanitary pads!' Red-caped 'Menstrual Avengers' in Sydney chanted, 'Get your bleeding tax off

---

442   Verbal communication from my younger sister, Mary Magarey.

443   Dorothy Darroch, Maria Miranda, Angelica Marx, Lucy Parish, Anne Stanton, Frances Sutherland, Carolyn Traill and Helen Williams, *The public secret: a story about menstruation*, Canberra, 1981, copy in my possession.

our Tampax'. In Canberra, women wearing red scarves and T-shirts proclaiming 'I bleed and I vote' gathered in the city centre.[444] Menstruation may never be something that young women delight in. But it is not, now, any kind of secret, it would seem. It might even have ceased being useful to prevent women being employed in certain kinds of work, like flying planes. And some feminists think differently about making dichotomous oppositions between sex and gender, nature and nurture, biology and culture.

Conclusion

During the 1980s, some feminist philosophers in Australia began calling into question the traditional primacy that their discipline accorded to the mind. This was the beginning of a school of feminist philosophy that came to be named the New Australian Feminisms.[445] It was no accident that their title echoed an earlier, very famous United States collection of articles called *New French Feminisms*.[446] As Judith Allen and Elizabeth Grosz noted in their editorial to a special issue of the journal *Australian Feminist Studies* on 'Feminism and the Body' in 1987, such work was being influenced by the development of post-structural theories in Europe, North America, Britain and Australia.

> Post-structural critiques of the historical privilege of the mind over the body within the West are also preoccupied with issues of corporeality. Foucauldian genealogy, Derridean grammatology, the writings of the French feminists, poststructural historians, anthropologists, literary theorists all share this much: they reintroduce the question of the body to the intellectual traditions within which each works.[447]

---

[444] Marita Borton, 'Government officials in hot water over planned new tax on tampons', *Dateline Australia*, April 2000, on http://www.socialism.com/drupal-6.8?q=node/1160, accessed 25 July 2012.

[445] See *Hypatia*, vol. 15, no. 2, Spring 2000, Special Issue titled 'Going Australian: reconfiguring feminism and philosophy'. The Australian philosophers in this issue were Genevieve Lloyd, Moira Gatens, Clare Colebrook, Robyn Ferrell, Rosalyn Diprose, Linnell Secomb, Penelope Deutscher, Zoë Sofia and Barbara Bolt.

[446] Elaine Marks and Isabelle de Courtivron (eds, with Introductions), *New French feminisms: an anthology*, Schocken Books, New York, 1981.

[447] Judith Allen and Elizabeth Grosz, 'Editorial', *Australian Feminist Studies*, vol. 2, no. 5, Summer 1987, p. viii.

In 1983, Australian feminist philosopher Moira Gatens had challenged the distinction that Oakley, and others, had drawn between sex and gender, arguing that the body was not the fixed, neutral receptor of 'social lessons'. Instead, she emphasised the unity of mind and body, arguing that sexual embodiment is inseparable from gender identity.[448] I had no difficulty, at this time of my life, in accepting such a case; half of the time my mind felt like mush from lack of sleep as my (female) partner and I spent nights hurling bedclothes on and off in response to hot flushes. In 1989, in another special issue of *Australian Feminist Studies*, this one on 'Sex/Gender', Gatens noted that each human being lives with a balance of feminine and masculine, and went on to argue that

> the way we live out our particular balances (or imbalances) of masculine and feminine traits is crucially connected to our bodies: the meaning and significance of our own bodies for us and — what cannot be separated from this — the meaning and significance of the sexed body in culture.[449]

Nevertheless, the sexed female body still menstruates, and during our menstruating years — at least in Australia — most will encounter the tampon.

Considering the tampon always reminds me of an entry that I encountered in the Canberra Women's Liberation Archives when I was reading them in the Jessie Street Library in Sydney. I was reading the minutes of a group called the Red Fems, minutes which still reduce me to hysterical joy and tearful reminiscence. This group, which lasted from late 1979 to the end of 1980, was about serious discussions. It appears in the pages of *Worth her Salt: Women at Work in Australia*, the publication of papers presented to the second Women & Labour conference in Melbourne in 1980, with a paper titled 'The implications of technological change for women workers in the public sector'.[450] We undertook a further paper to present to the Political Economy Conference held, also in Melbourne, in August 1980. A serious group, then. With serious concerns about the crisis in capitalism, technological innovation, de-skilling workers, especially women workers, and ways of organising against such injustices.

---

448   Moira Gatens, 'A critique of the sex/gender distinction', in Moira Gatens, *Imaginary bodies: ethics, power and corporeality*, Routledge, London and New York, 1996, first published in Judith Allen and Paul Patton (eds), *Beyond Marxism? Interventions after Marx*, Intervention Publications, Sydney, 1983.

449   Moira Gatens, 'Woman and her double(s): sex, gender and ethics', *Australian Feminist Studies*, vol. 4, no. 10, Summer 1989, p. 34.

450   Red Fems, op. cit.

Figure 10: Jenny Macklin and Julia Ryan, members of the Red Fems in Melbourne for the Political Economy Conference, 1980
Photograph by Susan Magarey

But no-one reading the minutes that the group kept could consider it entirely serious. The decision to rotate minute-taking, for instance, was taken because of Daphne Gollan's 'dereliction of duty, general negligence and lapses into housewifely fussing'; Daphne, a lecturer in History at the Australian National University, also a brilliant cook, used to insist on making cakes to feed the group. She was also the author of these minutes. The minutes show, as well, consideration of other problems: should one wear a bra to Tai Chi classes or to squash matches, or not? What does one do about a diaphragm which won't stay with its applicator and bounces all about the room? A discussion that lapsed into a conversation about gardening includes this: 'Daphne: has become fond of shit if Sara can spare any'. And Sara Dowse, a novelist, formerly Director of the Office of Women's Affairs in the Whitlam and Fraser governments, that same evening 'reels from chair with too much rosé'. It is in that context that I encountered an entry in capital letters with many exclamation marks, reporting with delighted mock-horror that Dorothy Johnston, also a novelist, had gone with her (male) partner to a fancy-dress party dressed as a MENSTRUAL CYCLIST, and with tampons decorating her clothes and her bicycle.[451] A moment when the menstruating female body was so far from trying to hide that it was celebrating itself.

Ironically, my own first encounter with the tampon, when I was twenty, had nothing to do with the menstruating female body. On the contrary. In a relationship with a woman old enough to have ceased menstruating herself, I found myself — hopelessly ignorant — embarrassed by the vaginal juice which my desire and pleasure produced. So I bought a packet of Meds. But even for my lover, the significance of the sexed body in culture meant that, when she encountered the string attached to the tampon, she enquired tenderly about menstrual pain.

---

[451]   Canberra Women's Liberation Archives, Jessie Street National Women's Library, Sydney.

Part II

Women's Studies: Introduction

Unlike social movements which have formed religious sects or trades unions or political parties, the Women's Movement has not itself become an institution, and it never had a readily identified membership. Rather, it was, and remains, an amorphous, shifting collection of groups and individuals whose objections to aspects of the subordination of women bring them together at particular junctures to argue around particular issues, to campaign for particular goals related to those objections, or to celebrate women's creativity, energy and humour. English feminist journalist Beatrix Campbell had occasion early in 2012 to reflect on what had happened to Women's Liberation. 'After the 1970s', she wrote:

> Women's Liberation lived on not as a thing, a place, an address — it had no institutional moorings — but as contingent politics: as ideas, as coalitions, as challenges to the professions, political parties and the academy, in women's services, and in popular culture; it created new political terrain.[452]

As she notes, 'the academy' — one of the locations in which Women's Liberation could still be found — was in Women's Studies.

I was employed to teach Women's Studies at the Australian National University from 1978 until the end of 1983, and I was employed to establish and run a Research Centre for Women's Studies at the University of Adelaide from 1983 until 2000. I

---

[452] Beatrix Campbell, 'Speak up for feminism', in 'Letters', *London Review of Books*, 26 January 2012, p. 4.

have written about these activities and reproduce (most of) five of those conference papers, lectures and articles here. They are each a product of the time at which they were written, so there are references specific to those times. I mention the Tertiary Education Assistance Scheme in Chapter Eleven, for instance; issues around fees for students and schemes to assist students have changed mightily over the years. In Chapters Twelve and Thirteen, I give examples of some of the difficulties that I encountered among colleagues and administrators, but I decided not to elaborate on these in this Introduction. Accordingly, all of these pieces need a little historical and autobiographical background. First, though, a general introduction.

Often, when I was asked to explain why we would want Women's Studies in a university, I would tell an abbreviated version of a short story written by the North American, early twentieth-century, Pulitzer-Prize-winning author Susan Keating Glaspell. It is called 'A Jury of her Peers'; it was published in 1917. It is available on the Web, but it is little known in Australia, and as it offers a telling justification for Women's Studies I will include that abbreviated version here.[453]

> Five people have gone out in the freezing north wind of a rural north American winter to visit an empty house. In that house, on the previous day, the neighbouring farmer had found Minnie Wright sitting in a rocking chair in the corner of her kitchen, looking worn out and pleating her apron. He asked to see her husband, and she told him that he couldn't — because he was dead. She fell to pleating her apron again. He asked, 'Why, what did he die of?'
>
> 'He died of a rope round his neck', says she; and just went on pleatin' at her apron.
>
> The neighbour went upstairs and discovered, to his horror, that Minnie's husband was indeed dead — in his bed, with a rope around his neck. He fetched the local sheriff who arrested Minnie Wright and took her into custody.
>
> The next day, he, Sheriff Peters, and his wife, accompanied by the county attorney, called at the neighbours' farm and asked them, Mr. and Mrs. Hale, to accompany them to the Wrights' house to investigate. The five arrived at the desolate house, and first stood around in the kitchen to hear Mr. Hale tell about his visit and discovery the day before. He called in, he said, because he wanted to put a telephone in his own house, but would only be able to

---

[453] Susan Keating Glaspell, 'A Jury of her peers', 'A Jury of her peers', in Lee R. Edwards and Arlyn O'Fermond (eds), *American voices, American women*, Avon, New York, 1973, www.learner.org/exhibits/literature/story/fulltext.html.

afford it if he could persuade Minnie's husband, John Wright, to share the cost of a party line with him.

' ... I thought maybe if I went to the house and talked about it before his wife, and said all the woman-folks liked the telephones, and that in this lonesome stretch of road it would be a good thing ... though I didn't know as what his wife wanted made much difference to John —.'

He had told Minnie Wright that that was why he'd come ...

' ... and at that she started to laugh, and then she stopped and looked at me — scared.'

When Mr. Hale had finished his account, the county attorney decided that the men would go upstairs first, and then to the barn, to investigate. He looked about the kitchen and asked the sheriff: 'You're convinced there was nothing important here?'

The sheriff looked around, too.

'Nothing here but kitchen things,' he said, with a little laugh for the insignificance of kitchen things.'

The young attorney poked about briefly, observing that the preserved fruit had leaked all over the cupboard, that the roller towel was dirty, and so were the pans stacked under the sink. Then he and Sheriff Peters and Mr. Hale went upstairs.

The women had exclaimed over the preserved fruit, at the pity of the waste of all Minnie's work during the hot summer. Minnie had been worried about it, Mrs. Peters said, when the sheriff had brought her in and the night had turned so cold. 'She said the fire would go out and her jars might burst.' The sheriff and the attorney had laughed at the idea of a woman held for murder worrying about her preserves. Mrs. Hale had protested, too, at the attorney's criticism of the dirty roller towel:

'Those towels get dirty awful quick. Men's hands aren't always as clean as they might be.'

Left to themselves in the kitchen, the women slowly begin to notice — the cover off the bucket of sugar, and a half-full paper bag of sugar beside it, as though Minnie had been interrupted while filling it; the worn made-over clothes they fetched for her, which moved Mrs. Hale to exclaim:

'Wright was close! ... I think maybe that's why she kept so much to herself ... you don't enjoy things when you feel shabby. She used to wear pretty clothes and be lively — when she was Minnie Foster, one of the town girls, singing in the choir. But that — oh, that was twenty years ago.'

They noticed, as well, the table half-wiped, with the dish cloth left in the middle; the bad stove which would have been so difficult to bake in; the pieces for a quilt — half-made.

'Do you suppose she was going to quilt it or just knot it?' one of them asked, a question which prompted more indulgent mirth from the men passing through the kitchen on the way to the barn. They'd gone again when Mrs. Peters exclaimed to Mrs. Hale over one of the pieces of sewing in the quilt.

'All the rest of them have been so nice and even — but — this one. Why it looks as though she didn't know what she was about!'

Their eyes met — something flashed to life, passed between them; then, as if with an effort, they seemed to pull away from each other. A moment Mrs. Hale sat there, her hands folded over that sewing that was so unlike all the rest of the sewing. Then she unpicked the ragged stitches and sewed them up neatly. Mrs. Peters, wife to a sheriff, protested weakly, but then sat, her eyes having 'that look of peering into something.'

It was Mrs. Peters, looking for paper and string to wrap up Minnie Wright's clothes, who found the bird-cage. It was empty, and, she observed, its door was broken.

Mrs. Hale came nearer.

'Looks as if someone must have been — rough with it.'

Again their eyes met — startled, questioning, apprehensive.

Mrs. Peters hadn't known John Wright, beyond his reputation as a good man. Mrs. Hale, his neighbour, reflected on that view.

'He didn't drink, and kept his word as well as most, I guess, and paid his debts. But he was a hard man, Mrs. Peters. Just to pass the time of day with him — ' She stopped, shivered a little. 'Like a raw wind that gets to the bone.' Her eyes fell upon the cage on the table before her, and she added, almost bitterly: 'I should think she would've wanted a bird! ... She — come to think of it, she was kind of like a bird herself. Real sweet and pretty, but kind of timid and — fluttery. How — she — did — change.'

To distract themselves with everyday things, the women had the happy thought of taking the quilting to Minnie Wright in gaol, to take her mind off her plight. They investigated the sewing basket, a pretty box which, Mrs. Hale guessed, Minnie had had a long time ago. She opened it. Instantly her hand went to her nose.

'Why — !'

Mrs. Peters drew nearer — then turned away.

'There's something wrapped up in this piece of silk,' … She raised it with an unsteady hand. 'Oh, Mrs. Peters!' she cried. 'It's —'

Mrs. Peters bent closer.

'It's the bird,' she whispered.

'But Mrs. Peters!' cried Mrs. Hale. '*Look* at it! Its *neck* — look at its neck! It's all — other side to.'

She held the box away from her.

The sheriff's wife again bent closer.

'Somebody wrung its neck,' said she, in a voice that was slow and deep.

And then again the eyes of the two women met — this time clung together in a look of dawning comprehension, or growing horror. Mrs. Peters looked from the dead bird to the broken door of the cage. Again their eyes met. And just then there was a sound at the outside door. The men passed through on their way upstairs again. The two women sat motionless, not looking at each other, but as if peering into something and at the same time holding back. When they spoke now it was as if they were afraid of what they were saying, but as if they could not help saying it. Mrs. Peters protested that it was an awful thing to have killed a man while he slept, 'slipping a thing round his neck that choked the life out of him.'

Mrs. Hale's hand went out to the bird-cage.

'His neck. Choked the life out of him.'

'We don't *know* who killed him,' whispered Mrs. Peters wildly. 'We don't *know*.'u

Mrs. Hale had not moved. 'If there had been years and years of — nothing, then a bird to sing to you, it would be awful — still — after the bird was still.'

It was as if something within her not herself had spoken, and it found in Mrs. Peters something she did not know as herself.

Again they distracted themselves, preparing bundles to take to Minnie Wright, returning to the world in which it was the men who were looking for evidence of a motive for murder, and mocking themselves for getting so upset over a dead canary. But as the men are returning, still without the evidence they have been seeking, both women, on the same unspoken impulse, hide the little sewing box containing the dead bird in Mrs. Hale's pocket. The three men come back into the kitchen.

'Well, Henry,' says the county attorney facetiously, 'at least we found out that she was not going to quilt it. She was going to — what is it you call it, ladies?'

Mrs. Hale's hand is against the pocket of her coat.

'We call it — knot it, Mr. Henderson.'

At one time, this story could have been cited as an illustration of feminist standpoint theory. (Perhaps it might be again in the second decade of the twenty-first century.) A quarter of a century ago, when it was first formulated, Women's Studies had established a place on most tertiary campuses in Australia.

Here is the historical and autobiographical background that I promised.

I did not leap into the job of teaching Women's Studies. On the contrary. In the early 1970s, I maintained a firm separation between the work that I did in the Women's Movement and the work that I did in the academy. This was not a distinction between practical work and fun, on one hand, and intellectual work on the other: listening to psychologist Hazel Steiger presenting to our Women's Liberation group a paper titled 'The Haves and the Have-Nots: the Penis-less People' may have reduced us to hysterical delight, but it also taught us a lot about Freud. The discussions in our Women's Liberation group, and at some of the national feminist conferences that we went to, provided far greater intellectual excitement than could usually be encountered at a postgraduate seminar or academic conference. The Women & Labour Conferences of 1978, 1980 and 1982, for instance, produced three published collections of articles which remained among the best material available to Women's Studies students for a couple of decades. The separation that I made was, rather, a distinction between work (and play) that I engaged in as a feminist, and work that I did in an institution where patriarchal imperatives seemed unassailable. It was a campaign for Women's Studies at the Australian National University [ANU] where I was still a postgraduate in History that began to dismantle the separation between the two most consuming involvements in my life.

In 1974 at ANU students mounted what has since been called, euphemistically, an 'education campaign' during which they occupied the Chancelry for twenty-four hours demanding *inter alia*, a Women's Studies course.[454] Committees were formed. Debates and discussions ensued. Three issues surfaced and a number of difficulties.

---

[454]   *ANU Reporter*, 24 May 1974; Gwenda W. Bramley and Marion W. Ward, *The role of women in the Australian National University*, internal publication, Canberra, 1976, pp. 115-16.

One issue was the question of ghettoisation or mainstreaming. Women on a committee of academics included two who had for years included material about women in their courses: comparisons of the voting behaviour of women and men in a course in Political Science, for instance, and a focus on the family in a course on Ancient Rome in Classics. They argued eloquently that consideration of women and gender needed to be an integral part of *all* university courses. By setting up a separate course, they maintained, we would not only ghettoise consideration of women but also remove any impetus towards its inclusion in other courses. A second committee of students (I was one of them) countered that feminist teaching and research needed to be concentrated to develop the concepts and what we would learn to call the critical mass of monographic scholarship that would, when introduced into other courses, do more than add an occasional seminar on women. Women's Studies, we argued, meant much more than adding women and stirring. It was developing perspectives, approaches and bodies of material that would ensure that whole courses would need to be rethought and reshaped. You can't simply add the notion that the world is round to the belief that it is flat. Besides, we urged, more pragmatically, integrating consideration of women into existing courses would depend on the political will of the people — still predominantly men — teaching them.

It was probably the pragmatic argument that won the day. The academic women knew their colleagues only too well. But the university would be careful; Women's Studies, like Women's Liberation, some hoped, was a passing fad. They advertised for an appointment limited to three years. A Women's Studies course was offered at that university for the first time in 1976.

A second issue was about academic credentials. At Flinders University in 1973, for example, groups of feminists from both inside and outside the institution set up a course which operated on the principles of 'participatory democracy'. This meant 'no appointed teacher to give lectures or seminars, involvement of anyone who wishes to participate, and group assessment'. 'There is a very strong feeling in the course', some of its participants noted,

> that these principles are necessary for the course to serve the interests of women, and that no compromise would ever be possible for the sake of academic recognition of the course.[455]

---

455 Penny Ryan (ed.), *A guide to Women's Studies in Australia*, Mulgrave, Melbourne, 1973, p. 41.

In the following year, participants in the course were concentrating on matters that were, they held, 'probably a lot more relevant to the women in the groups who have come from outside the university' than matters which — and you have to hear the sneer at the university in the rest of their sentence — could produce '"good solid academic work"'. Most radically, participants in this course were distinguishing assessment of work — carried out readily by the whole group, collectively — from grading — done only for those students enrolled in the university, and only to 'satisfy the Registry's requirements'.

> Increasingly, we are critically assessing the work that people submit to the group, but giving them the grade that they feel they need. If a person wanted to go on to Honours, for example, and needs a credit to do so, her group might well decide to give her a credit, as well as assessing her work quite separately from that grading submission.[456]

This course continued to operate on these principles for more than a decade, supported by a grant from the International Women's Year funds provided by the federal government of Labor Prime Minister Gough Whitlam, and protected by Flinders University's Philosophy Department, where it was based, because it was Philosophy's most popular second- and third-year course. I'm not aware of any other Women's Studies courses attempting to emulate Flinders University's, and I know that at ANU we wanted Women's Studies students not only to conform to the university's assessment requirements, but also, in doing so, to show how exceptionally good they were.

A third issue was: what would a Women's Studies course teach? Most often such a question was answered pragmatically by who was available and willing, and what they knew. Kay Daniels taught a pioneering Honours History seminar at the University of Tasmania on 'Women in English Society, 1791-1928'. At Sydney University, the Philosophy Strike in 1973 brought forth a course on 'Women and Philosophy'. A year later, other feminist colleagues at Sydney, among them brilliant political economist Margaret Power, organised an interdisciplinary unit called 'The Political Economy of Women'.

At ANU, Ann Curthoys was appointed to establish and teach the later-year, full-year Women's Studies unit.[457] She enlisted other academics from both the

---

[456] ibid., p. 42.

[457] See Ann Curthoys, 'Women's Studies at the Australian National University: the early

undergraduate teaching section of the ANU, and the postgraduate and research section, and they organised themselves into groups which offered half-year research courses during the second half of the year. I was, by then, tutoring in History; I taught in one of those Women's Studies research courses, on Capitalism and the Family, together with sociologist Cora Baldock and Marxist feminist Jenny Macklin (who would become a federal parliamentarian in the late twentieth century, and in the twenty-first, a minister in the Labor governments of Kevin Rudd and Julia Gillard).

Figure 11: Ann Curthoys, with Ned Curthoys, mid-1970s
Photograph by Susan Magarey

Ann's initiatives were so successful that enrolments grew to 100 in only two years. But at the end of that second year, Ann moved on to another, tenurable, post in Sydney. ANU had funds committed for the third year, and students already on the books. The Dean of Arts telephoned me. 'Please would you come and take over Women's Studies for its last year?' he pleaded.

I was flattered. But I was also reluctant to abandon the new Australian Social History course that I had designed. And I was challenged: I did not think that I'd read carefully enough the books and journals that we discussed at our Women's Liberation meetings, so how could I teach an even greater range of such material? More fundamentally, perhaps, I was apprehensive about bringing together my work as a feminist and my work as a scholar. Would this not amount to allowing my feminism to be co-opted into, perhaps neutralised by, a patriarchal institution? Would my colleagues in History ever speak to me again? Looking again into the rear-vision mirror at this crossroad in my life, I can only be thankful that I agreed to take it on.

A year or so later, when the university conceded both the successes of Women's Studies and the extent of continuing student demand, and advertised a tenure-track post to run the course, I applied for it and gained what was the first post in Australia

years', *Australian Feminist Studies*, vol. 13, no. 27, 1998, pp. 75-80.

Figure 12: Julia Ryan, Master Teacher
Photograph courtesy of Susan Magarey,
gift from Julia Ryan

to be *named* a Women's Studies position. I was very proud. At the same time, we gained a full-time tutorship, a position which we filled with brilliant and engaging Master Teacher Julia Ryan.

In the beginning, in 1978, I was allowed funding for a succession of visiting lecturers. This meant that my concerns could be primarily intellectual and pedagogical. Listening to different visiting lecturers each week served me as a form of intensive in-servicing in the array of subjects which — in the 'renaissance woman' days of feminist scholarship — we believed that any Women's Studies course should address (and I am quite extraordinarily indebted to all of the people who gave lectures during that year). But it also brought me face-to-face with a problem — one which I think is often still encountered in interdisciplinary teaching, especially when it's carried out by an array of scholars from different disciplines — of addressing inevitable student confusion about the differences in the core assumptions of one intellectual discipline and another.

When I designed the two full-year units to replace the single Women's Studies course in 1979, I attempted to take this difficulty on. This was ambitious, something I could not have attempted without the examples given to me during my first year of teaching Women's Studies, and it was a staggering amount of work. Each course would draw on four disciplines: one would canvas issues derived from Biology, Anthropology, Cultural Studies and Philosophy; the other would consider issues drawn from Psychology, Sociology, History and Political Science. And, in each case, there would be time and space to reflect upon the dominant assumptions operating in the analysis drawn from each discipline, as well as the substantive issues that we wanted to consider. The students would gain not only the consideration of specific issues but also a perspective on the ways in which those considerations were shaped by the ways in which different disciplines formulated such issues. In the late 1970s, I called this mode of working 'transdisciplinary', a term redolent of the emancipatory discourses which also informed much socialist and radical feminism then. This is the subject of Chapter Ten. I wrote an article about it for the *ANU Reporter*.[458] The university would see, I thought, how intellectually serious — and challenging — was the enterprise to which it was giving a temporary place.

I was also, and primarily, concerned with Women's Liberation's emancipatory desires. The overall goals of both units were to examine explanations for the differences in power between women and men — as a step towards eliminating them, of course. In the first unit, we considered critically such issues as the biological basis (or lack of it) for gender differentiation and current debates about genetics; theories of evolution and their ability (or lack of it) to explain gender differentiation; the absence of women's writing from the established canons of literary value, the sexist criteria governing those canons, and the slowly emerging evidence of valuable literary productions by women; and the critique that Genevieve Lloyd (then still at the ANU) was developing of the 'maleness' of Reason in philosophy.[459] In the second course, we began with psychology's theories of gender differentiation, and their inadequacies when asked such questions as, 'Why are we not, then, all the same?'; moved on through role theory and critiques of its ability to explain the power differences between women and men; historical challenges to conceptions of 'the family' as timeless; and the success (or lack of it) of challenges to the established political order through the established channels. I was gratified to find marked similarities in range and approach in the rainbow-coloured books of the first British Open University course in Women's Studies when they were published in 1982.[460]

The first of my courses was titled 'From Bodies to Minds'; the second 'From Consciousness to Organisation'. The leftist echoes were intentional. In both cases, the goal was to foster the revolution that I thought the Women's Movement was

---

[458] *ANU Reporter*, 28 November 1980. On the term 'transdisciplinary' see also Shulamit Reinharz, *Feminist methods in social research*, Oxford University Press, New York, 1992, p. 4.

[459] Genevieve Lloyd, *The man of reason: 'male' and 'female' in Western philosophy*, Methuen, London, 1984.

[460] *The changing experience of women, 16 Units*, Open University Press, Milton Keynes, 1982, repr. 1983.

bringing about and, while I knew that I could not spell out such a goal to curriculum-approving bodies within the university, I was sure that it would gain recognition among students, and among a broader feminist community outside the university.

Some students objected, of course. But this led to lively debate, and enrolments in these courses grew. (Indeed, they grew so rapidly that at the beginning of — I think — 1980, I learned from disgruntled students wanting to enrol that the Faculty Office had been trying to contain our numbers by sending out notices saying that the courses were already full! The Faculty Office was embarrassed when I went to ask what was going on; there was no official quota on enrolments in Women's Studies.) We were able to add the Honours year that Ann Curthoys had recommended, and offered as its core unit a course that Ann had designed: 'A History of Feminist Thought'. Undergraduate essays submitted for Women's Studies courses were appearing in print in a variety of publications.[461]

We still had some lectures by invited experts. They included an outstanding cast: distinguished sociologist Dorothy Broom, postgraduate student Marcia Langton (now a professor at Melbourne University), Sara Dowse (a writer, but at that time Assistant Secretary of the Office of Women's Affairs in the Department of the Prime Minister & Cabinet), Margaret Thornton, a learned and inspiring legal academic from Melbourne, just for instance. But by then, Julia and I gave most of the lectures, and in order to encourage students to debate with each other and with us, we divided each lecture-hour into two: the first forty or so minutes for the lecture by one of us, and then the last ten or so minutes for a commentary on that lecture by the other, suggesting an alternative analysis, or an elaboration, or attention to a different body of material.

I have presented this account in some detail because someone who had encountered Women's Studies at ANU after I had left told me, in tones of total certainty, that the early days of Women's Studies at the ANU were characterised by consciousness-raising and 'all that touchy/feely stuff'. Does such a story arise from the quite widespread delusion that feminists did not do any theoretical work before the advent of everything lumped together under the label 'post-modernism'?

---

[461] Lesley Barclay's essay appeared in *Australian Family Physician*. Christine Fernon's discussion of the support shown for Vida Goldstein in her campaign for election to the Australian Senate in 1903 and Merawan Scowcroft's critique of Mary Daly's *Gyn/Ecology* were published in *Refractory Girl*. Two other students, Christine Fernon and Frances Sutherland, made a film.

Figure 13: Sara Dowse, on holiday from the Australian Public Service, early 1970s
Photograph by Susan Magarey

Is it simply an import from someone who first encountered Women's Studies in, say, the United States? I don't know. But I do know, with matching certainty, that if such a characterisation is accurate for the first eight years of Women's Studies at the ANU, then it passed right by me. No doubt consciousnesses were raised. And I do recall intense engagement and passionate debate. But I thought that these were spin-offs from the central focus of the work that we did in Women's Studies classrooms, which was determinedly cerebral, and included quite a bit of theoretical work — derived from Marx, Althusser, Freud, and Foucault, those grand old men, and from Beauvoir, Mitchell, Millett, Firestone, Joan Kelly, Eleanor Maccoby and Carol Jacklin, Michelle Rosaldo and Louise Lamphere, Michèle Barrett and Mary McIntosh, Christine Delphy, Luce Irigaray, and, at home, as well, Carole Pateman, Bettina Cass, Rosemary Pringle and Ann Game, Genevieve Lloyd, Moira Gatens … (I must stop — this is a list that could go on and on, as the articles and footnotes in this collection show).

Slowly, I began to consider just how enormous was the subversion that Women's Studies offered. Were we, I asked — here in Chapter Eleven — changing the paradigms that governed all the knowledge we had learned? It was, I reflected, more than two centuries since Alexander Pope, observing that '[t]he proper study of Mankind is Man', summarised that great shift in the direction of intellectual inquiry in the Western world away from contemplation of the works of a deity, and towards investigation of the physical and social world. It was only twenty or so years since pioneering French feminist Simone de Beauvoir, in *The Second Sex*, remarked that men had observed the world from their own point of view and then confused what they saw with Absolute Truth. In Women's Studies we were engaging in an epistemological revolution, a revolution in the study of knowledge, one that others would follow, as Chapter Fourteen suggests.

It is not surprising, then, that we should have run into a number of difficulties. At ANU, these were mostly endeavours at financial efficiency and seldom conveyed hostility to the concept of Women's Studies, or to me personally. When I moved on — or back; I had attended Adelaide University as an undergraduate — to Adelaide University in 1983, to a post that required me to set up Australia's first Research Centre in Women's Studies, I encountered difficulties of a different order. A few of these appear in Chapters Twelve and Thirteen. I have decided not to burden these pages with an account of the gratuitous and sexist insults and the distrust that I encountered at that university during the subsequent twenty years.[462] Times have changed. Those who held personal fiefdoms have now retired; personal 'interest' would not any longer be allowed to weigh against transparent and accountable procedures in job-selection; 'student choice' would not be allowed to prevent sensible recommendations of works for students to read; it is not only academics, I learned, who can be as mean as dried spiders. Finally, Adelaide University academics are not the only men who, thinking that they might need 'a woman' for some grant-application or project, fail to recognise that 'a woman' reduces the individual concerned to an item of sex, rather than a person with intellectual capabilities that are nothing to do with her sex. Looking into that rear-vision mirror again, I see how the sexism bewildered me, and the insults startled me, sapping my confidence. Ultimately, though, this misogyny made me indignant and rendered me all the more determined to do the job to which I had been appointed, a job which I had to make up as I went along.

It must be said, though, that there were also aspects of this job which brought me immense satisfaction, among them the support that I gained from feminists throughout the community of Adelaide, and from feminist scholars throughout Australia — indeed, eventually, across the world — to say nothing of all that they taught me.

The chapters in Part II of this collection all suggest that my aspiration for Women's Studies was to make it a permanent feature of tertiary education. Perhaps I did hope for such an effect, at one time. But the changes in nomenclature, context,

---

[462] At the time of writing, a more detailed narrative about these difficulties has been lodged with Special Collections in the Barr Smith Library.

costume and substance that have overtaken what were once called Women's Studies units in universities remind me that institutional survival was desirable primarily to keep alive an epistemological revolution, and not merely to preserve any old course or research project. And feminism's intellectual revolution is by no means confined to universities.

10

Women's Studies — towards transdisciplinary learning?

This article was first published in The Journal of Educational Thought, *Calgary, Canada, vol. 17, no. 2, August 1983. The version published here is an extract. I am grateful to the present editor, Ian Winchester, for permission to reproduce it.*

In 1983 we are drawing close to the end of the ten years which the United Nations designated the Decade for Women. Halfway through that decade, in 1980, in Australia, the proportion of women in the population involved in some kind of post-secondary education had equalled the proportion of men. Only a year earlier it was possible to claim that 'Women's studies courses are at present offered at most Australian universities'.[463]

However, all the gains made by Women's Studies courses are affected by their relationships with the institutions in which they are offered. When funding, staffing, resources, requirements and procedures for enrolment and assessment are controlled by academic bureaucracies, the shape and nature of courses are inevitably affected by the attitudes of those bureaucracies. In general they have been, as Ann Curthoys observed in 1975, 'essentially conservative'. 'Universities', she went on,

> exist to provide skills for an authoritarian parliamentary-democratic society
> based on a capitalist economy, and can only develop into something else in

463   Beverly Walker and Margaret Smith, 'Women's Studies courses in Australian Universities', *Women's Studies International Quarterly*, vol. 2, no. 3, 1982, p. 375.

accord with fundamental changes in the society as a whole. The university is contained within the society around it, and is in many ways the perpetrator of some of its most conservative values.[464]

In a social formation whose government is prepared to concede equal pay for equal work in a gender-differentiated workforce, the universities follow suit by allowing Women's Studies courses to be established, but ensuring, or trying to ensure, that they are adequately contained within the established structure of the institution.

Courses which have conceded to the academic bureaucracies a broad conformity over enrolment and assessment requirements in return for their very existence can meet a far blunter containment. At the Australian National University, where the Women's Studies Program has offered two full-year courses since 1979, and an Honours course which began in 1982, the university's authorities have strenuously resisted any expansion in the Program's resources, despite consistently high enrolments. Indeed, for one semester in 1979, one seminar group was co-ordinated entirely by a group of feminists who were full-time lawyers and had no other connection with the university; they did this work voluntarily — the Program had no part-time teaching money left to pay them. And in 1982, after finally persuading the administration to concede funds for a second, full-time lectureship in the Women's Studies Program (a two-year post), and after interviewing candidates and selecting an appointee, the university 'froze' the position. Despite strenuous student protest, and letters from outraged participants in the Women's Movement all over Australia, the Program is limping through 1983 with only one full-time member of staff and three full-year courses.[465]

Likewise, at Melbourne University in 1980, after a protracted struggle in academic committee rooms, a Women's Studies course was finally approved and an invitation sent to a woman in London to co-ordinate it, a privilege for which — at least initially — the university apparently believed she would pay her own fare to and from Australia.[466]

Yet other courses can meet a form of containment more subtle than restricted resources and inadequate funds. Where Women's Studies courses are offered within

---

[464]   Ann Curthoys, 'Women's studies, the university, and the Women's Movement', typescript, June 1975. See also Curthoys, 'Women's Studies at the Australian National University: the early years', pp. 75-80.

[465]   Personal experiences as Program Co-ordinator since March 1978.

[466]   Patricia Grimshaw to Susan Magarey, 30 January 1980.

particular university departments, the issues discussed and the material considered are often restricted by assumptions prevailing within a department about the 'discipline' which that department teaches. Students attending a course on 'Women in History', say, complain when issues they want to discuss have to be set aside because they are 'not history'. Similarly, a course on 'Women in Australian Politics', which does not question definitions of 'politics' prevailing in university departments, could examine participation in various Australian parliaments, local government bodies, trade unions, and perhaps in pressure groups lobbying parliamentarians and bureaucrats. But it would not consider such concepts as 'the politics of everyday life', or 'personal politics', or 'sexual politics'. Both of these examples are hypothetical but they could — *mutatis mutandis* — describe a great many courses which relate to Women's Studies by focusing attention specifically upon the position or activities of women rather than men, but do this within the terms of reference determined by the paradigmatic assumptions of a particular discipline, or of a particular school of thought within a discipline. Such courses which can, not unfairly, be called 'compensatory' testify to the universities' success in containing potential intellectual disruption.

Nevertheless, the repressive tolerance of post-secondary educational institutions in Australia most often appears velvet-gloved, in commitment to a liberal ideology which professes to reject all kinds of 'political indoctrination' in education and to endorse free enquiry and unfettered research an analysis. These ideals can rebel in their own terms. Such ideals can, for instance, lead students of Sociology concerned with crime and social deviance to perceive the political and administrative assumptions permeating definitions of the criminal as innately wicked, or of the deviant as socially inadequate or socially deprived, and to press for a fresh consideration of crime or deviance as a process of transaction between the individual and a mutable conditional law or social norm. Such ideals can prompt Economics students to discern the political assumptions embedded in consideration of economic issues solely as mathematical models and to demand a return to, or revision of, courses in political economy.[467] Similarly, such ideals have allowed women to perceive the androcentric assumptions underlying all forms of social inquiry, and even the priorities governing the processes by which knowledge has been divided and subdivided through time. And their perception has led to expressions of a need, not only for compensatory

---

[467] See, e.g., Stanley Cohen (ed.), *Images of deviance*, Penguin, Harmondsworth, 1971, introduction; papers of the first-several national Political Economy conferences, Sydney, Melbourne, and Adelaide, 1976-82.

courses on women-and/in-this-or-that-specialism, but also for courses, research and analysis which may draw upon many of the established intellectual disciplines to find ways of understanding stasis and process in whole, as opposed to parts of, social formations. That need is usually expressed as a demand for 'interdisciplinary' or 'multidisciplinary' and 'transdisciplinary' Women's Studies.[468]

There is a distinction which is not unimportant to be drawn between the three. But first it is necessary to define a 'discipline' — no easy task when, in so many discussions, definitions are more often assumed than spelt out, and vary widely. Often, a discipline is thought to be defined by its object of inquiry: Physics is concerned with inanimate matter, Biology with living organisms, Psychology with the behaviours and psychic construction of human individuals (despite all the time it spends on rats), history with the past, and so on. But such definitions do nothing to explain why, for instance, Physics and Geology are considered distinct disciplines, or Politics and Sociology, or History and anything since everything has a past. Similarly, when J.P. Powell simply equates 'discipline' with 'established university department', he begs all the questions he began with.[469]

More epistemologically sophisticated definitions of a 'discipline' do address this question. Stephen Toulmin's for example, makes an 'isolable and self-defining repertory of procedures' the hallmark of a 'discipline'; Paul Hirst distinguishes any one 'discipline' from another by its 'dependence on some particular kind of test against experience' for its distinctive expression.[470] Such definitions are probably adequately summed up in Martin Trow's succinct phrase — 'a body of knowledge and characteristic ways of extending knowledge'.[471] Such definitions make any 'interdisciplinary', 'multidisciplinary', or 'transdisciplinary' enterprise into a 'field', not a 'form' of knowledge[472], and suggest that the distinction between the three must be drawn according to differences in methodology, technique and procedure.

---

[468] E.g. J.E. Branson, 'The nature of Women's Studies and its potential role within the university', typescript, Monash University, 1974, p. 36.

[469] J.P. Powell, 'Towards a definition of interdisciplinary studies', *Vestes*, vol. 17, no. 2, 1974.

[470] Stephen Toulmin, *Human understanding: the collective use and evolution of concepts*, The Clarendon Press, Oxford, 1972, vol. 1, p. 359; Paul. H. Hirst, *Knowledge and the curriculum*, Routledge and Kegan Paul, London and Boston, 1974, p. 45.

[471] Martin Trow, 'The American academic department as a context for learning', *Studies in Higher Education*, vol. 1, no. 1, p. 11.

[472] Hirst, op. cit., p. 46.

Accordingly, an 'interdisciplinary' enterprise adopts specific repertoires of procedures from the disciplines between which it has developed. A 'multidisciplinary' exercise must, then, be one which draws upon the procedures of a multitude of different disciplines, and will face enormous difficulty in establishing criteria for doing so, and deciding what to do with them once it has done so. Mere eclecticism will generate teaching and research that is either superficial, or chaotic, and probably reluctant to confront negative evidence. A 'transdisciplinary' enterprise, by contrast, endeavours to transcend a specific range of disciplines, and this must mean that it establishes criteria for assessing and selecting techniques and procedures from those disciplines, even if the criteria are chiefly of the rough and ready kind which determine selection according to their usefulness in illuminating a particular field of knowledge, or in facilitating synthesis of information from a variety of intellectual traditions.

If these definitions can be accepted, then the need for Women's Studies which are not merely compensatory research and teaching within established disciplines is a need for 'transdisciplinary' work. Their 'field' of knowledge and inquiry focuses upon the position and activities of women, but extends to whole social formations; their procedures derive from whichever of the disciplines is most appropriate for consideration of, or inquiry into, specific questions or issues raised within that field of knowledge. Research into the sexual division of labour in Canberra, for example, follows procedures developed by the social sciences — Sociology and Social Anthropology. Inquiry into the biological basis of gender differentiation follows, or examines, procedures developed by both natural and social sciences, Biology and Psychology. But in such instances, the procedures followed are themselves subject to scrutiny and the final result of such work is a logically coherent integration of information and discussion consistent with assessment of the procedures adopted, directed towards illumination of issues and questions posed, not by an incestuous scholasticism, but rather by the Women's Movement.

Courses attempting 'transdisciplinary' work, even in a conservative, penny-pinching, ideologically repressive institution, are — I would argue — subverting its patriarchal domination of learning, if not so much by an explicit challenge to its hierarchical material structure, then certainly by a clear and explicit challenge to its ordering and use of knowledge. The challenge of an endeavour of this kind is great, for it is extremely difficult. Some Women's Studies courses — those at Griffith University in 1979 and 1980, at Melbourne University in 1980, at the Australian

National University in 1978 and 1979, for instance — have attempted to meet the challenge through collective, co-operative teaching, undertaken by a group, each member teaching those aspects of the transdisciplinary course which relate to her own discipline. I think that these will eventually be seen as transition measures — enterprises to be sustained until all of us, those whom the university calls students and those it calls teachers, alike, have acquired the intellectual experience necessary to assess not only information but also procedures drawn from a range of disciplines, and to integrate their research and analysis.

To say all this may be simply to offer an elaborate version of Ann Curthoy's argument, in 1975, against people 'opting out of existing disciplines and into women's studies'. 'In my view', she wrote,

> unless women's studies draws from and feeds back into the traditional disciplines it will become an isolated enclave within the university, representing the intellectual ghettoisation of women. So far women's studies courses represent a content area and perhaps to some extent have some ideological/political unity, but I cannot see how they can develop methodological coherence. I see disciplines as essential to methodological coherence and intellectual depth, even though disciplines exist only to be transcended.[473]

Moreover, if the Australian publications which can be used in Women's Studies courses are any guide, such self-conscious and critical transcendence of disciplines and the boundaries between them still lies ahead of us. Most of the books that have appeared so far have been either firmly grounded in a single discipline, or are theoretically eclectic collections which draw together work carried out in a range of disciplines but make no attempt to integrate it. In the first category, the historians probably made the earliest impact with the publication in 1975 of Beverly Kingston's study of domestic work, and Edna Ryan's and Anne Conlon's *Gentle Invaders*, an examination of the dual labour market, women's wages and the fight for equal pay.[474] Historians have been well served, too, for in 1977 the International Women's Year research project published its two-volume annotated guide to historical sources about women in Australia, Beverly Kingston published a collection of historical documents, *The World*

---

[473] Ann Curthoys, 'Women's studies, the university, and the Women's Movement', typescript, June 1975.

[474] Beverly Kingston, *My wife, my daughter and poor Mary Anne*, Thomas Nelson, Melbourne, 1975; Edna Ryan and Anne Conlon, *Gentle invaders: Australian women at work 1788-1974*, Penguin, Ringwood, 1975.

Moves Slowly, and in 1980 Kay Daniels and Mary Murnane brought out another collection of historical documents, compiled from the extensive and wide-ranging research they had undertaken for the guide to historical sources about women.[475] But the appearance, in 1982, of *Women at Work* by Kaye Hargreaves, a sociologist, may indicate a challenge to the historians' precedence from the sociologists.[476] Anne Game's and Rosemary Pringle's *Gender at Work* was in the bookshops in mid-1983.

In the second category, an early assemblage such as *The Other Half*, edited by Jan Mercer, has yielded place to later collections.[477] One of these, edited by Norma Grieve and Patricia Grimshaw — *Australian Women: Feminist Perspectives* — set out to be 'an interdisciplinary reader for students pursuing studies of women in universities and colleges of advanced education'.[478] Those students may well gain much from a few of the individual articles in the book, but unfortunately the editors have neither integrated the articles into a coherent whole, nor addressed the question of what 'interdisciplinary' means. The collections compiled from the first two Women & Labour conferences, too, give little explicit attention to the conventions of intellectual disciplines. But the first, *Women, Class and History*, is a collection of predominantly historical articles, so that the editor's introduction can focus its discussion entirely upon the kinds of history represented, or to be aimed for in the future, without having to raise questions about other disciplines.[479] And the second, *Worth Her Salt*, a collection of thirty-one papers culled from over 200 offered to the conference held in 1980, divides into two sections, the first concerned chiefly with analysis of oppression, the second with struggles for change, so that it takes its intellectual touchstones directly from the Women's Movement rather than from any concern with disciplines.[480] Carol O'Donnell and Jan Craney have assembled ten articles which draw on a range of disciplinary expertise, solid scholarship and

---

[475] Kay Daniels, Mary Murnane and Anne Picot (eds), *Women in Australia*, 2 vols, AGPS, Canberra, 1977; Beverly Kingston (ed.), *The world moves slowly*, Cassell, Camperdown, 1977; Kay Daniels and Mary Murnane (comp.), *Uphill all the way*, University of Queensland Press, St. Lucia, 1980.

[476] Kay Hargreaves, *Women at work*, Penguin, Ringwood, 1982.

[477] Jan Mercer (ed.), *The other half*, Penguin, Ringwood, 1975.

[478] Norma Grieve and Patricia Grimshaw (eds), *Women in Australia: feminist perspectives*, Oxford University Press, Melbourne, 1981, p. xi.

[479] Windschuttle (ed.), op. cit.

[480] Margaret Bevege, Margaret James and Carmel Shute (eds), *Worth her salt: women at work in Australia*, Hale and Iremonger, Sydney, 1982.

practical experiences in *Family Violence in Australia*.[481] Even more than in *Women, Class and History*, the contributors share similar theoretical orientations to their work, and since this is sharply focused on a single — if many-sided — issue, the articles form a single coherent study. But they still do not address explicitly the assumptions in the wide range of disciplines which have helped form their contributor's ideas. As Anne Summers wrote, in her path-breaking synthesis, *Damned Whores and God's Police*, as long ago as 1975, it is most unlikely that 'a comprehensive picture of women's expectations and experiences can be gained by confining one's inquiry to narrowly defined conventional academic disciplines'.[482] But it is also unlikely that we will gain such a picture if we ignore the assumptions that we have learned to make without even thinking about them, and the intellectual disciplines which inform our schooling, even in institutions of tertiary education.

The Women's Movements' protest against patriarchal relationships has generated the recognition amongst feminist scholars that androcentric research has produced not merely analyses of societies and of ways of perceiving that present women as unimportant, but rather analyses that are substantially inaccurate. They have failed even to ask the questions which would produce accounts of whole social formations, instead of halves masquerading as wholes. They have failed even to ask the questions that would reveal the gender-lock of the ways in which they think and see. And this means that — to return to the questions with which I began — if the Women's Studies courses which are flourishing in post-secondary education are at least aiming at transdisciplinary inquiry, then the Women's Movement has good cause for optimism on this front in its struggle. For such courses work like 'revolutionary reforms', reforms which when once established cannot be reversed, so that they effect change as complete as a revolution would (a concept associated with the work of radical Left philosopher, André Gorz). And transdisciplinary inquiry informed by such learning will, eventually, shake the conceptual foundations of our knowledge.

---

[481]   Carol O'Donnell and Jan Craney, *Family violence in Australia*, Longman Cheshire, Melbourne, 1982.

[482]   Summers, *Damned whores and God's police*, p. 14.

11

Are we changing paradigms? The impact of feminism upon the world of scholarship

This paper was first presented to the Women's Studies section of the annual congress of the Australian and New Zealand Association for the Advancement of Science, Monash University, August 1985. It has not been published before.

Feminist research and Women's Studies courses have become a flourishing growth in Australia's academic jungle. This has occurred during a period of financial contraction and fierce competition for resources in universities. They probably owe something to the enactment of legislation outlawing discrimination on the grounds of sex, even if that something is no more than a few token gestures. They certainly owe a great deal, as does that legislation, to the continuing vitality and diversification of the Women's Movement throughout Australia. As they would suggest that the academic arm of the Women's Movement is making at least some impact on the world of knowledge.

There is other evidence that would support such a view, even if only negatively. The new science of socio-biology, scarcely ten years old, can be seen as having developed in reaction against questions raised by feminism; Janet Sayer's book *Biological Politics*[483] has contributed to that perception. Among psychologists, attention to gender differences and to questions about how gender is inscribed in individuals now occupies a place in teaching and research undreamed of twenty years ago. There is revived debate around psychoanalytic theory, and theories of gender

---

[483] Janet Sayers, *Biological politics: feminist and anti-feminist perspectives*, Tavistock Publications, London and New York, 1982.

formation; Juliet Mitchell's *Psychoanalysis and Feminism* and Nancy Chodorow's *The Reproduction of Mothering*[484] are only two in those rapidly growing fields. Scholars in disciplines as apparently distinct as Anthropology, Demography, History, Law, Sociology and Urban Planning have been exploring changes in the shapes, sizes and impetus towards coherence or disintegration of domestic units — households and families — and the connections between those changes and others in the social order that they constitute. The collection called *Families in Colonial Australia* edited by Patricia Grimshaw and her colleagues, Kerreen Reiger's book, *The Disenchantment of the Home*, and the papers given at the national Women and Housing conference held in March 1985 all add Australian examples to a field of enquiry already burgeoning in other places.[485] Feminist economists have been challenging the androcentric assumptions of the economics establishment: in their submission to the Committee of Inquiry into Labour Market Programs (the Kirby Committee) last year, Margaret Power and her colleagues argued that,

> [d]espite a growing body of literature on the economics of women and a smaller body of literature on the economics of home and family, economists have not come to terms with women's economic issues. This failure cannot be overcome by refinement of current methodological practices; there are serious gaps in the theory itself because male economists have observed the world [only] from their own point of view.

They go on to contend that realistic attempts to reduce unemployment require measures which will reduce labour-force segregation by sex.[486] Sociologists and the framers of social policy, likewise, increasingly recognise gender as a social division as important in their analyses as divisions by class, race, ethnicity and age; a host of Australian examples spring to mind, most notably perhaps the work of Bettina Cass, and Anne Game's and Rosemary Pringle's book *Gender at Work*.[487] Students

---

[484]   Mitchell, *Psychoanalysis and feminism*; Nancy Chodorow, op. cit.

[485]   Patricia Grimshaw, Chris McConville and Ellen McEwen (eds), *Families in colonial Australia*, George Allen & Unwin, Sydney, Boston, London, 1985; Kerreen Reiger, *The disenchantment of the home: modernising the Australian family 1880-1940*, Oxford University Press, Melbourne, 1985; First National Women's Housing Conference, Adelaide, March 1985.

[486]   Margaret Power, Christine Wallace, Sue Outhwaite and Stuart Rosewarne, *Women, work, and labour market programs*, prepared for the Committee of Inquiry into Labour Market Programs, August 1984, ch. 8, p. 1.

[487]   E.g. Cass, 'Women's place in the class structure', in E.L. Wheelwright and Ken Buckley

of culture and communications have been developing analyses which depict the very definition of their subject area as an arena of struggle between the feminine and the masculine, as the forum on feminist literary criticism at the annual conference at the Australian Universities Language and Literature Association demonstrated earlier in 1985.[488] So, too, have philosophers. As Jenny [Genevieve] Lloyd observed in her book, *The Man of Reason*:

> It is clear that what we have in the history of philosophical thought is no mere succession of surface misogynist attitudes, which can now be shed, while leaving intact the deeper structures of our ideals of Reason ... [T]he maleness of Reason goes deeper than this. Our ideas and ideals of maleness and femaleness have been formed within structures of dominance — of superiority and inferiority, 'norms' and 'difference', 'positive' and 'negative', the 'essential' and the 'complementary.' And the male-female distinction itself has operated not as a straightforwardly descriptive principle of classification, but as an expression of values ... Within the context of ... association of maleness with preferred traits, it is not just incidental to the feminine that female traits have been construed as inferior — or, more subtly, as 'complementary' — to male norms of human excellence. Rationality has been conceived as transcendence of the feminine; and the 'feminine' itself has been partly constituted by its occurrence within this structure ...
>
> The content of femininity, as we have it, no less than its subordinate status, has been formed within an intellectual tradition. What has happened has been not a simple exclusion of women, but a constitution of femininity through that exclusion.[489]

Analyses as thoroughgoing, useful and scholarly as this one, like all of the examples I've just given, would suggest that Women's Studies courses and feminist research are bringing about major change in epistemology.

(eds), *Essays in the political economy of Australian capitalism*, vol. 3, Australian & New Zealand Book Company, Sydney, 1978; Bettina Cass et al., *Why so few? Women academics in Australian universities*, Sydney University Press, Sydney 1983; Cora V. Baldock and Bettina Cass (eds), *Women, social welfare and the state*, George Allen & Unwin, Sydney, London, Boston, 1983; Bettina Cass, 'The changing face of poverty in Australia: 1972-1982', in *Australian Feminist Studies*, vol. 1, no. 1, December 1985; Game and Pringle, *Gender at work*.

[488] 'Feminist Forum', *AUMLA: Journal of the Australasian Universities Modern Language Association*, May 1986. (Panel discussion at AULLA 23rd Congress, 1985).

[489] Lloyd, op. cit., pp. 103-4, 106.

Does that mean that we are changing the paradigms of the disciplines into which most of our knowledge is organised? And is that what we want to do? There are several counter-examples, and a few questions which need to be considered before we can attempt answers to these questions.

It could be argued, for instance, that all of the examples I have chosen come from feminist research and Women's Studies courses, and that, while they constitute enlightenment for *us* about everything that we have been taught in our formal education, they are making little, if any, impact upon the assumptions and practices which govern production, reproduction and dissemination of knowledge in our overwhelmingly masculine universities. At the University of Adelaide I sometimes think that even if all 367 people listed in *The Violet Pages: The Women's Studies Research Directory*, published earlier in 1985[490], were employed as academics in that one institution, the rest of our colleagues would still find it difficult to notice that we were there, much less to hear what we might be saying. Can we claim to be changing paradigms when the maintainers and practitioners of any paradigm are unaware of even the questions that we are asking?

Nevertheless, it can be argued that the feminist challenges to which I have referred are only one kind of manifestation, among many, of changes already taking place in traditional disciplines. Women's Studies courses and feminist research derive much impetus from a recognition of the politics — the power relations — embodied in the processes of learning, and in the ordering and substance of what we learn.[491] Further, that process often set in train changes which might be regarded as shifts in presiding hypotheses and their priorities, or even paradigm shifts, in which feminist scholars participated, to which we contribute, and from which we continue to learn a great deal, but changes which owe nothing specific to critiques offered by feminism. That probably sounds entirely heretical. Here are two examples.

One comes from my own field of historical research. As early as 1970 the Australian historian Ann Curthoys argued that

> [a] 'history of women' ... should do more than restore women to the pages
> of history books. It must analyse why public life has been considered to be
> the focus of history, and why public life has been so thoroughly occupied by

---

[490] Bronwyn Davies, Shirley Fisher and Lenore Coltheart, *The violet pages: the Women's Studies research directory*, University of New England, 1985.

[491] See the argument advanced in Chapter Ten, p. 151.

men ... The concepts usually operating in historiography defining what is important, must be questioned.[492]

Feminist historians rallied to that challenge, contributing to the work which enabled the American historian, Joan Kelly-Gadol, to observe six years later that '[i]n seeking to add women to the fund of historical knowledge, women's history has revitalized theory, for it has shaken the conceptual foundations of historical study'.[493] Yet those same years also saw the development of what has been called 'the new social history', which defined itself — in contradistinction to Trevelyan's definition of social history as history 'with the politics left out' — as concerned with process and stasis in whole societies, with the relationships of power between each component of a social formation, with the politics of historiography. And that meant that women's history, or feminist historiography, could be seen as an important tributary to the stream of the new social history, but not as the stream itself.[494] As Elizabeth Windschuttle remarked, in her introduction to the published collection of papers from the first Women & Labour Conference, after discussing 'the new form of social history': 'Women's history, it is clear, can both benefit from and contribute to such a model'.[495]

The second example comes from a lecture which the English anthropologist, Marilyn Strathern, gave to the Research Centre for Women's Studies in 1984, a lecture published in the first issue of *Australian Feminist Studies* in December 1985. She argued that feminism's colonisation of most of the major areas of Social Anthropology during the 1970s challenged the very foundations of the subject, the way in which anthropologists conceived their subject matter. 'They were challenging', she said, 'the theoretical emphasis on group structures, on systems of authority, and on rules and norms. They were also challenging assumptions about ideologies, and about the description of total systems'. But she went on to observe that wherever those concepts had come under scrutiny most powerfully, it was as part of a systematic deconstruction process *internal* to anthropology, owing nothing specific to feminist critiques. The result of feminist Anthropology, she said, has been a deflection from its paradigmatic challenge to a concentration on putting women back on the map,

---

[492] Ann Curthoys, 'Historiography and women's liberation', *Arena*, no. 22, 1970.

[493] Kelly-Gadol, op. cit., p. 809.

[494] Eade [Magarey], 'Social history in Britain in 1976', pp. 38-52; Magarey, 'Social history in Australia in 1981', pp. 211-28.

[495] Windschuttle (ed.), op. cit., p. 31.

an enterprise which can readily be tolerated as yet another specialism, absorbed, or at least contained, within the discipline.[496]

Set beside the first cluster of examples that I gave, these two appear to leave us stranded between two diametrically opposed perceptions of the impact of feminism on the world of scholarship. This is not an opposition between feminist and non-feminist or anti-feminist projects; all of the examples come from feminist scholars. Nor is it simply an opposition between aims and achievements, between feminist aspirations and the obstacles that they encounter in an entrenched and intellectually supple patriarchal academy. Rather, I think, it is an opposition which arises *necessarily* from the terms in which I have posed the question.

The term 'paradigm', as I have been using it, comes from the work of Thomas S. Kuhn, a theoretical physicist turned historian of science, whose monograph, *The Structure of Scientific Revolutions*, first published in 1962, contributed importantly to the process which feminist scientist Evelyn Fox Keller describes as opening up understandings of scientific thought to a consideration of social, psychological and political influences.[497] Kuhn's principal target was the Whig, or Modernisation Theory, version of the history of science: a unilineal view of scientific discovery as an accretion of knowledge, moving ever closer to truth. Against this he proposed a model for scientific revolutions, passing through four stages: competing schools of thought; an anomaly which occurs when a normal problem resists repeated attempts to solve it by the established rules and procedures; extraordinary investigations leading to a scientific revolution; a return to normal puzzle-solving activities within the paradigm established by the revolution. It is not difficult to see the appeal of Kuhn's model as an analogy for changes in focus of attention, methodology and discourses of demonstration in fields well beyond those with which Kuhn was concerned. At least half a dozen writers, mostly in the United States, have seen Kuhn's model as describing a process familiar to feminists challenging approaches and practices in the humanities and social sciences. As Marilyn Boxer observes,

---

[496]   Marilyn Strathern, 'Dislodging a worldview: challenge and counter-challenge in the relationship between feminism and anthropology', *Australian Feminist Studies*, vol. 1, no. 1, December, 1985.

[497]   Thomas S. Kuhn, *The structure of scientific revolutions*, University of Chicago Press, Chicago and London, 1970 (1962); Evelyn Fox Keller, 'Feminism and science', in N.O. Keohane et al. (eds), *Feminist theory: a critique of ideology*, Harvester Press, Brighton, 1982, p. 116, n. 7.

[w]henever women seek to apply theories of human behaviour based on men's lives to their own experience, they confront what Kuhn terms the 'anomalies' that then lead to the challenge to and ultimately the reversal [Kuhn might prefer the term 'generation' or 'transformation'] of 'paradigms' in 'normal science'.[498]

And Sandra Coyner, in arguing for Women's Studies to be established as an autonomous academic discipline, finds Kuhn's concepts to be 'sufficiently plastic that everyone can find "paradigms" guiding work in their field, whether that work is scholarly, creative or activist'.[499]

However, there is a feature of Kuhn's model, spelt out in detail in the 'Postscript' to the 1969 edition of his book, which renders such easy analogies more difficult to accept. A crucial preliminary to his analysis of scientific revolution is the existence of a community of the practitioners of a scientific specialism. About such a community, Kuhn says this:

> To an extent unparalleled in most other fields, they have undergone similar educations and professional initiations; in the process they have absorbed the same technical literature and drawn many of the same lessons from it. Usually the boundaries of that standard literature mark the limits of a scientific subject matter ... As a result, the members of a scientific community see themselves and are seen by others as the men [*sic*] uniquely responsible for the pursuit of a set of *shared* goals, including the training of their successors. Within such a group communication is relatively full and professional judgement relatively unanimous ...
>
> ... Paradigms are something *shared* by the members of such groups.[500]

And 'paradigms' Kuhn characterises as shared and unquestioned 'symbolic generalisations', shared belief in particular models, shared values which — while they may also be common to larger social groupings — provide the community with ideological and social cohesion, and shared 'exemplars' which enable members of a scientific community to see particular situations as like each other and hence

---

[498]   Marilyn J. Boxer, 'For and about women: the theory and practice of women's studies in the United States', in Keohane et al. (eds), *Feminist Theory*, pp. 259-60.

[499]   Sandra Coyner, 'Women's Studies as an academic discipline: why and how to do it', in Gloria Bowles and Renate Duelli Klein (eds), *Theories of Women's Studies*, Routledge & Kegan Paul, London, Boston, Melbourne and Henley, 1983, p. 50.

[500]   Kuhn, *The structure of scientific revolutions*, p. 178, emphasis added.

susceptible to application of the same scientific laws.[501] Accordingly, the very existence of a paradigm depends, *by definition*, on the existence of a specific and quite extraordinarily closed and homogenous social group. Further, any change to a paradigm can occur, again *by definition*, only within that community.

This, I hope, provides us with the beginning of a resolution to the impasse I reached earlier, and the beginning of an answer to the question I have been addressing. Any community of the kind Kuhn described must, until employment practices have changed beyond recognition, consist predominantly, if not exclusively, of men. Women still occupy only 11 per cent of university posts in Australia in 1983[502], a figure which demonstrates that, whatever the other differences between women and men in our society as a whole, and however those differences may operate in tertiary education institutions, there is a major divide between women and men in universities, a division which positions each sex entirely differently in relation to the world of scholarship. Any woman must, therefore, submerge or repress gender-specific perceptions in order to be able to participate in a male community's shared values and beliefs, to say nothing of its shared symbolic generalisations and exemplars. And that must mean that a paradigm is, by definition, immune to even question, far less challenge, from any feminist quarter.

Of course, Kuhn's depiction of a scientific community sounds somewhat dated today. The appearance of Hilary Rose's and Stephen Rose's book *Ideology of/in the Natural Sciences* in 1980, if nothing else, signalled a range of ways in which at least some scientists had begun to question their places in such communities and the values dominant in them.[503] It might be more accurate now to describe scientific communities in ways similar to those in which we describe the social sciences and the humanities where, as Kuhn pointed out himself, competing or even coexisting schools of thought sustain continuing controversy. Scholars in the social sciences and the humanities form communities, if at all, that are far less tightly knit, with values and beliefs less uniformly shared, than in Kuhn's communities; and we usually prefer to discuss shifts in prevailing hypotheses, or hegemonic assumptions, rather than paradigms. Moreover, most of these collectivities of people are, as my second cluster

---

[501] ibid., pp. 182-8, 190-1.

[502] I am grateful to Maryan Beams, who located this statistic for me.

[503] Hilary Rose and Stephen Rose (eds), *Ideology of/in the natural sciences*, Schenkman Publishing Co., Cambridge MA, 1980, with an introductory essay by Ruth Hubbard.

of examples showed, open to at least some changes in focus and approach in response to events in the world beyond the world of the ivory towers, as well as those within.

Nevertheless, there is still a sense in which a looser, or sloppier, version of Kuhn's description of a scientific community can be read as a description of most university communities. The proportion of academic posts held by women may be higher in the social sciences and humanities, but they are still a marked minority. Only about 10 per cent of Australia's population even gain places as students in universities, I'm told. And of that 10 per cent, despite scholarships, the Tertiary Education Assistance Scheme and the — now threatened — abolition of fees, a disproportionate number of students come to universities from the affluent middle class, from families able to send their offspring to private schools and to support them through their undergraduate years.[504] Universities are sanctuaries of economic and social privilege. It is inevitable that that fact will influence, if not determine, the priorities and the values expressed in their research and teaching. To the extent that feminism is prepared to challenge the perpetuation of privilege in any social group, feminists are precluded from full participation, full membership, in the academic community. And that, I think, explains how feminism's most conceptually radical challenges to a discipline's foundations can be so readily absorbed into the totality of a discipline, turned into a tributary or a sub-disciplinary speciality, and contained.

We have not the remotest prospect of changing paradigms. The way in which they are defined simultaneously defines that possibility out of existence. We *can* contribute to changes in prevailing hypotheses and hegemonic assumptions within particular disciplines. But we cannot effect these changes by ourselves. And that might be just as well. For if we could, surely we would be in the position of establishing Women's Studies in a position of disciplinary dominance, with all the pressures towards conservation that dominance engenders? Attractive as such a thought of dominance might be, it is in contradiction to the most fundamental aspirations of all feminist politics.

If we are not changing paradigms, or the dominant hypotheses in the academic disciplines, what are we doing? How are we to understand any credit-list of achievements for feminist research and Women's Studies courses? I think that we

---

[504] See, e.g., Margaret Truscott, *Women's access to universities: a pilot study*, Research Centre for Women's Studies, University of Adelaide, 1985.

are doing two things, both of them more epistemologically challenging than any old paradigm change.

Firstly, we are at last, just as men have for generations, allowing ourselves to ask questions which arise from our positioning in the world and our distinctive experiences of it. That is not to say that all women, or even all feminists, are asking the same, or even similar, questions; we know too well how profoundly we are divided, just as, if not in the same way, men are, by race, class, ethnicity, age, physical fitness, sexual preference, and the condition of being married or single. It *is* saying, however, that there is a difference within all those distinctions between women's and men's experiences of them. And the questions arising from our perceptions of that difference are seldom adequately answered by the received wisdom or established procedures for research within any one discipline. That does not mean that we may not spend a long time — years, perhaps — exploring the possibilities of answers within a particular discipline, nor that such exploration may not enrich that discipline considerably. But it does, ultimately, lead us to perceive that the way that knowledge is divided and sub-divided into disciplines is politically shaped by the domination in the academy of privileged men. And that impels us beyond disciplinary boundaries in search of answers to our questions. This is not simply the occasional venture into an interdisciplinary field which any good researcher engages in. Rather, it is a search which leads us to transcend disciplinary boundaries, ranging the disciplines and selecting from them the information, methodologies, techniques and procedures most fruitful for answers to our questions. It is a search which keeps us constantly on the boundary of the particular discipline in which we have been trained. It is also a search which gives an edge to our contributions to change within a particular discipline, for it introduces into the discussions and debates through which such change occurs the foreign element, the piece of grit around which an oyster forms a pearl.

Secondly, I would suggest that our ability to ask such questions emerges from our participation in at least two worlds, not merely the one in which paradigms rule. That is not to say that all of the research that I touched on at the beginning of this paper — ranging from research in Biology and Psychoanalysis, through Anthropology, Demography, Economics, History, Law, Sociology and Urban Planning, to Communications, Cultural Studies and Philosophy — is not informed by those disciplines. On the contrary, it makes extensive and fruitful use of their tools and concepts. But it is also shaped and coloured by participation in the Women's

Movement, where we learn to give attention to our positioning *as women*, to the conditions of our lives and the relationships that we form with the world — an attention which our formal education in established academic disciplines effectively prohibits.

Feminist research and Women's Studies courses give us, to steal a title from North American feminist historian Joan Kelly, 'the doubled vision of feminist theory'.[505] It was the doubled vision which enabled Margaret Power and her colleagues to perceive that both radical and orthodox economists had reached conclusions which were not only inadequate but also 'misleading and erroneous'.[506] It was the doubled vision of feminist theory which informed Susan Sheridan's reading of Geoffrey Serle's discussion of three Australian nineteenth-century women novelists in his book *From Deserts the Prophets Come*. Serle found all of those novelists infuriating for the contrast, as he experienced it, between their acute intelligence and intellectual depth on the one hand, and on the other their romantic, tripey plots. And he wondered if they were, perhaps, bound by the conventions of polite female fiction, and were, perhaps, more satirical than we know, 'we' in the context clearly referring to a community of literary men. Sheridan considered this a disarming confession of bewilderment, and went on to remark:

> But how odd the female version sounds, if I say: perhaps Boldrewood and Clarke were writing mainly for men, for this might explain why they accepted the distorting heroics of male adventure fiction, within which limitations they may, for all I know, be making profound metaphysical comments on life as men experienced it ... Of course [she continued] I cannot pretend to be so ingenuous, for I have been schooled to recognise metaphysical profundity when confronted with it.

'Now', she concluded,

> having taught myself to read women's books, I am blessed with double vision and can see that there are indeed two literary cultures.[507]

---

505   Joan Kelly, 'The doubled vision of feminist theory', in Judith L. Newton et al. (eds), *Sex and class in women's history*, Routledge & Kegan Paul, London, Boston, Melbourne, Henley, 1983.

506   Power et al., *Women, work and labour market programs*, p. 1.

507   Susan Sheridan, 'Ada Cambridge and the female literary tradition', in Susan Dermody et al. (eds), *Nellie Melba, Ginger Meggs and friends: essays in Australian cultural history*, Kibble Books, Melbourne, 1982.

It is the doubled vision of feminist theory which enables Elizabeth Gross to observe not only that 'feminist theory can afford to ignore the history of and contemporary [men's] conceptions of power at its own peril', but also that '[f]eminist theory does not have to commit itself to the values and commitments of patriarchal theory, but in order to go beyond them, it must work through them, displace them and create a space of its own'.[508]

All feminist scholars, whatever their kind of feminism and whatever the discipline in which their scholarship was formed or is forming, participate in the doubled vision of feminist theory. There is, inevitably, a tension between the two worlds in which we learn to see; we often experience a schizophrenic conflict of demands. Yet anyone who has worked in a Women's Studies course or undertaken feminist research knows how creative that tension can be. A French philosopher, Gilles Deleuze, has suggested that while 'majority' implies a state of law and domination, 'minority' implies potential — 'creative becoming'.[509] Women may be a numerical majority in many human societies, but we are not a majority which can be associated readily with law and domination. Rather, we appear most often as subordinate — in the position of minority groups. Perhaps that is why the creative tension of the doubled vision of feminist theory gives us so strong a sense of potential, of 'creative becoming'. Who would sacrifice that to arrive at the condition of majority, confined to a one-eyed paradigm?

---

[508] Elizabeth Gross, 'Contemporary theories of power', in Deakin Women's Studies Course Team (comp.), *Feminist knowledge as critique and construct*, Study Guide, parts A & B, in production 1985.

[509] Gilles Deleuze, 'Philosophie et minorité', *Critique*, no. 369, February 1978. I owe this reference, and translation of the article, to Jenny Lloyd, to whom I am most grateful.

12

Setting up the first Research Centre for Women's Studies in Australia, 1983-86

An earlier and longer version of this article was first published in a guest-edited issue of Australian Feminist Studies, *vol. 13, no. 27, 1998.*

In November 1997, the Research Centre for Women's Studies [RCWS] at Adelaide University celebrated its fourteenth birthday. Structurally, it is now affiliated with the new Adelaide Research Centre for Humanities and Social Sciences in a recently created Division of Humanities and Social Sciences. It seems to have established its intellectual respectability by winning large grants from the Australian Research Council [ARC], by producing a fully refereed international journal, *Australian Feminist Studies*, by running a regular seminar series to which an array of international, interstate and local feminist scholars have contributed, and by organising a succession of conferences and workshops, some supported by no less a body than UNESCO.[510] None of these

---

[510] The conferences organised by the RCWS are: 'The Sixth International Interdisciplinary Congress on Women', 1996; 'The Body Politic, an Historical Conference Commemorating the Achievement of Women's Suffrage in South Australia', 1994; 'Women, Work and Control of Household Expenditure', a Regional Workshop funded by UNESCO, 1994; 'Women and Restructuring: Work and Welfare', a workshop organised in conjunction with the Academy of Social Sciences in Australia, 1992; 'Women and Development', a Workshop funded by the Australian Commission to UNESCO, 1992; 'Women's Studies in Asia & the Pacific', funded by UNESCO, 1991; 'Australian Feminist Biography & Autobiography', 1989; 'Feminist Enquiry as a Transdisciplinary Enterprise', in conjunction with the Humanities

factors *guarantees* its continued existence, though. Restructuring within institutions of higher learning continues to effect major change with increasing frequency; ARC grants run out; memories of seminars and conferences fade. But, for the moment, the oldest Research Centre for Women's Studies in Australia seems to be secure, more secure than at any other moment in its fourteen years. In this article, I'm concerned only with its first three years, 1983-86, possibly — as with most infancies — the time of its greatest insecurity. I will outline these under three headings.

Intellectual erasure

When I moved to Adelaide at the end of 1983, I found it a very different environment from the one in which I had become a feminist and an academic. Just as the Women's Movement in a city of around a million people had markedly different complexions from that in Canberra, a city of around 250 000 with an exceptionally high proportion of university-educated women, so the established sandstone Adelaide University was a very different institution from the ANU. There were students wanting Honours-level courses that would teach them something about feminism, and students wanting supervision for feminist topics for both Honours and postgraduate theses. There was a small core of committed academics, chaired by Jean Blackburn who was then attached to the Education Department in the university, who had conducted the campaign to secure the funding for the post to which I came. In the wider community, there was an array of feminist groups and organisations, many of them connected, however distantly, with the state: bodies like the Working Women's Centre, the Women's Studies Resource Centre, the Women's Information Switchboard, the Rape Crisis Centre, and Women's Advisors in a number of government departments. But, at Adelaide University, there was no groundswell among the students for undergraduate units in Women's Studies; the numbers seeking Honours-level or postgraduate supervision were very small and firmly located in their discipline-of-origin; the small core of committed academics included more people trying to finish postgraduate qualifications and gain secure academic posts in established disciplines than it included tenured academics or anyone else, so it was very unlike the predominantly non-university anarchist intellectual adventurers in the discussion groups I had known in Canberra; the territoriality of university departments, reinforced by the dependence

Research Centre, Australian National University, 1986; 'Crucible of Feminism: Women in the Nineteenth Century', 1985; 'Women and Tertiary Mathematics', 1985.

of funding on student numbers, militated strenuously against even interdisciplinary research, far less anything that could be called 'transdisciplinary'; and there seemed to be confusion about whether or not the Director of the new Research Centre for Women's Studies should be functioning as some kind of Equal Opportunity Officer.

There had been pioneering undergraduate Women's Studies courses at both Flinders University and at the South Australian College of Advanced Education [SACAE]. But, in 1983, both were in a state of transition: at Flinders, there was a struggle underway about the future of undergraduate teaching in Women's Studies at all, and at the SACAE the academic staff involved were still straddling a divide between their fields or disciplines of origin and their specifically Women's Studies courses. In those feminist groups that I encountered beyond the institutions of higher learning, preoccupations seemed to be far more practical and concerned with theatre, therapy or policy. Or, as time passed, and the legendary Dunstan years faded, with maintaining any feminist services at all. Not with the kinds of learning and debate that had occupied us in Canberra.

At Adelaide University, beyond the group that had appointed me, there was some curiosity about what I might say or do, though a far greater readiness to *tell* me what I *should* say and/or do; widespread and complacent ignorance about what Women's Studies was doing in other places; and significant hostility. I felt deprived of the undergraduate constituency that had driven the establishment of Women's Studies at ANU, and its subsequent efforts at 'transdisciplinarity'. Ultimately, too, my experience of all of these differences included a sense of personal intellectual erasure.

Let me illustrate this last point with one light, but symptomatic, story. I choose this one because it hit me where I was most vulnerable. This story concerns my early connections with the discipline in which I had gained both of my postgraduate qualifications at ANU, in which I was still endeavouring to research and publish. Historians had been among the strongest, and simultaneously humblest (they did not assume they knew better than we could what feminist scholarship should be about) champions of Women's Studies at ANU. Historians, I had thought, were my academic fathers and brothers, mothers and sisters. But, then, familial relationships can also be the most careless.

I had been invited to write an extended review of four works concerned with the debates over history versus theory that had been raising such a political and intellectual dust in Britain for a North American journal.[511] I offered this to the staff/postgraduate seminar in the History Department, specifically because it was *not* concerned with feminism and I wanted to establish some local credibility in other fields as well. Imagine my chagrin, then, when I arrived to present the paper to a crowded room to find that the historians had not been able to remember my name when they had advertised the seminar, and had announced it as being given by an entity called simply 'Women's Studies'. My personal intellectual identity had effectively been erased.

Scrounging for paperclips

The funding that had enabled Adelaide University to advertise for a Director of a new Research Centre for Women's Studies had been secured from what, in the language of the times, were called 'windfall monies'. But those monies were sufficient only to provide my salary and a very small setting-up grant. On a preliminary visit to Adelaide, during the mid-semester break in 1983, I learned that the first thing I would need to do was to raise other money to fund activities that the Centre would need to undertake. The university's Office of Research suggested that I apply immediately to the University Research Scheme; the deadline for applications was in two days' time, and the application would have to be for a research project. It also provided me with the application forms for an Australian Research Grants Scheme [ARGS] large grant. My training as an historian had been only in individual research, immersed in archival collections by myself with notebook and pencil. This was the beginning of what others have taught me to call 'a steep learning curve'.

The University Research Scheme [URS] provided funds for a Research Assistant for six months. The ARGS large-grant application was a dismal failure: 'over-ambitious' and 'greedy' are the terms that I recall from its assessments. But these were also the days of the federally funded Community Employment Program [CEP]; feminists in the bureaucracy in Adelaide let me know that there were still funds to be allocated for competitive projects. Soon after I arrived in Adelaide, then, I knew that I had money for three research projects. Successful as these wild early efforts might

---

[511] Susan Magarey, 'That hoary old chestnut, free will and determinism: culture vs. structure, or history vs. theory in Britain. A review article', *Comparative Studies in Society and History: an International Quarterly*, vol. 29, no. 3, July 1987, pp. 626-39.

have been, they generated major problems of space and time, and failed to assist the Research Centre's needs for basic infrastructure.

I am sure that the lessons that I learned in these years are now familiar throughout the tertiary education sector. Successful project grant applications meant people, and people meant office space. In the University of Adelaide, office space was (and still is) a highly contentious matter. The Faculty of Arts had allowed me a room in the History Department's corridors, and had suggested that I might be allowed to join the queues for the secretarial services of the History Department's office. The URS Research Assistant used my room for the duration of that project's funding; we shared it during the last two months of 1983. But I was about to have to engage no fewer than four new full-time research assistants and a full-time typist, and there was simply no room for them anywhere in the building. Eventually, we found some unoccupied space in another building, but the room which at first housed three research assistants, subsequently two research assistants and a professional writer, then three postgraduate students, was always overcrowded. The Research Centre was to move three times during its first seven years.

The successful grant application also meant time. The accountability requirements for the CEP funds meant that, even if I had devoted *all* of my time to training and supervising the researchers I employed, I could not have clocked up enough hours to satisfy the CEP's requirements. Indeed, given the other demands on my time, I provided so little supervision that one project depended crucially on the skill and initiative that the researchers already had, and never produced even a list of the research material that they compiled — a sad waste of good work. My learning curve now included what I can only call 'creative accountability-reporting'.

All of these funds were for projects. They could not be used for the Research Centre's infrastructural needs, which, with increasing urgency, included at least some secretarial support, a typewriter, and access to a photocopier. I cannot recall now the means by which I eventually secured funding for one of the best half-time Secretaries in the world — Maryan Beams, a university medallist in Sociology from Flinders — or for what became a regular maintenance budget of around $1500 a year from 1984 until 1996. But I was reminded recently of the day when I came upon an unused typewriter in a store-room and, being desperate and institutionally indigent, simply took possession of it.

Political will

The windfall monies that provided my salary were to last for only three years; my appointment at Adelaide University was temporary. The small core of committed campaigners for the Research Centre made it clear that the most important, though unwritten, item in the brief to which I had been appointed was to ensure the continuation of the Research Centre for Women's Studies beyond that time. In the beginning, I thought that all I would need to do was to make a good job of the written items in my brief. I organised a regular seminar for academic staff and postgraduates. I organised a series of public lectures under the general heading 'Changing Paradigms', at which about 100 people each time listened to such speakers as Human Rights Commissioner Dame Roma Mitchell, English feminist anthropologist Marilyn Strathern, feminist historian Kay Daniels, feminist economist Meredith Edwards, and feminist sociologist Bettina Cass.[512] I gave a term's worth of lectures in a later-year course in the History Department, and co-taught an Honours option on Sexualities in the Anthropology Department. I offered 'A History of Feminist Thought in the English-Speaking West' to Honours students from the Departments of Education, English, History, and Politics, and supervised the theses of more than one prize-winner. I began to co-supervise postgraduate students — jointly, though, because I might be around for only three years. My second attempt at an ARGS grant succeeded. I organised a couple of small conferences, and arranged that the third of the conferences to be held during the year on 'Feminism and the Humanities' at the Humanities Research Centre at ANU in 1986 would be held at Adelaide and organised by the Research Centre for Women's Studies. (This was the conference which, being thoroughly into difference, finally laid to rest my commitment to feminist scholarship being able to be so synthesising as to be 'transdisciplinary'.) I even presented papers of my own at conferences both in Adelaide and interstate. I accepted a consultancy at Griffith University. I chaired the South Australian government's review of the Working Women's Centre. Like a dog with a well-chewed shoe, I presented these achievements to the Research Centre's Management Committee, wagging my tail and demanding approval. It was not enough.

All of our enquiries about what was to happen to the Research Centre after the end of 1986 met polite rebuff: 'Don't worry about it'.

---

[512] All were published in *Australian Feminist Studies*, vol. 1, no. 1, Summer 1985.

But we did. The chairperson of the Management Committee at the time was Fay Gale, Professor of Geography and, at the time, the only woman to hold a senior appointment in the university. She knew that as early as 1984 negotiations were already underway over the university's submission to the Commonwealth Tertiary Education Commission [CTEC] for funding for the triennium to follow 1986; if continuing provision for the Research Centre for Women's Studies were not included in that submission the Research Centre would simply disappear and I would go back to ANU. A concerted campaign was necessary.

This felt like being back at ANU, where the very existence of the Women's Studies course resulted from what became known as the Student Education Campaign of 1974. I had had plenty of practice. Late in 1984, we wrote letters to prominent feminists throughout Australia, suggesting that they write to the Vice-Chancellor, Don Stranks, asking him to ensure the Research Centre's continuation. When we ran into him early in 1985, he said that if he had $10 for every letter he had received he would be able to guarantee the Research Centre's future from that fund. Carol Johnson, a member of the Research Centre's Management Committee and a postgraduate student in the Politics Department, had strong connections with the Postgraduate Students Association and, through that body, with the (undergraduate) Student's Association. They began organising a demonstration, and for an occasion on which they could ensure maximum embarrassment for the university. In April 1985, Adelaide University was to celebrate the centenary of the graduation of its first female graduate. The students planned the demonstration for that day.

But there was also a strand to this campaign that was entirely unfamiliar to me. The negotiations about the submission to CTEC in this university which took pride in its collegial form of management depended crucially upon agreement by the deans of the various faculties. Fay Gale went to each of them in turn, to try to persuade them to support the Research Centre's future. In a climate of parsimony generated by knowledge that funding from Canberra was already shrinking, she was asking them for unprecedented altruism, and it is probably only because she was personally held in such high esteem throughout the university that she gained a hearing at all. She was not able to persuade them to support us, but, exercising her very considerable diplomatic skills, she did persuade them not to oppose us.

Only days before the threatened demonstration by the students, the Vice-Chancellor acted. He had always been markedly supportive of the Research Centre, but collegial management meant that he could not override the deans of the faculties; funding for the Research Centre was at the bottom of a long list of other posts to which the deans gave priority, and the 1986 submission to CTEC would not move the Women's Studies post from anywhere but the bottom of that list. So Don Stranks resorted to an inventive and quite extraordinary measure. First, he summoned me to ask if I would stay at the University of Adelaide if he were able to make my post tenured. Of course I said yes. Then he sent a circular letter to all senior academic staff pointing out that the recent salary rise had moved them into a different tax-bracket, increasing their income tax. He went on to suggest that a regular donation to the University Foundation to secure the Research Centre for Women's Studies would be tax-deductible, thereby ameliorating the tax disadvantages that they had just incurred. He invited them to make such donations, as he did himself, and put out a press release announcing that the future of the Research Centre for Women's Studies was ensured.[513]

I was embarrassed at having, in effect, become a university charity. But I was pleased at the acknowledgement that this measure implied, that the Research Centre for Women's Studies was doing a good job. And I was even more pleased, as we had been when the Student Education Campaign at ANU eventually succeeded in establishing a Women's Studies post, at the thought of what concerted political will could achieve — though I could not avoid an additional strong sense of the irony over the changes in time and place, for this victory had depended crucially on political will at the top, as well as at the grassroots of the system.

Of course there have been other times when the Research Centre's closure seemed imminent, though never as inevitably so as in 1984. We are now housed in a space built specifically for us. I am no longer a university charity; responsibility for my salary was moved to the Faculty of Arts in the early 1990s.

Women's Studies is now established as a field of serious academic endeavour across the three universities in Adelaide. Since 1986, a fully fledged Women's Studies Unit has been developed at Flinders University with what was, for a time, the most senior appointment in Women's Studies in Australia, Lyndall Ryan's Readership. The SACAE's Women's Studies Teaching Team moved into the University of Adelaide in 1990, under the Dawkins mergers, and combined with the Research Centre to

---

[513] 'Research Centre for Women's Studies confirmed', press release, 30 April 1985, in Special Collections, Barr Smith Library, University of Adelaide.

create the first Women's Studies Department in a university in Australia. What became the University of South Australia developed a Gender Studies Centre. In 1996 the Research Centre for Women's Studies (with a team drawn from Women's Studies at Adelaide and Flinders Universities and Gender Studies at the University of South Australia) organised the Women's Worlds Conference (the Sixth International Interdisciplinary Congress on Women), which brought no fewer than 1000 women to Adelaide from 57 different countries. Such strengths across the sector, and such inter-university collaboration, have ensured that Women's Studies is a distinctive presence in South Australia. And this is a presence that appears to find equivalent strengths in Women's Studies in the United States, in Britain, and in Europe.[514] The Women's Studies Department at Adelaide University has not only survived (though in 1997 it became part of a larger department, called Social Policy), but has also appointed a Foundation Professor in Women's Studies, Chilla Bulbeck. The variety and array of both undergraduate and postgraduate work under way in all three universities in South Australia ensures plenty of the intellectual ferment that I missed so when I arrived in 1983. Moreover, the Research Centre for Women's Studies continues — for now.

Still, as I indicated at the beginning of this summary account, there is nothing secure about being in Women's Studies — either intellectually or structurally. Even though the revolutionary aspirations that I assumed so unquestioningly fourteen years ago seem, now, extremely remote.

---

[514] For Women's Studies in the United States, see, for example, *Women's Studies Quarterly*, vol. 25, nos. 1 & 2, Spring/Summer 1997: *Looking back, moving forward: 25 years of Women's Studies history*, The Feminist Press at the City University of New York; for Women's Studies in Britain, see, for example, Jane Aaron and Sylvia Walby (eds), *Out of the margins: Women's Studies in the nineties*, The Falmer Press, London, 1991; Joanna de Groot and Mary Maynard (eds), *Women's Studies in the 1990s: doing things differently*, Macmillan, London, 1993; for Women's Studies in Europe, see the wealth of notices appearing in WISE-List on every subscriber's email daily.

13

The role of a Women's Studies Centre in the university

Paper presented at the invitation of the Equal Opportunity Unit and the Gender Studies Working Party at the University of Melbourne, 10 September, 1987. This has not been published before.

This is an exciting time in the deliberations which may set up a Women's Studies Centre at Melbourne University, and I am glad to be able to contribute to them. What I want to spend most of my time talking about now are answers to the question, why have a Women's Studies Centre?

I would like to assume that, in 1987, it is no longer necessary to argue the prior question, why have Women's Studies at all? But I will pause over it for just a moment, because it is a question I am still called upon to answer from time to time at Adelaide University. Earlier this year, I was asked to give a seminar paper to the Botany Department on what Women's Studies is and does. Last year I had to perform a similar exercise for the Department of Plant Pathology at the Waite Institute of Agricultural Research. In both, it emerged that there was a previously formed expectation that Women's Studies must either be about ensuring more jobs for women in universities, or be concerned solely with — in their view — 'soft' humanities waffle about representations of women in literature. On the first count, the Botany Department had hoped to demonstrate that there was no need for Women's Studies at Adelaide because they already employed several women —

though, as usual, clustered in the lowest paid and least secure jobs. On the second, the Plant Pathologists simply could not believe that questions about gender could have anything to do with their research. One of them, who had listened to me talking about the masculinity of the work culture established in some laboratories and classrooms (to say nothing of industries) with care and, I think, no special lack of sympathy, finally said:

> Well, I can see how considerations of gender might alter your research agenda, the priorities determining what you will investigate next. But I can't see what difference it would make to The Scientific Method.

This response came as quite a shock. Any historian of the Philosophy of Science knows that the last twenty to thirty years have seen profound and far-reaching discussion in scientific communities about the social and political formation of scientific values. As North American feminist scientist Evelyn Fox Keller wrote:

> As long as the course of scientific thought was judged to be exclusively determined by its own logical and empirical necessities, there could be no room for any signature, male or otherwise in that system of knowledge. Furthermore, any suggestion of gender differences in our thinking about the world could argue only too readily for the exclusion of women from science.[515]

But when Fox Keller wrote that, in an article published five years ago, she was already able to assume that the so-called value-neutrality of the sciences was a myth that was well and truly dislodged. I had assumed that my colleagues in Botany and Plant Pathology were evincing precisely that awareness when they asked me to talk to them, and were ready to hear about the gendered signatures that scholars like Fox Keller, Sandra Harding and Ruth Bleir have discovered in supposedly value-neutral scientific enquiry.[516] Indeed, the papers I prepared for my colleagues had included Genevieve Lloyd's critique of the masculinity of the rationality which lies at the heart of The Scientific Method, what she called 'the maleness of Reason' (see Chapter Eleven, pp. 158-9). Some of the botanists were able to recognise this, though with some surprise, and what then emerged as the masculinity of the language in which they talk about plants. The Plant Pathologists, however, were still so wedded to belief in the

---

[515] Fox Keller, 'Feminism and science', pp. 116-17.

[516] Evelyn Fox Keller, *Reflections on gender and science*, Yale University Press, New Haven and London, 1985; Sandra Harding, *The science question in feminism*, Cornell University Press, Ithaca and London, 1986; Ruth Bleir, *Science and gender: a critique of biology and its theories on women*, Pergamon Press, New York & co., 1984.

universality and value-neutrality of The Scientific Method that they could not even hear Lloyd's argument.

Both responses, I thought, furnished good reasons for the existence of Women's Studies in universities. The botanists may go on to explore the more interesting questions about how considerations of gender might alter not merely their research agendas, but also their assumptions, methodologies, perhaps even their findings. And the students and laboratory assistants from departments like Plant Pathology, including students from the misogynist Faculty of Engineering, are beginning to come to Women's Studies seminars, are even offering papers about the processes of working in non-traditional occupations. The Plant Pathologists may have dismissed me. But they will not so easily remain deaf to their own colleagues.

I find it difficult to imagine, though, that you here at Melbourne University would have to argue such an elementary and already dated case. After all, in this university you already have at least some undergraduate courses which focus specifically upon women and gender relations. Your Gender Studies Working Committee includes people from Psychology, Pathology, Economics and Psychiatry as well as from departments more often perceived as receptive to Women's Studies issues. This would suggest that you can already offer postgraduate supervision to students wanting to do research concerning women in a wide range of disciplines. And members of this university have already published two of the principal and bestselling Women's Studies texts produced in Australia — Norma Grieve's and Pat Grimshaw's *Women in Australia: Feminist Perspectives* and the *New Feminist Perspectives* volume which Norma Grieve and Ailsa Burns edited, published last year.[517] Amid such an established wealth of achievement, the most fundamental question becomes — why establish a Centre of Women's Studies? What could a centre achieve that you are not achieving already?

I would note, in passing, that you are not entirely alone. Macquarie University hopes to attract funding from the Commonwealth Tertiary Education Commission to establish a centre of undergraduate teaching in Women's Studies, and is in a strong position — in terms of staff and students already committed to the project, and courses and research projects relevant to it — to do so. Sydney University, likewise, offers a range of undergraduate courses, some of which could be grouped

---

[517] Grieve and Grimshaw, op. cit.; Norma Grieve and Ailsa Burns, *Australian women: new feminist perspectives*, Oxford University Press, Melbourne, 1986.

into a coherent Women's Studies program. Deakin, Murdoch and Queensland Universities already, jointly, offer an undergraduate major in Women's Studies. And the Universities of New South Wales and Western Australia offer coursework Masters degrees in Women's Studies. Despite economic stringencies in tertiary education, Women's Studies is clearly making enormous gains in Australia. It is probably an ideal time to establish a Women's Studies Centre.

Of course, you are far from the first to propose that a centre be set up. Universities seem constantly to be establishing centres — to facilitate a concentration of research effort around a particular theme, a particular cluster of issues. Examples range from the Centre of Research in Environmental Studies, the Humanities Research Centre, the Social Justice Project, and the Aging and the Family Project — all at ANU — to the Social Welfare Research Centre at the University of New South Wales and the Special Research Centre in Gene Technology at Adelaide University. And there are many more. Arguments for a centre are, in principle, very much the same. I'd have thought that your established strengths in the field of Women's Studies would make such arguments for a Women's Studies Centre particularly forceful.

But there are also more specific arguments in favour of a Centre in Women's Studies, arguments which arise from the Women's Studies endeavour itself. I would like to dwell on these a little. People engaged in Women's Studies — students, teachers, researchers — are always working in four dimensions, with four sets of focus, facing in four directions at once (difficult if there are fewer than four of you), working with a recognition of four distinct (though often overlapping) communities of involvement.

The first is the world of feminist scholarship. As North American feminist scholar Catharine Stimpson noted: 'Casual observers of Women's Studies may underestimate how large and how refined it has become as an intellectual enterprise'.[518] Of course, as it has grown, feminist scholarship has developed internal theoretical debates of very considerable sophistication. They are not, by any means, hermetically sealed against influences from fields of scholarship and critique that are not specifically concerned with feminist issues. On the contrary. One current debate, over the relative usefulness for feminist research of the Marxist-derived concept of agency, or the

---

[518]   Catharine R. Stimpson with Nina Kressner Cobb, *Women's Studies in the United States*, Ford Foundation, New York, 1986, p. 34.

Freudian-derived concept of subjectivity, clearly draws from theoretical discussion in circles other than those concerned exclusively with feminist issues. Yet another debate, also current, over the question of difference — not merely between women and men, but more complicatedly *among* women — has arisen from critiques which are largely internal to feminism and feminist scholarship, critiques of the silenced or subjugated Other within the feminist texts and practices of most of the 1970s. Issues of race, ethnicity, class, sexuality and age (at least) now render discussion of gender infinitely more complex than it was even ten years ago. At Princeton University, where undergraduate Women's Studies courses are taught by a team which can include Natalie Zemon Davis and Elaine Showalter, one course initially emphasised cultural and historical specificities to an extent that, by the end, they had lost sight of women as an identifiable social and subjective category of analysis altogether. Now they tread a fine line between attention to difference and attention to the commonality of women's experiences in different cultures through time.[519] These are only two examples of a host of issues under debate amongst feminist scholars and in Women's Studies courses.

The second focus of attention, community of involvement, for Women's Studies practitioners is the world of non-feminist scholarship which usually forms our most immediate intellectual environment: the academic disciplines into which our knowledges have been divided. Feminists working within the established disciplines have developed critiques of their androcentricity, their incapacity to encompass the positioning and experiences of women. In Economics, for instance, in 1984, the Australian Political Economist Margaret Power, and her colleagues, reported to the Committee of Inquiry into Labour Market Programs (the Kirby Committee) that 'economists have not come to terms with women's economic issues' because 'male economists have observed the world [only] from their own point of view' (see also Chapter Eleven, p. 158).[520] And in another of the non-scientific, so-called hard disciplines — Law — feminist critiques led, in 1986, to a conference at Macquarie University on 'Feminist Legal Issues' at which more than 200 people listened with approval to a Canadian feminist legal academic, Mary Jane Mossman, urging in a

---

[519] Professor Davis told me about this when I was in Princeton University as part of my journey around the United States as a visitor of the United States Information Agency in 1986; see Chapter Sixteen.

[520] Power, Wallace, Outhwaite and Rosewarne, op. cit., p. 1.

new way of looking at law, with a view to disengaging from conventional forms of legal analysis which, she argued, are inherently patriarchal both in form and in substance.[521]

Feminist critiques of the established disciplines have begun making a considerable impact upon the intellectual landscape. In 1982 the North American literary critic Wayne C. Booth analysed the works of Rabelais and Bakhtin from what he had learned of a feminist perspective and concluded:

> I finally accept what many feminist critics have been saying all along. Our various canons have been established by men, reading books written mostly by men for men, with women as eavesdroppers.[522]

In Australia, in 1983, that august body the Academy of the Social Sciences organised a conference which it called 'Women in the Social Sciences: New Modes of Thought'.[523]

For many thinking in new modes, feminist critiques of the established disciplines have led on to arguments that their androcentricity renders them incapable of accommodating research on and discussion of the issues that feminism raises. In Women's Studies, such arguments maintain, we need to transgress, to transcend the established disciplinary boundaries.[524] As the English anthropologist Marilyn Strathern observed last year:

> Much feminist discourse is constructed in a multiple or plural way … Arguments are juxtaposed, many voices deliberately solicited in the way that feminists speak about their own scholarship. There are no central texts, no definitive techniques. And the deliberate transdisciplinary enterprise plays with context. Perspectives from different disciplines are held to illuminate one another; historical or literary or anthropological insights are juxtaposed by writers at once conscious of the different contexts of these disciplines and refusing to take those contexts as organising frames.[525]

---

[521]   See Regina Graycar, 'Feminism comes to Law: better late than never', *Australian Feminist Studies*, vol. 1, no. 3, Summer 1986.

[522]   Quoted in Stimpson, op. cit., p. 43.

[523]   The book resulting from this conference is Jacqueline Goodnow and Carole Pateman (eds), *Women, social science, and public policy*, Allen & Unwin, Sydney, 1985.

[524]   See Chapter Ten, above.

[525]   Marilyn Strathern, 'Out of context: the persuasive fictions of anthropology', Frazer Lecture delivered at the University of Liverpool, 1986, pp. 45-6. I am very grateful to Marilyn Strathern for sending me a copy of this lecture.

The transdisciplinarity of Women's Studies has implications for all the institutions whose very buildings represent the materiality of discipline boundaries in tertiary education institutions. But it should be noted, I think, that even as Women's Studies endeavours to transcend these boundaries, it depends upon the existence of the established disciplines as much as it depends upon feminist critiques developed within them.

The third direction in which Women's Studies practitioners face is outwards to the world outside the institutions of higher learning. From this direction we learn many of the issues that become central in feminist scholarship. To this world we look for many of the political implications of concepts being discussed and refined in Women's Studies courses, of the findings being generated by feminist research. One example is the debate during the last few years over the new reproductive technologies, in which Robyn Rowland, senior lecturer in Women's Studies at Deakin University, has taken a leading and controversial part.[526] Another is the now horrifying visibility of child sexual abuse, newly recognised during the 1970s in feminist shelters and refuges, disseminated through discussions of violence and power in Women's Studies courses, now — finally — gaining acceptance in the medical and social work professions to such an extent that front pages of the British dailies were filled with raging, and still unresolved, debate about it for most of July this year.

Another, and more difficult, example is furnished by the notorious Sears Roebuck case in the United States, in which feminist scholarship was brought to the aid of each of the contesting parties. In 1979 the Equal Employment Opportunity Commission filed a charge of sex discrimination against the massive general retail chain, Sears Roebuck. By mid-1985 the case was being heard in a courtroom in Chicago. Among the expert witnesses for Sears Roebuck was the feminist historian Rosalind Rosenberg. She claimed that history teaches us that a female culture has created women who have values other than those of a masculine, competitive marketplace. They *choose*, she said, to take less well-paid, less competitive jobs.

---

[526] See, for example, Robyn Rowland, 'Reproductive technologies: the final solution to the woman question?', in R. Arditti, R. Duelli Klein and S. Minden (eds), *Test tube women: what future for motherhood?*, Routledge & Kegan Paul, London and Boston, 1984; Janet Ramsay, 'Liberation or loss? Women act on the new reproductive technologies', *Australian Feminist Studies*, vol. 1, no. 3, Summer 1986; Rebecca M. Albury, '"Babies kept on ice": aspects of Australian press coverage of IVF', *Australian Feminist Studies*, vol. 2, no. 4, Autumn 1987.

Appearing for the plaintiff was another feminist historian, Alice Kessler-Harris. She argued that the lessons of history show the structure, ideology and practice of the marketplace discriminating against women. Given the opportunity, she maintained, women will choose to pursue well-paid and competitive jobs. In February 1986, the judge, a Republican appointee, ruled Sears not guilty, and in his judgement explicitly cited Rosenberg's testimony as a reason for his ruling.[527] The tremors from the case are still travelling through Women's Studies in North America, as any reader of the journals *Signs* or *Feminist Studies* would know. As Kate Stimpson observed, 'it asks severe questions about the relationship of scholarship to action'[528] — questions which are severe for good reason but, nevertheless, bring fresh emphasis to the connections between the world of women and work, and that of feminist scholarship.

The fourth direction in which Women's Studies practitioners look is towards the future (and, therefore, also towards the past). We explore the shrivelled tissue of the past for understandings that will inform our present and future. We badger friends and colleagues in labour market research programs in government departments, or in Working Women's Centres, or in trades unions, for information that will enable us to shape our research towards strategies for transforming the world into a better place for women to live and work in. We read future-vision fiction — Marge Piercy's *Women on the Edge of Time*, or Ursula Le Guin's *The Left Hand of Darkness* and *The Dispossessed* — for visions of possible futures, and Margaret Atwood's novel *The Handmaid's Tale* for nightmares to avoid.[529] We scour university reports or publications to find out what gene technology is making possible in the animal labs, possibilities which might surface abruptly, like *in vitro* fertilisation, in clinics for humans. To quote the preamble to the constitution of the National Women's Studies Association of the USA:

> Women's Studies owes its existence to the movement for the liberation of women; the women's liberation movement exists because women are oppressed. Women's Studies, diverse as its components are, has at its best showed a vision

---

[527] This account is taken from Catharine R. Stimpson, 'Women's Studies: the state of the art (1986)', paper delivered to a conference on Women's Studies as a Transdisciplinary Enterprise organised by the Research Centre for Women's Studies at Adelaide University, August 1986.

[528] ibid., p. 20.

[529] Piercy, op. cit.; Le Guin, *The left hand of darkness*; Le Guin, *The dispossessed*; Margaret Atwood, *The handmaid's tale*, Jonathon Cape, London, 1986, see above, Chapter Eight, and Introduction, pp. 10-13.

of the world — from all the ideologies and institutions that have consciously or unconsciously oppressed and exploited some for the advantage of others.[530]

Marilyn Strathern voiced a similar aim, though in a very different way, when she observed:

> [I]f feminist scholarship is successful … then its success lies very firmly in the relationship between scholarship (genre) and the feminist movement (life). Play with context is creative because of the continuity of purpose between feminists as scholars and feminists as activists. Of course purposes may be diversely perceived and talked about. Yet the scholarship is in the end framed off by a special set of social interests. It is scholarship for a cause.[531]

If these four dimensions, directions of attention and commitment can be accepted as an adequate summary of the nature of the Women's Studies endeavour, then it would, I hope, be clear that a centre is probably the most appropriate environment in which such an endeavour can be pursued. A centre can be more flexible than a university department. It can house freelance scholars, and visiting academics from interstate or overseas. It can provide fellowship programs, as well as maintaining its own core of academic staff. It can co-ordinate undergraduate and postgraduate courses in Women's Studies so that they are properly integrated, team-taught, transdisciplinary programs, rather than the incoherent succession of specialist contributions so often to be found around Australia now. A Women's Studies Centre can experiment with new ideas, collaborate on research, and run pilot programs that serve as models to be adopted elsewhere. It can train administrators. At the very least, it can provide a base for women and their concerns in an institution which might otherwise prefer to ignore them.

More concretely, a Women's Studies Centre can bring together the 'critical mass' of personnel that would make possible such collaborative research, such experimentation with ideas, such co-ordination of coursework components provided by people who remain partly or wholly within established departments. It could supervise postgraduate students from a range of academic disciplines. It could, indeed undoubtedly would, become a source of policy advice for unions, governments, and private enterprise. It could become a centre for postgraduate vocational training for women moving into jobs as teachers in schools which, increasingly, offer Women's

---

530   Quoted in Stimpson, op. cit., p. 27.
531   Strathern, 'Out of Context: the persuasive fictions of anthropology', p. 46.

Studies courses, or into equal opportunity and affirmative action positions in the bureaucracies of both government and private enterprise. And it should become the centre of advice and co-operation for other academics wishing to integrate consideration of gender into courses in established departments.

But — and this may seem a bigger 'but' in Adelaide than in Melbourne — if a Women's Studies Centre is to achieve all this, it will need a physical place, with enough space to accommodate everyone working in it, or attached to it. The ability to form innovatory concepts can be deeply affected by who it is you chat to in the corridor. It will also need the commitment of at least the equivalent of three or four full-time academics, with consonant clerical and administrative support, and at least one position of sufficient seniority to provide authoritative references for grant applications and promotions. Joint appointments and honorary attachments simply do not work unless specific commitments to the Centre's work are written into the initial agreements. And, even though the Centre will not be a Department, someone will always have to shoulder the tedious responsibility of representing the Centre on the various administrative and policy-determining committees/councils of the institution — a responsibility which could be educative, rather than boring and burdensome, if it were shared.

I would not want these caveats to reflect upon the Research Centre for Women's Studies at Adelaide University; though my four years back in that institution has certainly taught me — a very impatient person — something of Adrienne Rich's 'wild patience'.[532]

The Research Centre for Women's Studies at Adelaide University was founded in November 1983. It emerged from the work of a loosely formed committee, like yours, which propelled Adelaide University into a statistical analysis of the position of women within the institution, an analysis which shocked most people in that smug and complacent body; produced a policy statement on the use of non-sexist language, with guidelines more honoured in the breach than the observance; and, in response to pressure to introduce Women's Studies in some form or other, secured to the Faculty of Arts an allocation of what are called 'windfall monies', funds for a three-year appointment to establish and conduct a Research Centre for Women's Studies. I don't know why they determined upon a research centre rather than a program of

---

[532] Adrienne Rich, *A wild patience has taken me this far: poems 1978-1987*, W.W. Norton & Co., New York, 1981.

undergraduate courses, which they still need. But they certainly had large ideas for a research centre. The brief to which I was appointed was six-fold:

- to initiate individual and group research projects
- to facilitate cross-disciplinary research
- to supervise higher degrees in the field of Women's Studies
- to organise seminars, conferences and publications
- to attract outside grants and commissions
- to offer its collective and diverse expertise to other departments.

I have always wondered how a research centre with only one member of staff was to offer collective and diverse expertise to anyone. But perhaps we have managed that through our journal.

It is our proudest publication, one which does offer 'collective and diverse enterprise', though from all over Australia rather than from one institution: our twice-yearly journal, *Australian Feminist Studies*. This has established a national presence in the fields of feminist scholarship and Women's Studies courses, partly, at least, through its national editorial advisory collective. And it is gaining a toe-hold in the international market as well, partly through individual networks, but partly, too, as a result of the international conferences which the Research Centre has organised.

Given the constraints and inadequacies within which the Research Centre for Women's Studies at Adelaide University was set up, I think it is doing fairly well. I am acutely conscious, though, of how much more could be achieved. But this, of course, does not depend upon one such centre. What if there were seven? Or at least two? My goals, at present, are modest and pragmatic. But there is no reason for yours to be. Why not aim for something of the order of Wellesley College's Centre for Research on Women? It occupies a whole house, has an annual budget of between US$1 million and US$2 million, employs over fifty people, and produces, among many other things, that laudable paper the *Women's Review of Books*. If they can do it, you surely could, too?

14

Outsiders inside? Women's Studies in Australia at the end of the twentieth century

A paper delivered to a conference titled 'Winds of Change: Women & The Culture of Universities' held at the University of Technology, Sydney, 13-17 July 1998, published in the Conference Proceedings *(eds) Dinah Cohen et al, Equity & Diversity Unit, University of Technology, Sydney, 1999.*

Metaphors

There are many ways in which to figure the world of higher education and developments within it. All are metaphors, though often they are so embedded in the language in which we speak every day that we regard them as simply descriptions of 'how things are', the discourse of common sense. The pursuit of knowledge is imaged at some times, particularly in the sciences, as colonial exploration and heroic discovery; at others, particularly in such fields as Communications Technology, Computing or Gene Technology, as ingenious invention and manufacture; at yet others — and such metaphors are to be found in such fields as the humanities and social sciences, too — as a boom in a building industry, with foundations being laid and frameworks being constructed. The metaphor most commonly used in the late 1990s about the pursuit of knowledge in any field is that of the identification of commodities which can be sold in an increasingly global market.[533]

In this paper, I want to mobilise a different metaphor, drawn from the field of ecology, an image of an ecosystem in which the pursuit of knowledge will flourish best where there is concern with the preservation of biodiversity in a balanced and interdependent environment.[534]

Since my subject is the state of Women's Studies, and — more broadly — feminist scholarship in Australia at the end of the twentieth century, I want to image three stages of being in ecological terms. The first is an image of luxuriant, if often struggling, growth — a way of figuring Women's Studies in universities in the 1970s and 1980s. The second is an image of a flattened landscape, with whole forests decimated to supply markets in construction, palm oil production and paper-supply, hills razed by mining companies, the hole in the ozone layer growing larger while citizens in so-called northern economies fail to modify their use of domestic heating, cooling, or hydrocarbons — an image for Women's Studies in the 1990s, in particular, the mid-to-late 1990s. The third image is a particular, stubborn, and adaptable kind of plant — wisteria, say — insisting on growing even in inhospitable terrain, and by doing so, helping to transform it — a stubbornly optimistic vision of Women's Studies for at least the beginning of the next century.

Luxuriant, if often difficult, growth: Women's Studies, 1970s-1990s

This is an origin narrative, an example of institutional memory, one of the ways in which Women's Studies helps contribute to the symbolic capital of the broader Women's Movement. As in many cultures, Women's Studies in Australia began as a reflex of the social movement upon the world of learning. The exuberant and ambitious Women's Liberation Movement of the 1970s was always an educational movement. Meetings of Women's Liberation groups were informal classrooms. National conferences which

---

[533] I owe this discussion, and the illustrations, to Penny Boumelha, 'Culture in the age of information: knowledge and research in the humanities and social sciences', in Susan Magarey (ed.), *Social justice: politics, technology and culture for a better world*, Wakefield Press, Adelaide, 1998.

[534] For this metaphor, Penny Boumelha acknowledges Ken Ruthven, 'The future of disciplines: a report on ignorance', in *Knowing ourselves and others. The humanities in Australia into the 21st Century*, 3 vols, prepared by a Reference Group for the Australian Academy of the Humanities, Australian Government Publishing Service, Canberra, April 1998, vol. 3, ch. 6.

were primarily political — on Feminism and Socialism, Feminism and Anarchism, Feminism and Marxism, Women and Labour — produced papers of impeccable scholarship, as well as political analyses.[535] It is hardly surprising that such energy and intellectual ferment should have turned to the principal knowledge-producing and knowledge-controlling institutions in our society, demanding that they pay attention to our work, demanding that they honour their own liberal education principles by allowing us space, quite literally, in their buildings and in their curricula, to cultivate our own forms of knowledge and enquiry — Women's Studies courses.

Further, when the Whitlam Labour government of 1972-75 abolished fees for university education, there appeared on university campuses a host of women looking for courses which spoke specifically to them about their place in the world.

Since most universities, particularly the older traditional universities (now referred to as the 'sandstone universities'), still bore marked resemblances to the monastic Oxbridge colleges from which they had been transplanted about a century earlier, they did not automatically furnish hospitable soil for a growth so unruly, and so undisciplined (and I mean that in every sense of the term 'un-disciplined'). The first course to be named 'Women's Studies', established at Flinders University in 1973, gained approval only after opposition from the Professor of Spanish had been quelled; he attempted to ridicule the proposal out of existence by proposing an alternative course on 'tauromarchy' — bull-fighting.[536] A course on Women and Philosophy gained a place at the University of Sydney only after a strike of both

---

[535] There were several conferences on Feminism and Socialism in the early 1970s; the one that I have in mind was held at the University of Melbourne in 1974; the Feminism and Anarchism Conference was held at the Australian National University, Canberra, in 1975; the Feminism and Marxism conference was held at the University of Sydney in 1977. These conferences were held in university premises because such premises could, in those years, be engaged for such purposes free of charge, and offered meeting-spaces large enough to accommodate all of the participants; as institutions, the universities offered no official endorsement of these conferences. Papers from them were not published; some are held in The First Ten Years Collection, in the Mitchell Library. Papers from the first three Women & Labour Conferences were published, though: see Windschuttle, op. cit.; Margaret Bevege, Margaret James and Carmel Shute (eds), *Worth her salt: women at work in Australia*, Hale & Iremonger, Sydney, 1982; Women and Labour Publications Collective [Margaret Allen, Jean Blackburn, Carol Johnson, Margaret King and Alison Mackinnon] (ed.), *All her labours*, 2 vols, Hale & Iremonger, Sydney, 1984.

[536] See Susan Sheridan, '"Transcending tauromachy": the beginnings of Women's Studies in Adelaide', in *Australian Feminist Studies*, vol. 13, no. 27, 1988, pp. 67-73.

students and many of the academic staff over students' rights to determine the content of their courses in 1973.[537] The Women's Studies course at the Australian National University found a foothold only in the wake of what was later, and euphemistically, called 'The Student Education Campaign' of 1974, during which students occupied the university's central administration buildings for roughly a week.[538]

Such growths necessarily took some of their shape from the surrounding environment furnished by each of the institutions in which they endeavoured to take hold — so Women's Studies courses in the 1970s varied. Some kinds of course found crevices in traditional universities in which to grow without the same order of disruption to the sandstone walls around them. A course on 'Women and Politics' at Adelaide University, and an Honours seminar on 'Women in English Society' at the University of Tasmania, were both seen as specialisms within the assumptions of particular disciplines, rather than as disruptions to them. But, as in the first of these examples, they depended on teaching provided by junior academics or postgraduate students, usually on top of other work for which they were paid, so they could last only as long as those people were able to contribute their voluntary labour. And, as in the second of these examples, such a course offered to students the opportunity to ask why it was necessary to have a course focusing specifically on women — where were women in the other courses taught in mainstream historiography? — such questions, necessarily, leading to a critique of assumptions and priorities in that mainstream.[539]

Like wisteria sucklings from beyond, taking hold within, all of these courses pushed at the sandstone walls, producing fissures and dislodgements — a focus on women which was very largely unprecedented in tertiary education, and a challenge to the long-established assumptions and practices of the sandstone disciplines. The Women's Studies course at the Australian National University developed into a program of courses in which one of the goals was specifically to challenge these

---

[537] See Alison Bashford, 'The return of the repressed: feminism in the quad', *Australian Feminist Studies*, vol. 13, no. 27, 1988, pp. 47-53.

[538] *ANU Reporter*, 24 May 1974; Bramley and Ward, op. cit., pp. 115-16. See also above, Chapter Twelve; Curthoys, 'Women's Studies at the Australian National University: the early years', pp. 78-80.

[539] Susan Magarey, Lyndall Ryan and Susan Sheridan, 'Women's Studies in Australia', in Norma Grieve and Ailsa Burns (eds), *Australian women: contemporary feminist thought*, Oxford University Press, Melbourne, 1994, p. 288.

assumptions.[540] Off-campus teaching courses established, at least initially, through co-operation between Women's Studies course teams at Deakin, Murdoch, Queensland and (after 1987) Flinders Universities, grew into two publications edited by Sneja Gunew, specifically named *Feminist Knowledge as Critique and Construct*.[541]

Looking back from the end of the twentieth century, it is possible to see such challenges as shoots on a larger growth which would produce even more extensive challenge, from within as well as without, to the conventions maintaining the sandstone disciplines. Within, challenges to those conventions erupted also into growths of what has been called 'The Studies': specialist fields such as Literary Studies (rather than English Language and Literature); Cultural Studies, Communication Studies, Australian Studies, Aboriginal Studies. The three-volume report prepared by the Academy of the Humanities in Australia and released earlier this year surveys an array of teaching and research activities far more varied than would have been considered thinkable even ten years ago.[542] In this respect, if I may change my metaphor for a moment, Women's Studies — and feminist scholarship — was on the crest of a wave which has clearly broken right across the humanities and social sciences in universities in this country.

But this story is not simply one of triumphal growth. For the nature of the institutions in which such growths have taken place has also changed. In 1987 the Australian government unified the university sector, a process which, almost overnight, doubled the number of universities by reorganising existing universities, colleges of advanced education and institutes of technology into a single national system, and increased the number of university student places by more than 50 per cent.[543] Then, just as the reorganised institutions were settling into their new arrangements, a new conservative government proceeded to make savage cuts to the funding which has, traditionally, maintained the universities. This brings me to the second metaphor that I want to develop for the environment in which Women's Studies has struggled for nourishment.

---

[540] See above, Chapter Ten.

[541] Sneja Gunew (ed.), *Feminist knowledge: critique and construct*, Routledge, London and New York, 1990; Sneja Gunew (ed.), *A reader in feminist knowledge*, Routledge, London and New York, 1991.

[542] *Knowing ourselves and others*, see especially vol. II, 'Discipline Surveys'.

[543] Roderick West (chair), *Learning for life: review of higher education financing and policy, a policy discussion paper*, Australian Government Publishing Service, Canberra, May 1998.

The flattened landscape of market-supply — Women's Studies in the 1990s

The metaphor for the pursuit of knowledge being the identification of marketable commodities has never before been so dominant in Australia (though I understand it to be familiar in Britain, northern Europe, Canada and the United States). Funding-cuts have been accompanied by government requirements that universities earn more of their income in the market. In all of these institutions, whole departments are being closed down; the number of academic staff is being cut; students are being crammed into large and often overcrowded lecture-halls with the kind of individual attention associated with the term 'tutorial' becoming a dim memory; so student numbers are shrinking; fees, in various forms, have been reintroduced, initially targeting overseas students; funding for scholarships has been reduced so that it is increasingly difficult for working-class Australian students to afford it; academics are being required to engage in fundraising activities of a kind for which most are entirely without training or ability.

This is an environment severely smitten by a market-imperative, with additional occasional bursts of poison being administered to eliminate those growths deemed unprofitable, so that their resources can be transferred. Those that *are* considered profitable — research and teaching in Communications and Information Technologies, financial services, and administration — are those best placed to make links with partners in the industries which they will serve. An analogy with the hole in the ozone layer growing, while the citizens of so-called northern economies increase their use of heating, cooling, or hydro-carbons, seems not inappropriate. The 'northern' economies that are gaining in the present regimen are *not* the fields among or between which 'The Studies', including Women's Studies, have flourished.

The growths of the 1970s and 1980s have not simply lain down and died, though. They have diversified in ways which demonstrate quite remarkable imaginative power and energy. As the Review of the Humanities points out:

> Humanities scholars are increasingly … involved in the work of public history, business ethics, medical ethics, tourism, town planning, heritage issues and their like, [and] a very great deal of the content and the skills of the practitioners of the rapidly growing communications industries derives from the knowledge and competency base of Humanities research.[544]

---

[544] *Knowing ourselves and others*, vol. I, p. 8.

At the University of Adelaide, where I work, one of the most successful research projects currently underway specifically in Women's Studies is Margie Ripper's on domestic violence.[545] But overall, the present market-driven ecology of higher learning militates actively against much of what is called the 'curiosity-driven' research and teaching, and that includes work which feminism found politically useful, work which characterised the early years of Women's Studies in Australia. And this has occurred at the same time as government commitment to equal opportunity — marked in the 1980s by the passage of the *Sex Discrimination Act 1984*(Cth) and Australia's endorsement of the United Nations' Convention to Eliminate Discrimination Against Women [CEDAW] — has fallen so low that Australia was recently named in the United Nations for failing to sustain its efforts in relation to CEDAW. It would be surprising, therefore, if I could report optimistically on the conditions of Women's Studies now.

This brings me to my final metaphor.

Adaptability helping to transform an inhospitable environment

Surprising though it might be, Women's Studies and — more broadly — feminist scholarship seemed to be slated for survival even in so inhospitable an environment. Many of the Women's Studies courses established amid the stormy politics of tertiary education in the 1970s have grown into fully fledged centres, even departments. At the Australian National University and at Sydney University, for instance, Women's Studies now have no fewer than three full-time academic staff each, and offer full undergraduate majors including Honours programs, and postgraduate supervision. As Gretchen Poiner reported in 1992, 'an overwhelming number of Australian universities now offer Women's Studies as a field of inquiry leading to the award of a degree'.[546] The Australian Women's Studies Association established in 1989 has held annual or biennial conferences ever since, attracting between 100 and 200 registrants, and in 1996 was affiliated with the Worldwide Organisation of Women's Studies launched at a conference in Adelaide with participants from the National Association

---

[545]   Margie Ripper, Chief Investigator, 'An evaluation of perpetrator programmes in stopping domestic violence', a research project funded by the Australian Government Public Health Research and Development.

[546]   Gretchen Poiner, 'Report on Women's Studies at Macquarie University', unpublished paper, 1992, appendix 3.

of Women's Studies in the United States of America and Women's International Studies, Europe.[547]

One or two would seem to have bitten the dust. But this is more appearance than fact. The Department of Women's Studies established at Adelaide University in 1992, as part of the tertiary education amalgamations of the late 1980s, for instance, has now been further amalgamated with the former Centre for Labour Studies to form a new Department of Social Inquiry, so that the first Department of Women's Studies would seem to have disappeared. But the new department not only maintains an undergraduate major and postgraduate coursework in Women's Studies, and supervision of postgraduate students specifically in Women's Studies, but has also, in this process, gained the appointment of the second full professor appointed specifically in Women's Studies in Australia, and she presently heads the new department.[548]

In institutional terms, then, Women's Studies appears to be weathering the bleak environment offered by universities in the late 1990s. As Ann Curthoys noted in a review of 'Gender in the Social Sciences':

> It has recently been observed of Women's Studies in the United States with some insight, which in my view can be applied to Australia also, that Women's Studies has wanted to be marginal and non-marginal at the same time. It has probably achieved both aims. It remains marginal in the sense that most departments, units or centres of Women's Studies are small and in times of cuts and restructuring therefore vulnerable. It is non-marginal in the sense that many of its practitioners have achieved intellectual recognition and influence.[549]

---

[547] See, e.g., Margaret Allen, 'Inaugural Australian Women's Studies Association Conference', *Australian Feminist Studies*, vol. 4, no. 10, 1989; Chilla Bulbeck (ed.), *Proceedings of the Australian Women's Studies Association Seventh Conference*, Adelaide, April 1998; *The Australian*, 26 April 1996; Susan Magarey, 'Women's Worlds: The Sixth International Interdisciplinary Congress on Women, Adelaide, 21-26 April 1996', *Australian Feminist Studies*, vol. 11, no. 24, 1996, p. 324.

[548] This is Chilla Bulbeck. The other full professor of Women's Studies is Rosemary Pringle, at Griffith University.

[549] Ann Curthoys, 'Gender in the social sciences in Australia — a review essay', prepared for the Review of the Social Sciences by the Academy of the Social Sciences in Australia, *Challenges for the social sciences and Australia*, 2 vols, Australian Government Publishing Service, Canberra, July, 1998. I am grateful to Ann for sending me a prepublication copy of this essay. It was her observation about Women's Studies wanting to be both inside and on the margins at the same time, together with Ann Froines, 'Outsiders within — outsiders without?', *Women's Review of Books*, vol. 15, No. 5, February 1998, pp. 20-1, which gave me the title of this paper.

A glance at the people on the International Editorial Advisory Collective of *Australian Feminist Studies* amplifies her last point. When this journal was launched in the summer of 1985, its editorial advisors included only two professors and nobody else above the rank of senior lecturer. In 1998, it includes no fewer than sixteen professors (including two at universities in the United States and a third at a university in Canada; a deputy vice-chancellor and the dean of a faculty), and several associate professors. The expanded list of editorial advisors now includes, as well, younger practitioners who have postgraduate qualifications specifically in Women's Studies.

I would like to argue a further case, and that is that Women's Studies has offered a significant site for the development of feminist scholarship in tertiary education over the last quarter century, and that feminist scholarship has made an impact on all scholarship far beyond the realms named 'Women's Studies'. I do not refer here to the journals which publish specifically feminist scholarship — *Refractory Girl*, founded in 1973; *Hecate: A Women's Interdisciplinary Journal*, founded in 1975; *Australian Feminist Studies*, established in 1985 — though I could, since all three continue to flourish. Nor do I refer to the huge compilation of feminist scholarship which will be published as the *Oxford Companion to Australian Feminism* later this year. Rather than detailing these triumphs, I would like to draw attention to two surveys commissioned by the Australian Research Council and carried out by reference groups appointed by the Academies of the Humanities and of the Social Sciences in Australia. The review that Curthoys undertook, from which I have just quoted, was carried out for the Academy of the Social Sciences, not yet, unfortunately, published. And I referred earlier to the review of the Humanities, published in three volumes, entitled *Knowing Ourselves and Others: Humanities in Australia towards the 21st Century*. It is the second of these works that I would like to consider now.

Even a decade ago, it was possible to argue that feminist work was very well in evidence in books and articles published across a range of academic disciplines, and the new fields developing between or beyond those disciplines. Moreover, such work was carving out new fields of its own. Early debate over definitional distinctions between sex and gender had yielded place to a new philosophy of the body[550], work with great intrinsic importance, which also, by reconceptualising the

---

[550]   The best known of such work is Moira Gatens, 'Towards a feminist philosophy of the body', in Barbara Caine, E.A. Grosz and Marie de Lepervanche (eds), *Crossing boundaries: feminism and the critique of knowledges*, Allen & Unwin, Sydney, 1988; Moira Gatens, *Feminism and philosophy: perspectives on difference and equality*, Polity, Cambridge, 1991; Moira Gatens,

sexed female body, has important implications for policy-making on such issues as reproductive rights, women's health, sexual autonomy and strategies for combating violence against women.[551] Such work had also deconstructed the universality of the masculine, bringing recognition that men are gendered, too, recognition which reverberates through a host of fields from criminology to health to mathematics to cultural studies.[552] New scholarship on relationships between feminism and the state had brought into prominence 'the femocrat' (feminist bureaucrat) as a uniquely Australian phenomenon[553], and had engendered, literally, new analyses of the operation of welfare and the economy.[554] Recognition of difference among women, as well as between women and men, together with an imperative to render Australian scholarship useful to scholars in other countries, had begun expanding the scope of Women's Studies to include attention to differences of race, ethnicity, culture, and religion. Yet, for all the wealth of these developments, there was little evidence that the majority inhabiting the sandstone disciplines were even reading it, much less giving heed to its implications for their own work. Being invited, over and over again, to give a guest lecture on women, or feminism, in a course otherwise innocent of any such consideration, prompts cynical disillusion. Reading the Humanities review offers a quite different, and very welcome, experience, on three counts.

Firstly, it includes a review of 'Gender Studies and Women's Studies' by Terry Threadgold which, after charting the disorderly growth of Women's Studies, and

---

Imaginary bodies: ethics, power and corporeality, Routledge, London and New York, 1996; Elizabeth Grosz, 'Notes towards a corporeal feminism', *Australian Feminist Studies*, vol. 2, no. 5, 1987; Elizabeth Grosz, *Volatile bodies: toward a corporeal feminism*, Allen & Unwin, Sydney, 1994.

551   Magarey, Ryan, and Sheridan, op. cit., p. 293.

552   E.g. R.W. Connell, *Masculinities*, University of California Press, Berkeley, 1995.

553   Dowse, 'The Women's Movement fandango with the state'; Suzanne Franzway, Diane Court and R.W. Connell, *Staking a claim: feminism, bureaucracy and the state*, Allen & Unwin, Sydney, 1989; Sophie Watson (ed.), *Playing the state: Australian feminist interventions*, Verso, London, 1990; Anna Yeatman, *Bureaucrats, technocrats, femocrats: essays on the contemporary Australian state*, Allen & Unwin, Sydney, 1990; Hester Eisenstein, *Gender shock: practising feminism on two continents*, Allen & Unwin, Sydney, 1991.

554   E.g. Lois Bryson, *Welfare and the state: who benefits?*, Macmillan, London, 1992; Bettina Cass, 'The feminisation of poverty', in Caine, Grosz and de Lepervanche, *Crossing boundaries*; Anne Edwards and Susan Magarey (eds), *Women in a restructuring Australia: work and welfare*, Allen & Unwin, Sydney, 1995.

more recent developments in Gay and Lesbian Studies and Queer Theory, reaches the cautiously optimistic conclusion that

> [t]here is not a single discipline in the Humanities, and probably not in the Social Sciences, which has remained untouched by the feminist work of the past thirty years. Gender is now on the agenda of all of the disciplines.[555]

Secondly, of the twenty-seven chapters of the volume devoted to 'Discipline Surveys', no fewer than twenty refer to 'Studies' rather than to the more traditional sandstone disciplines. While some of these may well say more about the impact of restructuring and 'down-sizing' than about any new transdisciplinarity among them, some are relatively new area studies, representing the development of post-colonial approaches in, for instance, Aboriginal and Torres Strait Islander Studies, or African Studies, or Australian Studies, or a new emphasis on multiculturalism in, say, European Studies; and some make a clear case for their field being transformed by interdisciplinary collaboration and what one calls 'theorisation of the discipline'.[556] These last two represent developments in which, as I've argued already, feminist scholarship led the way. Thirdly, reading the whole review shows just how extensive has been the impact of feminist scholarship in fields and disciplines which had previously ignored it. The chapter on Cultural Studies states that '[f]eminist concerns have marked the development of Australian Cultural Studies from the outset in ways that have had a lasting influence on its formation'[557]; the chapter on English Studies maintains that '*Feminist Criticism* might be claimed as a movement that is genuinely redrawing the whole map of English literary studies'[558]; and the chapter on History announces that '[a]bove all, Aboriginal history and women's history recast the study of Australian history'.[559]

Accordingly, and to conclude, I would suggest that feminist scholarship has shown itself quite remarkably adaptable, not only to the imperatives of ecologically damaging economic rationalist strategies in universities, but also, and far more

---

[555] Terry Threadgold, 'Gender Studies and Women's Studies', in *Knowing ourselves and others*, Vol. II, p. 138.

[556] Robert White, 'The State of English Studies in the 1990s', in ibid., p. 101.

[557] Tony Bennett, 'Cultural Studies', in ibid., p. 83.

[558] Robert White, 'The State of English Studies in the 1990s', p. 101, emphasis in the original.

[559] Stuart Macintyre, 'History', in *Knowing ourselves and others*, Vol. II, p. 142.

importantly, to new currents of thought in intellectual and political life. One result of that has been that, for many, those new currents of thought are already imbricated with feminism at the time when they encounter them; feminist scholarship has been central in them. Leading figures in Cultural Studies such as Meaghan Morris, in Philosophy such as Moira Gatens and Elizabeth Grosz, in Film Studies such as Barbara Creed, in Post-Colonial Studies such as Sneja Gunew and Marcia Langton have introduced their students and readers to their feminism in the same sentences as they write or speak of cutting-edge theoretical work associated with the 'posts' — post-modernism, post-structuralism, post-colonialism. The centrality of feminism, as assumed, in the current media beat-up over a so-called generation war gives a popular culture instance of the impossibility of any longer ignoring feminist scholarship.[560] Wisteria can tip a house over; it can also, just as ivy can, keep a cracked wall standing upright. Such adaptability will ensure the survival of Women's Studies, intellectually at least, no matter how harsh and drought-stricken our institutional environments become. And even if a small number of the perpetually marginal, the outsiders, should find a more permanent place nearer the centre, inside the universities, then it may be that we can help to sustain the intellectual biodiversity that is essential to survival of Australian universities if they are not to dwindle into service-points for a globalised tertiary education provided by the media-monopolies on the Web. Then, of course, Women's Studies would have another set of worries — about maintaining those on its own margins.

---

[560] See, e.g., press coverage of Mark Davis, *Gangland*, Allen & Unwin, Sydney, 1997, and Jenna Mead (ed.), *Bodyjamming*, Vintage/Random House, Milson's Point, NSW, 1998.

Part III

Around the World

In Women's Liberation and in Women's Studies, both, we were always conscious of being part of a global scholarly community as well as a local polity. Making up my job at Adelaide University allowed me to foster both. International visitors rolled in like waves on an incoming tide, from the United States, Britain, The Philippines, New Zealand, Sweden, Canada, Germany, and that was only those who came to give seminars. We organised conferences and workshops, a major conference every two years, on average, ranging from one in 1986 organised in conjunction with the Humanities Research Centre at ANU, to a workshop on Women's Studies in Asia and the Pacific organised in conjunction with UNESCO in 1991, to another workshop, this one in 1992, in conjunction with the Academy of the Social Sciences in Australia on Women and Restructuring: Work and Welfare, and a major conference, the Sixth International Interdisciplinary Congress on Women in 1996 at which we hosted almost 1000 participants from 57 countries. Local participants came from all over Australia, and in Adelaide the Research Centre was involved with the Working Women's Centre, the Women's History Task Force, the government's Tertiary Education Authority, and a conference on Women and Housing. In Chapter Twelve I have a footnote listing all the conferences that the Research Centre for Women's Studies at Adelaide University organised between 1985 and 1996. The reasons for such boasting are that these conferences were an immense amount of administrative, as well as intellectual, work (and such work included applications for funds), and

Figure 14: Robyn Archer, Susan Sheridan and Susan Magarey launching
Australian Feminist Studies, **summer 1985**
Photograph courtesy of Susan Magarey

these were times when we undertook that work ourselves — we did not have recourse to professional conference-organisers then, any more than we had access to email (still to reach us).

However, the achievement of which I am still proudest is the establishment of the journal *Australian Feminist Studies*, which I edited from 1985 until 2005. In the last issue that I edited — before *AFS* went off to Mary Spongberg to be edited from Macquarie University for the ensuing ten years — I announced that

> [f]rom the moment in January 1986 when Robyn Archer launched our first
> issue, I conceived of *Australian Feminist Studies* as providing a platform for the

appearance of work that connected along two axes: one travelling from the global to the local, showing the mutual implication of each in the other; the other moving between the political and the scholarly, again showing the two to be as closely related as the palm and the back of your hand. I wanted to provide a forum for the appearance of feminist research, scholarship, debate, critique and enthusiasm developing within Australia for a global readership. At the same time, I wanted to introduce some of the most theoretically exciting feminist material appearing in other countries to a predominantly Australian readership. The balance between the two — theory from overseas; research and scholarship at home; and vice versa — has shifted through our 20-year history. Or has shown it to be multi-directional from the beginning.[561]

And for this to happen, a good deal of travelling was called for.

It was at the suggestion of Sue Sheridan, my life-partner since 1981, that I set about *AFS*; she joined me as the journal's reviews editor for its first twenty years. Even before we initiated that enterprise, we had begun travelling together, and publishing accounts of what we had discovered.[562] And we continued to do so. But I also undertook a number of journeys without her. The first of the traveller's stories in this section, Chapter Fifteen, makes it clear that I was travelling with a group — which included the peerless Daphne Gollan — from the ANU, and Sue and I were both at the conference described in Chapter Eighteen, in San José in Costa Rica. The other four are about journeys that I undertook alone.

Given the close connections between the Australian Left, in its various manifestations, and the Women's Liberation Movement (see especially Chapter Four), Australian feminists were immensely curious about how women were faring under specifically socialist regimes, especially as we knew so little about one (behind the Iron Curtain) and another (closed to foreign visitors and undergoing the Cultural Revolution). Similarly, given how very much the Women's Liberation Movement in Australia had adopted and adapted from the United States of America, Australian feminists were intensely engaged with the feminisms developing in the north of the

---

[561]   Susan Magarey, 'Editorial', *Australian Feminist Studies*, vol. 20, no. 47, July 2005, p. 148.

[562]   Susan Magarey and Susan Sheridan: 'Greenham Common — 12 December 1982', *Canberra Women's Liberation Newsletter*, n.d.; 'Women's Studies in Northern Europe', *Hecate*, vol. 9, nos. 1 & 2, 1983, pp. 183-91; Women's Studies Conferences in Australia in 1985', *Women's Studies Quarterly*, The Feminist Press, City University of New York, vol. 14, nos. 3 & 4, Fall/Winter 1986, pp. 35-6; 'The Seventh Berkshire Conference on the History of Women', *Australian Feminist Studies*, vol. 2, no. 5, Summer 1987, pp. 149-54.

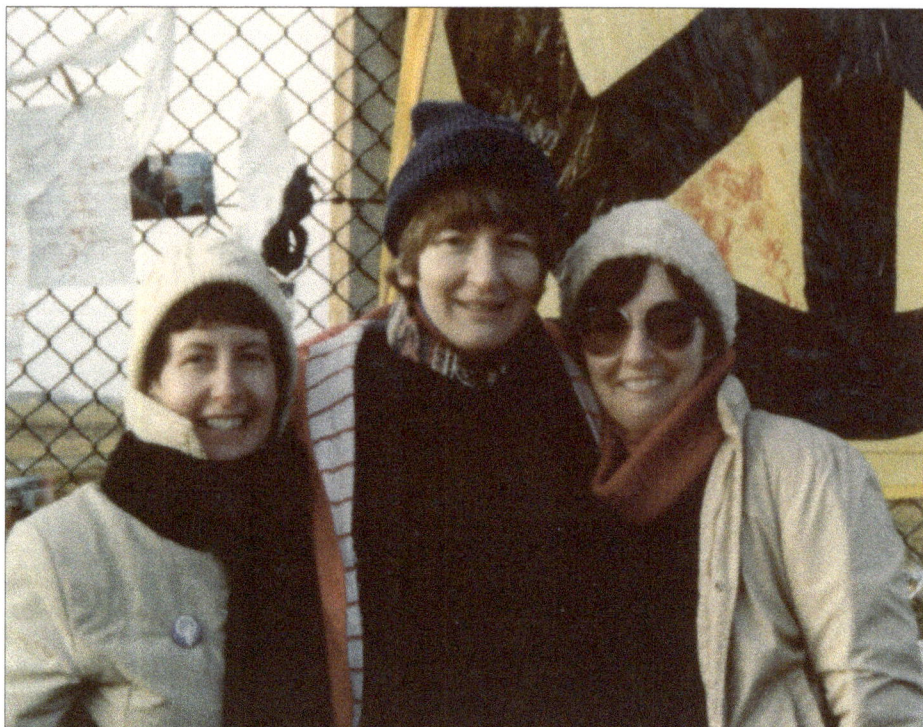

Figure 15: Jenny Oswald, Susan Magarey and Susan Sheridan at Greenham Common, 1982
Photograph courtesy of Susan Magarey

American continent. Exploration of feminism and Women's Studies in Greece, a country to which so many Australian feminists owed their origins, seemed logical. And an encounter with the feminisms of a third-world country like Costa Rica could not be anything but educational.

But these accounts are as historical and political as they are geographical. There were changes of a quite extraordinary magnitude over the period of time that they cover (getting on for twenty years). They are book-ended by two reports focused on China, inviting comparison between those two moments. At the time of the first, the Cultural Revolution was over in only some parts of the nation; foreign visitors to 'mainland China' were still rare and extremely carefully monitored (we had to fill out the forms about what we wanted to see about four times — to check for consistency, we were told — and we could not go anywhere without our guides); we still referred to places and people by the anglicised names that we had learned from the anglophone press; and our discussion with members of the Shanghai branch of the All-China Women's Federation took place before the introduction of the One-Child Policy. So eager were China-watchers in Australia to hear what we had learned in 1978 that when we returned we were invited to give papers to such august bodies as the Contemporary China Centre in the Research Centre for Social Sciences at ANU.

In 1995, by contrast, the conference that I attended in Huairou was associated with the United Nations' World Conference on Women in Beijing, and was an immense gathering of women from all over the world. The One-Child Policy and the consequent gender imbalance were beginning to prompt worries about social and reproductive disjunction: lots of boys, not many girls. The roads that I recalled having been crowded with bicycles, bullock-drawn carts, with only a very occasional bus honking deafeningly, were now packed with trucks, cars and taxis. And you could take a taxi, without having to get permission from anyone. People were not, now, wearing Mao-jackets. It was even possible to buy tampons, something that we had been told was impossible in 1978. This was only three years before the People's Republic of China hosted the Olympic Games.

Change was the central concern of the conference that I attended in Moscow, too, a conference held at the last minute of the existence of the USSR, a time at which I discovered my carefully purchased roubles to be useless as the economy collapsing all around wanted only American dollars from tourists. This one, like the conferences which are the focus of my reports on going to Costa Rica and Greece, were different from most of the conferences that I was accustomed to attending within Australia, or in Britain, at least until around then; they were different because they were so international. They brought me my most overwhelming experience of feminism as a global movement.

We have been extremely fortunate. We have lived in a period of history when air-travel was not only technologically possible, but also economically available on a fairly democratic scale. My parents could never have travelled by air as much as I have. And I wonder if it will be possible for my great nieces and nephews to do so, given the rising financial costs of air-travel and the growing recognition of just how much it contributes to the pollution of the earth's atmosphere. There were people at the conferences that I attended in San José, on the Sounion Peninsular, and in

Huairou who had all arrived by air, even the woman who, coming from an island in the Pacific, had begun her journey on a canoe. At that time, the devices that have enabled the development of social media, and the consequent speedy global reach of political protests like the Occupy movement, were still in their infancy. The internationalism of the Women's Liberation Movement was evident in China in 1995 primarily because of the physical presence of so many women, from all over the world, in the one place at the same time.

The reports presented here give the names of the people to whom I was listening, and I could usually record the titles of their presentations from the programmes supplied. But we were not given copies of papers presented; these were not academic conferences, aiming at producing a publishable collection of papers afterwards. The substance of people's presentations given here, and quotations from them, come entirely from my notes taken at each event; I did not compose them from published sources, and I did not keep those notes after I had written the reports.

The final paragraph of the last chapter of this book quotes Aung San Suu Kyi. Her speech for the UN conference in China reached us on video; she was still under house-arrest in 1995. Now, twenty years later, she is free, able to travel to receive her Nobel Peace Prize, and to participate in the politics of her country, Myanmar. It was possible to be optimistic about the strength of the international Women's Movement then. Could it be at least as possible, now?

15

The position of women in China: 1978

This report was first published in John Reid and Anne Gollan (eds), Visiting China, *Waverly Offset Publishing Group, Canberra, 1979, pp. 43-9.*

All of our group of sixteen — eleven women and five men — were interested in the position of women in China, though the questions we wanted to ask varied greatly from one individual to the next. One of our number was primarily concerned with sexuality and sexual satisfaction among Chinese women, a matter he gained little information about. Others brought to China questions arising directly from issues concerning the Women's Movement in Australia, issues which assumed somewhat different shapes when translated into a different language and society. But we all wanted to learn how women's lives had changed with the huge changes in Chinese society during this century, and what their lives are like now. We gathered answers to our questions wherever we went: at the Lung Tan neighbourhood in Peking, at the Chiang Chiao people's commune on the outskirts of Shanghai, in conversations with our guides on the bus or train, but principally in a three-hour discussion organised for us with representatives from the Shanghai branch of the All-China Women's Federation.

Our guides had asked us to prepare a list of questions for that discussion before it took place. The discussion then began with a long and beautifully constructed response to our list. The speaker was Mrs Wu, head of one of the departments in the Shanghai branch of the Women's Federation, a stocky woman whose greying hair suggested that she was probably between forty and fifty years old. She took the brunt

Figure 16: Daphne Gollan in China in 1978
Photograph courtesy of Susan Magarey

of our later questioning, too, answering us seriously but not without humour. Parts of her opening reply summarised much of the information that we had been picking up piecemeal.

Before the liberation of 1949, she told us, all China had been oppressed by foreign imperialists and Chinese bureaucrats. But women had led a particularly bitter life, for as Mao noted as early as 1927, they were oppressed not only by the political, religious, and class authority systems which oppressed everyone, but also by the authority of men. There were limitations imposed on the employment of women, so that only 180 000 were employed in productive (as distinct from domestic) labour, and they — like children — were cheap labour, paid lower wages than men. This meant that women had no economic status; they were dependent on their husbands. They received no education — 'lack of talent is a virtue in a woman'. They had no political status. And, except perhaps as mothers-in-law ruling the domestic side of the sons' households, they had no status in the family. They were forced into marriage by their parents, who consulted professional matchmakers, not the prospective brides, about eligible partners, and, once married, they were wholly subject, first to their husbands, then to their sons. Women thought that their lives were governed by fate: it was a poor fate not to find a rich husband; if that happened, then all that a woman could do was hope that, on being reborn, she would be a man.

The grimness of the subjection of women in pre-liberation China is perhaps best conveyed in an anecdote related to us after we had returned to Australia. This concerned a group of people who approached a closed house, knocked on the door, and called out, 'Anyone at home?' A woman's voice replied from inside, 'No, no-one'. Other stories recounted the horrors of the widespread practice of foot-binding, a mutilation practised on even the peasant women in some areas, so that if their labour was necessary at harvest time, they had to work on their hands and knees. Foot-binding, however, was outlawed long before liberation, after 1911. Mrs Wu's illustration focused attention on the destructive effects of such wholesale oppression on human relationships, even the relationship between mother and daughter. She told us the story of Kung Ka Ching, a leading member of the Women's Movement in China, whose own mother had given her away when she was forty days old, and whose foster mother used to curse and beat her.

During the democratic revolution of 1911-17 and the wars of 1937-49, Mrs Wu went on, a lot of women worked against their own oppression by joining the struggle against the oppression of the whole class and the whole nation. They joined the revolution, and the armed struggle. Those in the rear worked to deliver grain to the front, and to prepare entertainments for the troops at the front. Those in areas occupied by the enemy joined the men in the underground struggle.

Their work was rewarded with liberation, and a constitution which gives full equality to women — politically, economically, culturally, and in the family. 'Now', said Comrade Wu, 'women are masters in our country'.

She illustrated the political equality of women by telling us that at the People's Representative Conference in Shanghai, attended by 1200 representatives, 330 of the representatives were women, that is, 27.6 per cent. In the leading body of 120 members, 22 were women, and the vice-chairman, too, was a woman. Later in the discussion, we congratulated the women of Shanghai on such proportions, proportions far nearer to equality than any we could muster for Australia. But then we asked them if they were content with such representation. Mrs Wu initially replied briefly: 'Women are half the population, and as Chairman Mao said, "Women hold up half the sky". So women have full confidence that we will do more in the future'. However, when we asked, 'But, as well as having full confidence, what else are you doing? What are women doing to achieve 50 per cent representation?', she answered at greater length, and made her fellow workers laugh by what she said.

She had explained to us earlier that emancipation for women was, in China, indissolubly linked to class and national emancipation. The Women's Federation was therefore — unlike several women's organisations in Australia which work independently (sometimes against) the government — linked closely to the ruling Chinese Communist Party. Mrs Wu described it first as the right hand of the Party, then as a bridge between the women masses and the Party, passing on the women's demands to the Party, propagating and implementing Party policy among the women masses. Accordingly, when Chairman Hua Kuo-feng had announced at the Fifth People's Congress in 1978 that the general task for the new period was to achieve the four modernisations by the end of the century, this became the principal objective of the Women's Federation at the same time. Our question suggested the possibility of a distinction between the aims of China's ruling organisations and its major women's organisation, and this, as Mrs Wu's reply made clear, could not — or not officially — even be contemplated.

'This', she said,

> is my personal opinion. The main goal for the women's movement in China is the realisation of the four modernisations, so the task of the Women's Federation is mainly to mobilise women to engage in socialist construction. But during that process, women can raise their ideology and the level of their knowledge of science and technology, so surely the number of women in positions at the top level will increase.

There are already some women 'at the top level': Teng Ying-Chao (Chou En-lai's widow), and a former textile worker, Mao Shing Sheng, are members of the Party's central committee. But they make up a small proportion of the whole. There are more women, Comrade Wu said, in the government organisations, and in Shanghai there are a lot of women among the representatives at each level of government, both in the cities and in the countryside. Nevertheless, as Mrs Wu's reply indicated, the women do not regard full political equality as something already won.

Women gained economic emancipation after liberation by joining the productive labour force. Of the 4 006 000 industrial workers in Shanghai, 1 740 000 now are women, working mostly in the textile, commercial, and trade industries. Fewer women work in building development and transportation. From 1958 on, the Women's Federation organised former housewives who were under the age of forty-five to join the paid labour force as well. We saw a group of about six of them in the Lung Tan neighbourhood in Peking, sealing plastic bags with electrically powered soldering irons. They worked an eight-hour day, five days a week.

There is, at least officially, equal pay for men and women in productive labour. But we found that, just as some kinds of work are more highly paid than others, so the work that women do might earn less than that done by men. At the Chiang Chiao people's commune just out of Shanghai, we were told that a woman could gain a minimum of 7 work points and a maximum of 9½, whereas men could gain a minimum of 10½ and a maximum of 12. The people on the commune said that this was because women had to take more time off than men, and because women are not physically capable of some of the tasks that men could perform. Perhaps this was realistic. Women in productive labour are specifically protected, throughout China, during four periods: menstruation, pregnancy, delivery and nursing. During such time their participation in productive labour is interrupted or reduced; the mother of a newborn baby does not return to work until fifty-six days after the birth. Nevertheless, when we asked one of our guides about the inequity of the work points at the Chiang Chiao commune, she hastened to assure us that it was always possible for women, as well as men, to gain extra points for piecework. And when we talked to people on the Tali commune, which we visited from Canton, about this, they expressed surprise and disapproval, and said that they hoped that the Chiang Chiao commune would improve. The women participating in our discussion in Shanghai did not mention such questions; they said simply that 'since most women participate in productive work, the Party had established equality'.

It had, they said, established cultural equality, too. By this, Mrs Wu apparently meant educational equality. 'Men and women both participate fully in education', she told us. 'There are equal numbers of both sexes in the schools.' She claimed that the only inequality in this sphere was in the universities: women make up only 40 per cent of the enrolments in universities, but they constitute 50 per cent of the enrolments in other tertiary institutions, such as the July 21 workers' colleges, and the 'spare-time colleges' [colleges that offered courses in the evenings and at weekends]. The first percentage matched that given to us at Peking University, but not that from Futan University, where the number of women students amounted to no more than 24 per cent of the total enrolment. However, there was another kind of gender inequality in existence at Peking University, one we meet often in Australia. At Peking University we were told that the 40 per cent of women enrolments was not evenly distributed throughout the university:

> There is a traditional tendency for fewer women to apply for enrolment in certain subjects, for example, geology. There are more women taking foreign languages, biology, and chemistry, for instance, than there are women taking mathematics.

This, they told us, 'is just a natural tendency'. When we asked the university staff if they were encouraging change in this area, they laughed. But then they said:

> Of course we are trying to improve the position of women, both politically and socially. But we have to admit that certain jobs are not suitable for women. Nevertheless, we try to encourage women by placing no restrictions on them. But such measures of encouragement have to be carried out throughout society, not just in the university.

The fourth sphere in which the Shanghai women claimed that liberation had brought equality was in the family. Forced marriage is now forbidden. 'And at home', Mrs Wu told us, 'men and women are equal; old ideas of male supremacy will be criticised'. Some of this equality must, of course, reside in the distribution of household chores. Many of them, particularly in the cities, have been rendered unnecessary by the 'socialisation of housework'. This was a matter to which the Party and the government had paid great attention, Mrs Wu said. 'Neighbourhood nurseries, factory nurseries, and kindergartens have been established. In neighbourhood service centres, there are canteens, laundries and places where clothes are repaired.' This was, it seemed, more than the communes provided; when we asked one person at the Chiang Chiao commune who did the household chores, she replied, 'Whoever gets home first'. Then, laughing, she indicated her small son and said, 'Sometimes he does them'. However, even the urban women did not think that the socialisation of housework had progressed far enough. 'It is still necessary to encourage further development of this kind', said Mrs Wu, 'and this is stressed in the Party'.

She may have been alluding, indirectly, to a discussion being conducted in the *People's Daily* at the time that we were in China. This concerned the establishment of 'modern bread factories' to save people from one of the most time-consuming of the household chores which, according to the paper, were responsible for the saying: 'tense Saturday, fighting Sunday, dog-tired Monday'. If she was, then the proposal for bread factories may have signalled a measure of defeat in the battle for gender equality in the family. Certainly, there was other evidence to support the view that struggle continues in this area. Mrs Wu said that it was necessary for education about household chores to be directed at men. And in one story that the Shanghai women told us, it was clear that the old ideas of male supremacy and the Party-sanctioned struggle for equality of the sexes could encounter each other on difficult terrain.

The story concerned an abortion. We had asked about the use of abortion in China. Mrs Wu replied, 'In China, since most women are engaged in productive labour, they don't want too many children; mostly they will have one or two children. They are allowed to have abortions, but they need their husband's consent. Both decide'. We then asked if the women were content with this situation. Mrs Wu said, 'Yes, because since liberation there has been free choice of marriage partners, so marriages are harmonious'. We replied, 'We have free choice of marriage partners, too, but we have found that there is still a possibility of contradiction between husband and wife on such an issue. In Britain recently, the contradiction was so serious that a man whose wife wanted an abortion took her to court in an attempt to prevent her having it'.

'Yes', Mrs Shao replied,

> we, too, have had such a case, in my shipyard. There was a contradiction between a couple over the second pregnancy: the first child was only eighteen months old, and the woman did not want the second, but the husband did. The woman told her factory committee, and asked them to persuade him to change his mind. They also visited the woman's neighbourhood committee, who talked to her mother-in-law, who wanted the second child, too. The mother-in-law gave in first — she would have had to look after the baby if it was born. Then, eventually, the husband changed his mind.

Mrs Shao concluded her story by saying, apparently without any irony, 'In this way, the family remains fairly harmonious'. China's progress towards political, economic, cultural, and domestic equality between the sexes seemed monumental. Criticism from inhabitants of a country so far less advanced in this respect could easily seem presumptuous. Yet some of us did wonder if the future in China, particularly if the endeavour to achieve full modernisation is successful, might not bring Chinese women into direct confrontation with two of the issues which concern the Women's Movement in Australia at present. These are: the sexual division of labour, and the autonomy of the Women's Movement.

The sexual division of labour is, some anthropologists tell us, the primary social division in all known societies, ranging from the hunter-gatherer to our own. This does not mean that men in all societies do one kind of work, and women another. But it does mean that in all societies the work that men do, and the work that women do, is differentiated on the basis of gender. And from this division follows the distinction between the public and the domestic spheres of life, the distinction between power (influence) and authority (recognised and legitimated power), and the supremacy of men, which is referred to, broadly, as patriarchy. Some theorists have argued that such inequality between the sexes originated in the development of private property; others maintain that its source is the female function of child-bearing. Yet, in China, where private property (as we understand the concept) no longer exists, and where child care has been extensively socialised, the sexual division of labour persists.

This was evident in the replies to our questions about women's participation in productive labour, about the enrolment of women in the universities, and about abortion. The women from the Shanghai branch of the Women's Federation attributed this simply to differences in physique between men and women. Mrs Shao said that, in her shipyard, the main cause of the sexual division of labour 'is the different physical constitutions of men and women. Women can't do some of the work'. Such a differentiation could be expected to disappear with modernisation, and Mrs Wu told us that '[i]n work where strength doesn't count, women are 60 per cent of the work force'. But even there, the four protections of women engaged in productive labour suggest that it is not so much physical strength which determines the sexual division of labour in China as the physical functions associated with reproduction. And this is a difference between the sexes which any program for population control and socialised child care seems unlikely to eliminate. Yet women's reproductive capacity is irrelevant to their numerical concentration in subjects like foreign languages and biology, rather than geology or mathematics, in the universities. Nevertheless, the staff members who talked to us at Peking University described such a concentration as 'just a natural tendency'. Accordingly, we wondered what would happen if the Chinese began to question such a correlation of cultural preferences with biological constitution. Would the whole society join in eliminating the cultural inequities developed from the sexual division of labour? Or would this be a struggle which the women would need to carry on alone?

Such questions related directly to the second of the issues with which some of us were concerned: the autonomy of the Women's Movement. It would in general be reasonable to expect that groups explicitly engaged in struggling for equality and justice in a society like ours would be able to make common cause of their aims. In particular, it would be reasonable to expect that sections of the Women's Movement and sections of the Left in Australia would unite in the struggle against exploitation based on gender, as well as that based on class. However, neither expectation is realistic, and women have found it necessary to carry out their own battle against oppression, independently of left-wing groups. About halfway through our discussion, Mrs Wu asked us to tell them about the Women's Movement in Australia. We told them about the necessity that we had found for the Women's Movement to be autonomous. Their response was a reiteration of their belief that 'with the full development of socialist construction, true equality between the sexes will be realised'. We remained sceptical, remembering Marx's observation that the demand for equal rights must, if it takes into account the fundamental inequality between one individual and another, actually be a demand for unequal rights, and recalling the Australian Women's Movement's call, not for equality, but rather for liberation. We wondered what would happen if the women masses of China should ever perceive their wishes and the Party's as being in conflict.

Answers to such questions must wait upon time. Perhaps the Party and the government in China will prove us impertinent for having voiced them. Certainly, the unity of the Party and the Women's Federation in this, the first year in which the Women's Federation has met for twenty-one years, appears unassailable. And the quiet, cheerful confidence of the women we saw and talked with made us all optimistic about the future of women in China.

16

A milkrun in the United States
of America: 1986

Report first published in Australian Feminist Studies,
vol. 2, no. 4, Autumn 1987.

Nearly ten years ago I visited the People's Republic of China for a three-week tour guided by Luxingshe, the China International Travel Service. China-watchers among my friends told me that such a trip was called a 'milkrun'. That term, with all its associations of haste, passing glimpses, picking up and dropping off bits and pieces, also seems the only appropriate description of the month that I spent in a very different society, the United States of America, in September-October 1986.

Any feminist going to the USA would have high expectations. North American feminism contributed so much to the formation of ideas and practices in the Australian Women's Liberation Movement, and continues to contribute to debates and strategies being explored by feminists in this country. Nevertheless, a feminist whose politics began forming in the Australian opposition to the USA's war against the Vietnamese people could hardly avoid being apprehensive as well. In December 1985 these politics had taken me to the Women's Peace Camp at Cockburn Sound to join the protest against the presence there of US warships and nuclear warheads. The contradiction between commitment of that kind and going to the USA as a guest of the US government was not lost on my friends who were making jokes before I left about 'Susan's CIA trip'.

I don't know what informal connections might exist between the CIA and the State Department. And, in spite of the horrific, and — in retrospect — comic possibilities with which I tormented myself before leaving for America, I did not personally encounter any such connections. Some North American feminists even responded with a combination of irritation and indignation to the suggestion that I might. 'The United States Information Agency [USIA] is the cultural exchange arm of the State Department', they informed me, 'and nothing to do with espionage and Irangate arms deals'. For those of us on the other end of an imperialism which has both cultural and armaments dimensions, the distinction between two sections of the US administration can seem less important than their combined effects. A major cultural event in Sydney while I was away was centred upon the US navy. However, I also met a number of other feminists in the USA who inquired with very proper suspicion about how I had fetched up on a State Department circuit; they relaxed with relief into discussion of the state of the Left and feminism when they discovered that my views of the USIA were even more ungrateful and suspicious than their own.

The USIA has offices in Washington. Its outposts in three or four other places in the USA, and dotted around the globe, are called the US Information Service [USIS]. It imports and exports some hundreds of people each year. Those exported, including several prominent feminist scholars, are expected to give lectures and seminars in the places they visit. Those imported are expected to observe, listen and meet people. It is not possible to apply to be imported. I eventually learned that my name had been put on a list of possible imports by an exported North American feminist academic who had visited the Research Centre for Women's Studies at Adelaide University, and thought that it might be useful for the Centre if I could see something of similar centres and Women's Studies programs in the USA. I also learned, once in Washington, that the USIA may have acted on her suggestion at least partly because Australia has been very slow to suggest women for such exchanges. Misogynist exclusiveness? I learned, too, that such cultural exchange visits are not for carrying out research. At the invitation of the USIS in Melbourne, and with valuable help from Martha Vicinus and Kate Stimpson, I submitted a proposed itinerary which included five days in the Schlesinger Library at Harvard. This produced two telephone calls from Melbourne expressing consternation and informing me that cultural exchange was meeting people and observing the American way of life, not reading books.

Visitor's itineraries are finalised in Washington, once they have arrived. The USIA contracts one of three organisations to do this, according to the broad field of a visitor's interests. My itinerary was prepared by the Institute of International Education, and the two young women who worked on it said that they had liked it because they enjoyed the chance to speak to many of the people I wanted to spend time with. One had had Louise Tilly's and Joan Scott's *Women, Work and Family* as a set text in one of her university courses, so she was particularly delighted about being able to talk with Joan Scott on the phone. They, and their counterparts in other places, also arranged for me to meet a number of people I had not known enough to include on my list; having spent time with Sarah Pritchard in the Library of Congress in Washington, with Rubye Jones, the Educational Director for the International Ladies Garment Workers' Union in New York, and with Pat Wulp who runs a Centre of Continuing Education for Women in Ann Arbor, I can only be thankful. They must also have done a great deal of talking with airlines, and some talking with railway companies, since they presented me with a fistful of tickets for getting from one place to another: along the Atlantic coast, west to Michigan, south to Austin (Texas), and to Tucson, then west again to San Francisco and north to Seattle. Having all of this, and accommodation, arranged for you, is an enormous luxury. And for all of that, it would be impossible not to be heartily grateful.

I embarked with two sets of questions: one concerned the state, security, morale and preoccupations of Women's Studies programs and centres; the second was the very open question, 'What are the burning issues for feminism here now?'

Generalising after a milkrun is foolhardy. But I'll risk it. I was impressed even more than I had anticipated by the number and variety of Women's Studies courses, programs, centres, projects and conferences in evidence all over the United States, and I made contact with only a handful of the forty-two listed in *Women's Studies Quarterly* for Spring 1985. Few of them are financially secure. Even Wellesley College's Centre for Research on Women, which inhabits a whole house in the countryside surrounding Wellesley and employs some fifty people, is finding that the large grants from bodies such as the Ford Foundation, which have supported much of its work since 1974, are now drying up. Its director, Susan Bailey, was writing lots of research proposals to raise further grants, and participating in an endowment drive to try to secure its future. Janice Monk, Executive Director of the Southwest Institute for Research on Women at the University of Arizona, told a similar story. Neither expected to fold up their tents and creep away, however; their accounts, rather, were about the strenuous work and shifts in its direction that continue to be necessary to sustain the institutions financially. Other kinds of struggle for a similar end were also evident. At Hunter College at the City University of New York, feminist academics were eager to argue for Women's Studies to be defined as a discipline (an argument which I contested), because this would gain their Women's Studies courses greater security and recognition within the university. And in at least one place I visited I could not avoid the impression that the Women's Studies Program had moved towards conformity with the requirements of conservative academic structures at the cost of its political edge and its broader community links. 'Cleaning up their act' was how one feminist academic I spoke with described it, in tones of regret.

Even so, morale in Women's Studies seemed high. Occasionally it was exuberant. An hour with Kay Warren at Princeton University would strike sparks from damp clay. Watching Evelyn Thornton Beck at a Women's Studies Assembly at the University of Maryland, drawing together a gathering of forty women, many of whom did not know each other, into a game which offered challenges to both ideas and inhibitions, was a chance to watch a gifted teacher at work. Listening to Donna Haraway, who teaches in the History of Consciousness unit of the University of California at Santa Cruz, talking about the politics of Women's Studies at that university was inspiring, even through the fog induced by my having to get up at 5 am to catch the bus to see her. If others were less dazzling, they were nevertheless committed and energetic. Talking with Roberta Spalther-Ross (University of Washington) about her research on women working on the streets, and about the principal issues concerning Women's Studies students and teachers, left me with a reading list and a rush of impatience to get to a library. Every feminist who visits Harvard should go and talk with Barbara Haber, who is now filling the Schlesinger Library with books as well as collections of manuscripts. At the Pembroke Centre for Teaching and Research on Women at Brown University in Providence, there were four postdoctoral fellowships being awarded each year for a three-year interdisciplinary, cross-cultural study of the formation, impact and transformation of cultural representations of women. Those four women, together with several other feminist academics, were spending each Friday morning working through a three-hour seminar which testified all over again to the solidity and conceptual daring of feminist scholarship. And this was no isolated experience for a visitor. I met it again on several occasions in New York, at lunch with a group of feminist scholars at the Institute of Advanced Study in Princeton, almost all the time I was in Ann Arbor, at lunch with a group of feminist historians at the University of Arizona, and at breakfast with Nancy Hartsock in Seattle.

The concerns of feminist scholarship in the USA — the nature and uses of a range of analytical discourses for illuminating the politics of sex and gender relationships, and the integration of analyses of the politics of gender with those of race, even, sometimes, those of class — almost inevitably shaded into the concerns of the Women's Movement at large, in many of the discussions I had. The burning questions for feminism in the late 1980s in the USA seemed to divide between the social policy issues which are still the subject of struggle: equal pay, comparable worth, parental leave and child care particularly, and, to a lesser extent, the unionisation of women in paid work; and vaguer but more apocalyptic questions about survival, sexuality, difference, and (to my ignorant surprise) religion. Most of these discussions were familiar, indicating yet again the extent to which feminists inhabit similar worlds of practice and imagination. I was startled, though, to hear one feminist reflecting despairingly on the state of the US economy, the growth of the military-industrial complex, and the lunatic defence strategies of the present administration, actually say, 'Well, the kind of solution that they might resort to could be another major war'. She's right, of course, but it was particularly chilling to hear it uttered. In a different discussion, another feminist argued the urgency of our analysis becoming more complex because, so far, our propaganda has not been working, and to prevent programs like Star Wars will require massive popular opposition to them. I did not encounter discussions of sexuality and difference that had any of the steam associated with the division among feminists in 1981 over questions about pornography and sexual freedom. And I did not pursue questions about feminism and religion, even though Barbara Haber told me of exciting new work which feminists are undertaking in the Harvard School of Divinity. (She told me, in passing, that Mary Daly is now allowing men to attend her classes.) However, the cluster of issues surfacing several times in discussion which surprised me most concerned feminism, love, loneliness and children.

Discussion of these issues had undoubtedly arisen partly in response to a number of recent publications about the increasing number of women, including married women, in paid work, their earnings (still only between 60 per cent and 70 per cent on average of men's earnings), their tendency to postpone marriage and child-bearing, the tendency of no-blame divorce proceedings to leave formerly married women unsupported, and at grave disadvantage in entering the labour market or trying to increase their earnings enough to support their children, and the persisting difficulties for women with children in finding child care. At least one of these books, Sylvia Ann Hewlett's *A Lesser Life: The Myth of Women's Liberation in America* (William Morrow & Co., New York, 1986), blamed all of these continuing disadvantages — *not* on persisting gender divisions in the labour market, *not* on a continuing sexual division of labour in relation to housework and child care, *not* on a misogynist state, *not* even on the fecklessness of men — but rather, on feminism.

It might have been easier to dismiss work like Hewlett's as the product of the new Right's anti-feminist backlash, rewriting the history of the Women's Movement to obliterate the early preoccupation of Women's Liberation with child care, and our continuing struggles to overcome gender divisions in paid work, housework and care of children. But it was clear that at least some feminists with long-standing commitment to the Women's Movement were finding the information and interpretations advanced by people like Hewlett profoundly troubling. And in the first tense discussion I heard, two feminists reviewing the questions that Hewlett and others raised had developed a historical account of second-wave feminism which described it as finished. The present, 'post-feminist' period of self-criticism, they argued, should allow us to develop from the second-wave's mistakes the lessons to be taken up by feminism's third wave. Those lessons, they thought, related to our continuing need for intimate relationships with men and with children.

This was not the only time I heard feminists in the USA saying that the Women's Movement is over. Using a definition of social movement particularly constrained by its origins in political science, Jo Freeman told Louise Tilly's seminar at the New School for Social Research that *as movement*, the Women's Movement had probably ended in 1974. That contention can readily be countered by using a more sociological and historically informed definition of social movement, one which recognises the plurality of feminisms which have gathered around the Women's Movement, and manifestly still do. But the earlier discussion of the work by Hewlett and others was, nevertheless, a moment when I heard feminists blaming feminism for the plight of women in North America today.

I would probably still be in catatonic shock had I not heard, simultaneously, an anguished critique of those feminists' review. Their arguments were class-bound, racist, and homophobic, urged their feminist friends. Further, they conveyed two entirely mistaken assumptions: firstly that feminism is singular and monolithic, and secondly, that feminism had been in a position of power great enough to dictate to all women what their satisfactions must be, and had then 'screwed up'. None of this is true. All of the subsequent discussions in which I heard such issues raised were troubled at the power of backlash publications like Hewlett's to capture, even for a moment, the hearts and minds of women still struggling against enormous odds for a decent living and for intimate relationships. But none of the feminists I asked were prepared to concede that feminism could be held culpable of anything but continuing, changing and many-fronted struggle for those goals.

I returned from this milkrun with a renewed sense of the urgency of feminists writing histories of our own times and of our own movement. How better can we combat misreading of our past, mobilised to deform our present? Feminist historians discover, over and over again, how extensive and varied, courageous and adventurous, were feminist ideas and actions in the past. We also discover how effectively they have been written out of the historical record. We cannot be subjected to such a silencing again.

I suppose the USIA might be surprised at the conclusions I drew from a month in their country. But I don't think that matters. I have written this report in gratitude to all the feminists from whom I learned about feminism and Women's Studies in the USA in the late 1980s. For hospitality, help in planning an itinerary, and in reaching at least a milkrunner's understanding of a different society and culture, I would like to thank particularly Desley Deacon, Heidi Hartmann, Florence Howe, Alice Jardine, Joan Scott, Kate Stimpson, Martha Vicinus and Liz Wood, and from the Institute of International Education, Jennifer Strauss.

17

'*Perestroika* has been bad for women': Russia 1991

This report first appeared in Australian Feminist Studies, *vol. 7, no. 15, Autumn 1992.*

For four days in November 1991 I attended an international seminar in Moscow. The letter inviting me to present a paper had arrived in July on the letterhead of the Academy of the Social Sciences of the USSR. That institution had been renamed by November: it is now called the Russian Academy of Management.

Speeches made at a small lunch on the first day, hosted by the Academy's new head and attended by one of the women in the People's Congress of Deputies, indicated that there was a struggle in process over who would control the Academy, now that the Communist Party of the Soviet Union [CPSU] had been banned. They suggested, too, that our seminar would play a major part in determining the outcome of such a struggle. What was less immediately clear, though, was why *this* seminar might have such determining power. Its subject was 'Gender Studies: Issues and Perspectives'.

We had been given a definition of 'Gender Studies' during the first morning. Dr Anastasiya Posadskaya, Director of the new Gender Studies Centre established in the Institute of Social and Economic Problems of Population in a different academy, the Academy of Science, told us that the Centre had introduced the term into the Russian vocabulary in a discussion that it had organised in 1989 under the heading 'How to Solve the Woman Question?' The principal social divisions between women and

men are not 'natural', she reminded us. They are socially constructed. 'Gender' refers to the social construction of the feminine and the masculine, and the allocation of socially differentiated kinds of work as part of such a construction. 'No single phenomenon can be gender-neutral', she declared. 'If gender is concealed, the task of the researcher is to discover and analyse it.' And this was particularly important in the USSR at present, she said. It would not have been possible to hold a seminar like this one in the USSR even as recently as two years ago.

Did this mean that *perestroika*, and moves toward a market economy — so celebrated as liberalising progress in the Western media — were improving conditions for women? Was there an upsurge of activist feminism across what was still, then, being called the USSR? If there was, what forms was it taking?

Figure 17: Susan Magarey at UNESCO conference on Gender Studies: Issues and Perspectives, Moscow, November 1991
Photograph courtesy of Susan Magarey

Was this what was prompting attention to 'Gender Studies' in the academies? Would a mere four days answer these questions?

The seminar had been sponsored by UNESCO. Serim Timur, of UNESCO's Population and Human Settlements Division in Paris, reminded us of the host of ways in which UNESCO had sought to spread awareness of the distinctive perspectives and experiences of women. These ranged from the United Nations Decade for Women (1975-85) and its major international conferences, to a series of regional seminars held in the years since 1985.

There were about 100 participants: 20 foreigners, 55 listed as 'Soviet Participants from the USSR', another 20 or so from the Ukraine, Byelorussia, Moldova, Azerbaijan, Uzbekistan, Tajikistan, Turkmenistan, Kyrghystan, Estonia and Tuva. We spent the first day and a half, and part of the last day, in plenary sessions. In between we divided into three Working Groups, one on 'Family, Household and Demographic Change', another on 'Women in Economic Life' and the third on 'Teaching and Training in Gender Studies'. There was also a 'Round Table' — with about 80 participants, on 'Women and Politics'.

The seminar was to be held in Russian and English, with simultaneous translation through those little earphones that you see in television clips of events in the United Nations. For a novice like me, this produced initial cognitive dissonance. I could both see and hear a woman speaking, but the only words I could understand were coming through the earphones in a man's voice.

There was another difficulty that I became aware of more slowly. Some of the Russian-language papers sounded, through the earphones, distinctly confused. Fortunately, though, many of them were also distributed as typescripts in English. A comparison of the written texts with notes taken from the simultaneous translation suggested that what gets lost under the pressure of high-speed interpretation is the distinction between the 'framing' and the substantive elements of a sentence. For instance, a Russian-speaker might say something like this: 'It is said that women should go back to the home, indeed that women yearn for domesticity and motherhood, but in fact women know that without jobs they face only increasing poverty'. The crucial 'framing' elements in that sentence — 'It is said that', 'but in fact' — often disappeared in the simultaneous translation, leaving puzzled listeners wondering at apparently internally contradictory statements.

One of the first things to emerge, very clearly, was a need for information. Over and over again, we heard calls for data, disaggregated by sex, and for literature that was 'not', I quote, 'stuffed with ideology, facts falsification and statistical data forgery'. Until 1990, we were told, statistics on women in the labour market had been kept secret.

This did not prevent citation of some chilling statistics, though. One speaker told us that women constitute 53 per cent of the population, a surprisingly small majority given other references to 'the shortage of men'. That speaker went on to announce that only 51 per cent of workers and office employees are women, and that 'more than 45 per cent of national income is created by women's hands'. Despite this, a woman's wage is one-third less than that of a man. And recent moves toward a market economy have exacerbated women's disadvantages. In 1989, 10 per cent of working men had increased their professional qualifications, but only 3 per cent of women had done so. As a result 20 per cent of women working in industry were still employed in hard manual labour. Further, what was called the 'disintegration of economic ties', closure of inefficient enterprises, privatisation of services and reductions in managerial staff had led to many women, particularly those who were also mothers, being dismissed.

This had occurred because enterprises endeavouring to operate under market conditions had acquired an interest in maintaining the most stable workforce possible. Since women continue to be assigned primary responsibility for the care of children, they are readily construed as 'unstable' elements in the workforce. Decades of sex-specific protections for women workers had led to such 'protections' operating against women. Current statistics show, we were told, that unemployment among women is four times greater than unemployment among men. Nowhere else in the world, said this speaker, is this differential so great.

Moreover, women constitute the elite of the unemployed, for they are far more likely than any men made redundant to have higher education and technical qualifications. Even so, they suffer from discrimination even in small businesses where they might find jobs as specialists, but hardly ever as entrepreneurs: only 0.4 per cent of entrepreneurs are women.

Losing your job means losing far more than your wages, too. For the enterprises order food and clothes for their workers, and furniture, things virtually unobtainable through shops. Losing your job means losing your ability to place orders through your work-committee. It can mean losing your place in a queue for housing, for a car, for a garden plot. You lose your right to stay in sanatoriums and holiday resorts owned by the enterprise. Losing your job means losing the whole fabric of your links with the world.[563] It is not fanciful to talk of 'the feminisation of poverty' in what used to be called the USSR.

Two years ago the Congress of People's Deputies had issued a fundamental pronouncement on the need for improvement in protections for women, the family

---

[563] Some of this information is also presented in Renfrey Clarke's interview with Anastasiya Posadskaya, published in *Green Left*, 11 September 1991.

and children, together with a directive to academics — 'scientists' — to conduct research to this end. The pronouncement had not even been published, though. And women, widely cast in the role of preservers of 'spiritual' health, were just as widely being blamed for current rates of suicide, alcoholism, juvenile delinquency, even for current rates of violence against women. Some speakers continued to invoke 'women-and-the-family-and-children' as a single set of issues, or, more often, 'problems'. But not many. More argued for a consideration of women and their needs and rights as distinct from the conglomerate unit into which they had previously disappeared, offering research about how women are positioned distinctly from men in relation to work, family, and politics; women therefore develop distinctive modes of decision-making, distinctive readiness to combat social and environmental disasters rather than, like men, to make wars. One speaker provided statistics comparing decisions made by committees that were composed entirely of men with decisions made by committees with 50 per cent female membership. Those decisions were far more humane when women participated in making them, she told us. Another spoke of the work that women had done towards clearing up destruction in the wake of what was here called 'the African war'.

Questions of reproductive control did not loom very large in our discussions, even though contraceptives are still unavailable in the USSR. The principal means of reproductive control is still, as it has been since the 1950s, abortion. Indeed, we were told, the number of abortions carried out in Russia each year is currently greater than the number of live births.

This information, though, was presented in the context of the alarm at the possibility of Islamic populations in some of the Republics out-breeding the Russians — a moment of nationalist, ethnic and religious tension — which effectively distracted attention from possibilities of discussing other forms of reproductive control.

This same paper, however, also pointed out that women are now suffering from additional discrimination, through their exploitation as sex objects — across a range of representations from advertising to pornography — rather than as fully human subjects. That speaker concluded by calling for women's right to self-determination in relation to sex and reproduction, and for recognition of the importance of solidarity among women.

Women's participation in officially recognised political bodies and government has plummeted. In elections in 1984, we were told, 50 per cent of the deputies in local Soviets had been women; 40 per cent of deputies in territorial, regional and republican Soviets had been women; and in the Supreme Soviet 33 per cent. But in elections held in 1989, women made up only 15.6 per cent of the People's Deputies of the USSR, only 5.6 per cent of the People's Deputies of the Russian Federation, and less than 3 per cent of the Deputies in the Supreme Soviet of 5 republics. 'There has never been such a situation in the whole history of the Soviet state', this speaker observed. 'What has happened?'

Answers came from two directions. Galina Sillaste, Professor of Sociology at the Academy of Management, pointed out that 74 per cent of women who had previously been members of the CPSU now rejected Party membership. Did this mean that they also rejected other political procedures like elections? Galina Sillaste urged attention to the developing women's organisations and Women's Movements.

We had, by then, already heard alarmed references to what Professor Rudolph Yanowski called 'negative trends in an ongoing feminist movement'. One such, he said, was the attempt to single out women's issues and from them formulate a separate women's policy. Another was the enlisting of women in — his words — 'extremism and destructive behaviour': popular fronts, nationalist organisations, organisations of women who are religious believers. Women stop traffic on roads, he told us. They stop work on construction sites. They picket military enlistment bureaux.

At the Round Table on 'Women and Politics' which Gallina Sillaste chaired, we heard two different views of women's organisations. One came from the editor of a new journal called *Business Woman*. She provoked laughter when she began by saying that she was happy to learn that there was a Women's Movement in the USSR because she had not noticed it. But she went on to exhort women to protest and action. We can't do anything until we stop being so obedient, she declared. You can't imagine women in the United States waiting in queues like we do. We need — and these are her words — 'a Ministry for Women's Rights like they have in Australia' (a reference to the Australian government's Office of the Status of Women?). She concluded: 'The women's organisations are not doing anything. We are not witnessing any Women's Movement. We need to make one!' She sat down to a storm of applause.

A different view of the women's organisations came from the chairperson of the recently formed Moscow Union of Women, established, she told us, to co-ordinate a host of smaller women's organisations. These had originally been charities, and their goal had been simply survival. But now, while that goal remained primary, the women's organisations were growing larger and more ambitious. The Moscow Union now embraces 91 organisations, and it is exploring ways in which women can maximise their capacity to earn.

The second direction from which we gained an answer to Rudolph Yanowski's question about the abrupt shrinkage in political representation of women was the Gender Studies Centre in the Academy of Science. Anastasiya Posadskaya said, simply: '*Perestroika* has been bad for women. *Perestroika* has been a male project'. Reconstruction in a patriarchal structure had maintained a separation between social and private life, and has progressively excluded women from the social. 'Women have been objects rather than subjects of change', she told us. 'The task that history has bestowed upon Soviet women now, therefore, is to formulate our own agendas for action on unemployment, reproductive rights and representation in government.' Her conclusion was also greeted with applause.

At least some of the questions I had brought to the seminar seemed to have been answered. Persisting patriarchalism meant that the position of women had grown far worse, despite political liberalisation and the beginning of transition to a market economy, indeed, possibly *as a result* of both. A range of women's organisations had been formed and are attempting to find ways of overcoming women's increasing disadvantage. And even state organisations, a few, were sufficiently concerned to contemplate support for teaching and research related to such disadvantages.

Courses in what some speakers called 'feminology' or 'social feminology' had already been established as shifts in emphasis in Soviet education had allowed questioning of earlier orthodox analyses exclusively in terms of class. Courses on sex education at the Youth Institute had become courses on women's rights. Courses in 'social feminology' provided a multifaceted and multidisciplinary analysis of women's position in society, including a history of the Women's Movement, all designed to change mental stereotypes of women and men, and to instil in women confidence in their abilities to become politicians, managers and teachers. There was still a long way to go, though. Several speakers reported opposition from male colleagues; their examples ranged across a familiar spectrum from chivalrous condescension through jocularity to outright hostility.

Our seminar offered opportunity for debate about future directions. One debate focused on ways of describing the ideology informing such work. Most speakers concurred that it represented progress from a 'paternalistic' ideology; the debate was about whether to label the current emphasis 'egalitarian' or 'humanist' or 'feminist'. A parallel debate concerned the terms 'feminology' and 'gender studies'. One speaker insisted that 'social feminology' was 'oriented to the positive experience accumulated by the multi-faceted feminist movement of the West'. Another contended that such a term sustains paternalist stereotypes of women and men. No-one explicitly challenged our seminar's title.

A third debate was concerned with what could be done next. In one form, this was a debate over autonomy for Gender Studies, and therefore the need to establish new programs and organisations, or the integration of Gender Studies into the mainstream of teaching, research, and policy-making. It was on the edges of this debate that questions about control of the Academy of Management also lurked.

Professor Alla Perminova, Secretary of our seminar's Organising Committee, argued for the Academy of Management to establish an international Gender Studies Centre that would co-ordinate research throughout the country and develop practical programs. When asked, she explicitly rejected the possibility of the Gender Studies Centre in the Academy of Science taking on such functions. That centre, she said, is isolated, like an island. It does not have the connections with other organisations, and with the Soviet parliament and government, connections that the Academy of Management already had.

By contrast, Galina Sillaste argued for a broad historical, social and psychological approach to Gender Studies to be implemented in wide-ranging programs, with non-government organisation. 'The Women's Movements are developing regardless of us (academicians)', she commented: 'we must be responsive to them'.

There were also at least eight proposals for new centres or institutes of Gender Studies to be set up, in different cities and regions, including one for a new inter-republic league to be called 'Women's Initiative'. Many were combined with references to the United Nations Convention eliminating discrimination against women and appeals to UNESCO for both guidance and material support. One speaker even proposed that we lobby the United Nations for a new convention mandating the introduction of Gender Studies in education systems throughout the world. Then, she said, national governments would have to report progress every three years, so they would be compelled to attend to research demonstrating persisting, indeed increasing, disadvantage for women, and to courses that would help empower women.

Who would guess what will follow from those four days' discussions? Only weeks later the USSR no longer existed as a political entity. But politics is concerned with food supplies as well as national boundaries, with human reproduction as well as control of armies — as the women I listened to made abundantly clear. Perhaps some of them are picketing arms enlistment bureaux as I write.

18

Scholarship for a cause:
San José, Costa Rica, 1993

This report was first published in Australian Feminist Studies, *vol. 8, no. 17, Autumn 1993.*

'Women's Rights are Human Rights!' we shouted in chorus with the woman with the megaphone in the van, 'Stop Violence Against Women!' One of the placards condemned the rape of women in Bosnia. Others called on the United States to ratify the United Nations Convention to Eliminate Discrimination Against Women.

Not the usual fare of an academic conference. But this was not a *usual* academic conference. It was the Fifth International Interdisciplinary Congress on Women. Most of the placards were in Spanish, because it was held at the University of Costa Rica. The main banner read 'La No Agresion Contra La Mujer es Tambien un Derecho Humano'. And the march from the university to the Plaza de la Democrazia in downtown San José (the capital of Costa Rica), which filled the streets with the 2000 participants from 43 different countries, was part of the program.

Other aspects of this congress gave it a flavour more like that of a United Nations gathering than the dusty scholasticism that can be associated with universities. Charlotte Bunch, of the Centre for Women's Global Leadership at Douglass College, Rutgers University, for instance, spoke of a current campaign to persuade participants at the UN Conference on Human Rights to take place in June this year that rape is torture (the UN has already outlawed torture, but not rape). Kazuko Watanabe, of the Kyoto Sangyo University, presented a chilling analysis of the continuum between

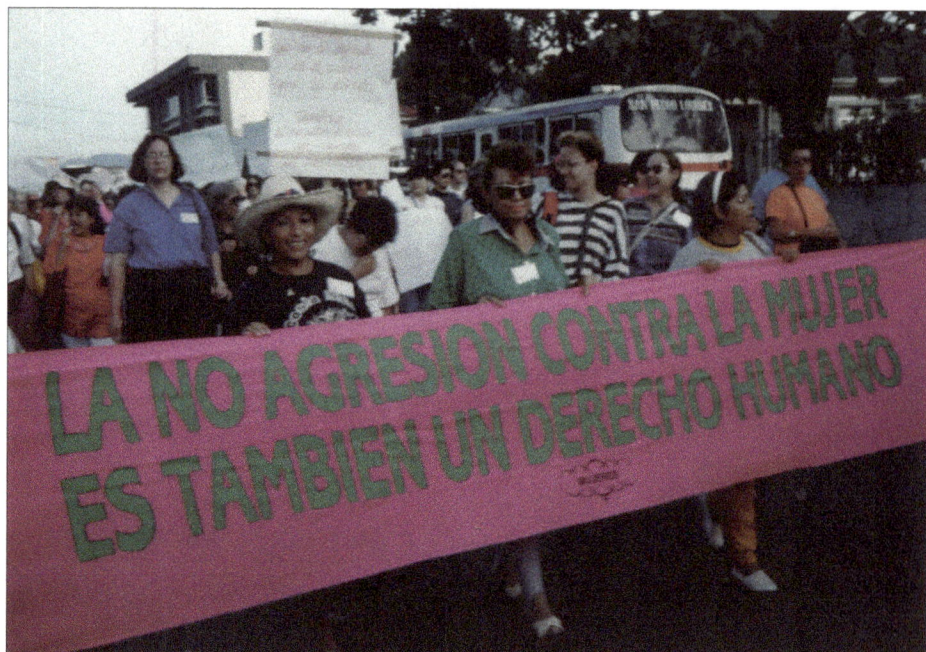

Figure 18: Fifth International Interdisciplinary Congress on Women, San José, Costa Rica, 1993
Photograph courtesy of Susan Magarey

the 'sex tours' that Japanese businessmen take in Asia today, and the 'comfort women' recruited in Southeast Asian countries to provide sexual services to the Japanese Imperial Army during the Second World War, information brought to international attention by a lawsuit that three Korean women brought against the Japanese government in 1992. Peggy Antrobus, of the Women and Development Unit in Barbados, speaking on Ecology to a packed lecture theatre, said that women in the developing world are sceptical of ways in which the feminist agenda had been 'mainstreamed' and thereby neutralised. She argued, too, that women are highly suspicious of the language and actions of government agencies: '*We* are not talking about "sustainable profits"', she noted, 'but that is what governments mean when they talk about "sustainable development"', an announcement which brought thunderous applause.

One of the principal keynote panels had been organised by UNIFEM and sponsored by the UN Development Fund for Women. Chaired by Achola Pala Okeyo of Kenya, on Black Women's Livelihoods in the Developing World, *that* crowded lecture theatre heard Sueli Carneiro of Brazil observe that even though Brazil is the second largest black country outside of the African continent it was not until 1988, the centenary of the abolition of slavery, that there was any extended discussion of the needs and rights of black women. And not only discussion but action is urgent: 'We are the women who were threatened with mass sterilisation', she told us, 'lest our numbers grow so great as to threaten political dominance by the year 2000'. Illiteracy is as high as 48 per cent among black women, double the figure for white women, and 85 per cent of black women live below the poverty line, even while they earn two salaries a month. Similar figures were appearing in other papers, which also observed that current policies for global economic readjustment depend upon the exploitation of the most economically deprived of the world's population — poor women extracting a bare survival from the Economic Free Zones of the transnational corporations, from domestic labour and/or prostitution in the cities, or from small farms where they live with almost no amenities and have to walk long distances to their plots of land.

All of these papers, and those in other keynote sessions as well, pointed towards a new era for international feminism, and the importance of grassroots women's organisations. They also pointed to important links between grassroots activism, teaching and research that recognises the centrality of gender and consideration of the position of women, and campaigns to change those government policies that — ignoring women — will accelerate global poverty and decimation of the global environment.

This is scholarship for a cause, research and teaching that is not only *about* women and their place in the world, but also *for* women and improving the worlds in which we live. It is a kind of scholarship that is characteristic of Women's Studies, which were also represented at the congress in daily two-hour keynote panels, with speakers from thirty countries ranging from Argentina to Russia, from Australia to Zimbabwe, from England to the Netherlands.

Yet, however different from conventional academic conferences this congress may have been, it is clear that universities around the world are not as opposed to scholarship for a cause as such difference might suggest. The majority of speakers held posts in universities; the papers offered a breadth and depth of research and analysis that would have impressed the professoriate of Oxbridge, the Ivy League institutions or the Australian National University; and this congress was welcomed enthusiastically by the Rector of the University of Costa Rica, who had provided substantial material support for it.

19

'Gender Studies: Towards the Year 2000': Greece 1993

This report first appeared in Australian Feminist Studies, *vol. 8, no. 18, Summer 1993.*

It wasn't actually *in* Athens, this gathering of scholars from parts of the globe as distant as Zimbabwe and the United States, China and the Caribbean, Canada and the Netherlands, Bulgaria and Brazil. Perhaps we were supposed to think that this was just as well. One of the conference-organisers told us — as she drove us south-south-east from Athens airport down the Sounion Peninsula — that the pollution levels in the city were now so high that the government had decreed that cars being driven into the city had to be rationed. Only cars with number-plates ending in odd numbers are allowed in the city on one set of alternate days; only cars with number-plates ending in even numbers on the other alternate days. (Of course, she said, this meant that most families kept two cars and made sure that their number-plates ended in alternate numbers — those families who could afford two cars, that is.)

We did go into Athens, though, for a reception at the Town Hall. And as the bus taking us back to the conference-locale rounded a corner, we were treated to the spectacle of a full moon above the Acropolis!

The conference, sponsored by UNESCO, and organised by Ketty Lazaris, the president of the Gender Studies Association of the Mediterranean [KEGME], was held in the Hotel Ilios, roughly twenty kilometres south of Athens. This hotel perches on a headland above the Mediterranean; it is a mere three minutes' scamper past the bougainvillea (and the trenches being dug for new plumbing) to the beach. It is a tribute to the program of papers that we were to hear — in a lecture theatre without windows, and with desks so distant from the seats that anyone wishing to take notes had to do so on her knee or risk rupture — that most of us attended most of the papers, rather than playing truant at the beach. But, then, this was also a conference about Gender Studies and its place in shaping a future world. (It was also a comment on the dirtiness of Greek beaches: potato-chip bags blew across bodies attempting an English version of sunbaking; a plastic chair rested upside down, in the rocks, just below the hotel's terraces. The beaches were stony — not like beaches in Australia: we — in Australia — have soft feet because our sand is soft.)

There was, perhaps inevitably, debate about the term 'gender studies', the title of the seminar, preferred by both Serim Timur of UNESCO and Ketty Lazaris, and rejected strenuously by many others. It was raised in the keynote paper during the opening plenary session by Nadia Serematakis, in a paper called 'Women's Studies: Theoretical and Pedagogical Issues, Aims and Directions'. The shift in nomenclature from 'Women's Studies' to 'Gender Studies' was, she said,

> assumed to be the recontextualization of Women's Studies in more relational and holistic framework that would in itself, not subtract but enhance Women's Studies … The turn to gender studies was meant to inhibit the ghettoization of Women's Studies in a self enclosed field of research and discourse that would be unable to impact on other disciplines and perspectives.

But such intentions have not always been fulfilled. Nadia then asked the question that focused this debate for much of the rest of the conference:

> [H]as the notion of gender studies expanded the discussion and awareness of women's issues or has it simply ended up creating a new restricting objectification of women? What ideological and methodological baggage accompanied the grafting of gender studies onto Women's Studies and how has that affected … the conceptualisation of women, gender, society and history?

For those committed to the term 'Women's Studies' rather than 'Gender Studies', the arguments were straightforward, and had been rehearsed often. The term 'Gender Studies' had all too often failed adequately to foreground the gendered specificity of the so-called human (male) subject in examinations of societies and histories; had denied gender specificity to women; and, in the worst cases, was simply a way of continuing to teach all the same old patriarchal courses without paying any attention to women. Moreover, as some conference-participants pointed out, in many languages other than English, there was no distinction between the terms 'sex' and 'gender', so that use of the term 'gender' was received either with mystification, or as an instance of cultural imperialism from anglophone cultures. As Jirina Smejkalova-Strickland observed, in her paper 'Gendered Thought: Birth of Revival? Gender Studies in Czech Academia':

> The terms 'gender', 'discourse', 'image' and 'representation' used by [English-speaking] feminist writers do not even have adequate equivalents in the Czech language. Furthermore, these concepts will probably continue to take on different political and social meanings in relation to the rapidly changing perspectives in both of the so-called Western and Eastern worlds.

On the other hand, Marina Morozova, in a paper called 'Women's Studies in Russia: Past, Present and Future', found no difficulty with the term 'gender studies', and offered an account of the establishment of the Centre for Gender Studies at the Academy of Sciences in Moscow in 1990, a Centre which brings together the state-supported academy and the energies of various informal Women's Movements. In November 1992, this Centre organised the Second International Women's Forum, at Dubna, attended by more than 300 women from various women's organisations and 100 foreign guests, she told us. Here, clearly, the term 'gender' — new in the Russian vocabulary, I had learned at a similar conference in Moscow in November 1991 — offered no difficulties for emerging feminist activism. Indeed, a body called the 'Group of Gender Experts' has been established at the Supreme Soviet of Russia to help legislators examine new laws for their capacity to take account of 'women's special and rightful position'. Though, Marina Morozova added, Russian laws are still without gender distinction, and the only difference between women and men recognised in Russian legislation is women's 'right of child-bearing'.

There were a number of papers that were not specifically concerned with the debate over the politics of naming 'Women's Studies', however. Highlights included Albertina de Oliveira Costa's paper, called 'Women's Studies in Brazil, or the Tightrope-Walking Strategy', in which she maintained that the social sciences in her country had been dragged out of the limbo in which they had existed since the 1970s specifically by the questions raised by the feminist movement. The principal trouble that Women's Studies in Brazil faces now, she told us, was that whereas high-quality research had been carried out in this interdisciplinary field, this 'had no connection with the implementation of systematic teaching and training'. Yue Daiyun, in a paper on 'Chinese Women in Traditional and Contemporary Chinese Literature', argued that in the twenty-first century a 'new system', characterised by collaboration between men and women in handling 'social affairs and family trivialities', will replace the traditional allocation of responsibility of the former to men and the latter to women; she quoted a 'young woman critic' writing:

> Since men and women share more and more in common with each other's feelings, experiences, and cultural mentality, a bisexual [*sic*] literature which belongs to both males and females will be bound to turn up. I should say that a new era is not far away from us when men and women equally share the world and jointly create a new culture.

And Patricia Mohammed, purportedly speaking to us about 'Gender in the Development of Caribbean Societies', read us a poem which brought her an enthusiastic ovation.

There were two points of tension at this conference, apart from the debate about 'Gender Studies' vs 'Women's Studies'. One was a question of process. Some participants found the organisation excessively formal, allowing space for people to speak to their papers, but far too little time and space for discussion. Peggy McIntosh (USA) dealt with this, in the session that she chaired, by arranging for her speakers to respond to a series of questions, rather than following the format of other sessions; those questions were then also thrown open for discussion from the floor. The other concerned the paper delivered by Sylvia Walby (England). She had been asked to address the question, 'Is the Women's Movement still necessary?' — a question to which, as she said, there seemed only one very short answer possible. We learned, after that session, that the reason for such a silly question being on the program was Ketty's hope — fortunately not fulfilled — that that session should have been a debate between Sylvia and Camille Paglia. We gathered that Paglia turned out to be too expensive.[564]

---

[564] See also my reference to Camille Paglia in Chapter Twenty, which says something about the cultural reach of celebrity, rather than anything about international feminism.

20

Looking at the world through women's eyes: United Nations in Beijing, 1995

This report first appeared in Australian Feminist Studies, *vol. 10, no. 22, Summer 1995.*

'Hail the Convocation in China the Fourth Non-Government Organisation [NGO] Forum on Women!' reads the huge red banner, beside the road to Huairou, about an hour's drive from downtown Beijing. Others, all written in both Chinese and English, wish 'A Complete Success to FWCW '95!', exhort the Chinese people to 'Be a Worthy Host' to the forum, and repeat the slogan 'Equality, Development and Peace!'

It is 31 August, and we are in a bus that left our Beijing hotel at 7.30 am, wearing our laminated registration cards on little chains round our necks. We are poring over the 28-page plenary program book, and another of no fewer than 200 pages, each divided into three columns, listing the workshops that will fill the next ten days. They are divided into thirteen themes: Economy; Governance & Politics, Human/Legal Rights; Peace & Human Security; Education; Health; Environment; Spirituality & Religion; Science & Technology; Media; Arts & Culture; Race & Ethnicity; and Youth. They begin at 9 am, finish at 9 pm, and we must choose between the plenary sessions and as many as 132 concurrent workshops at any one time. This will clearly be a marathon.

Since the maps inside the back covers of our books tell us that they are not drawn to scale, the marathon begins with everyone's efforts to find their workshops, in

271

locations ranging from air-conditioned halls in hotels where some of the participants are staying, through circles of metal chairs in a huge, multistoreyed but unfinished (roofless) concrete building labelled 'Willow Recreation Club (Plenary Hall)' on the maps, to the huge marquee (borrowed from the Malaysians) called the 'Golden Pavilion', an array of smaller marquees and tents set up between the buildings and linked by paths of concrete blocks laid on the ground, and several acres called 'The Sports Ground' studded with small round tables and chairs shaded by umbrellas. Chinese students wearing yellow t-shirts marked 'Translator' try to help read the maps at the chief access points to each area.

Everywhere there are women, in every variety of national dress, talking, pointing, laughing, hugging, hanging up banners on fences, posting notices on walls — at least 30 000 of us, from 180 countries, and representing more than 3000 NGOs, reports the *Independent Daily of the NGO Forum* on 8 September. We are attending the largest gathering of women to have taken place at any time, anywhere in the world, and this gathering is supposed to be committed to the continuing struggle for women's liberation, empowerment, dignity and equality.

Its purpose is spelled out on the covers of our program-books: 'To bring together women and men to challenge, create and transform global structures and processes at all levels through the empowerment and celebration of women'. The celebratory red and white logo, which appears everywhere, depicts eight women dancing. 'Each has her own energy and dynamism', the book explains.

> Each is tied to the other through a common centre. Thus they all together generate more energy and power than each of them could generate singly. The figure celebrates women as risk-takers, doers, and creative shapers of their own destinies.

That purpose is reiterated at the first of the plenary sessions which will spend the week presenting critical analyses of the powerful global forces currently affecting the quality of life of the human community, and the challenges those pose for everyone, women in particular. We are here to 'set the agenda for the Women's Movement around the world', proclaims Khunying Supatra Masdit, Convenor of the Forum, to the audience filling the seats, and packed in double rows in the aisles and against the walls of the main Convention Centre. We are here to 'network women's organisations of north and south, east and west' with each other, 'to lobby the Fourth World Conference on Women, Development, Democracy and Peace', and while 'recognising our diversity, to stand firm in our united purpose'. Irene Santiago, Executive Director of the Forum, elaborates. We are not presuming to lead the collective action of the Women's Movement, she tells us, since it is far too various for that to be possible. But we are aiming to create a common understanding among women throughout the world, particularly of the rights and claims made for women on the agenda of the United Nations' Fourth World Conference on Women, the conference of government delegates, which will begin in Beijing on 4 September.

The understanding that builds during the ensuing twenty plenaries is of an immediate global crisis, with immensely destructive implications for all human societies. This is a time of transition, says Charlotte Bunch of the Centre for Women's Global Leadership in the United States. The end of the Cold War signalled a beginning of the Hot Peace. There has been an escalation of gender-based conflicts and violence, linked with globalisation of the world's economy, and the undeclared, unaccountable world governance by the International Monetary Fund and its military allies. In the West, there has been a dismantling of welfare programs, matched by structural adjustment programs with similar effects in other parts of the world. Religious fundamentalism, she observes, demonises and reduces 'the other' in ways that function to control women.

A speaker from Croatia says that the Berlin Wall fell on the bodies of women; women's bodies have been integral in 'ethnic cleansing'; ethnic cleansing has been exercised by all sides in the war over the territory formerly called Yugoslavia; and the international community has been unwilling to do anything to prevent this war or bring it to an end. Hardly surprising, in her view: the armaments industry is big business, supported by the fact that there are at present no fewer than 150 wars going on all over the world. Who is selling arms to whom? she asks, a question that brings her tempestuous applause.

Helen O'Connor, from Ireland, notes that with the globalisation of the economy, countries in the 'south' cannot choose their road to development: the whole ethos is about maximising wealth, but not about distributing it. As another speaker points out, PanAm highways are being widened, while cuts in the economies of the countries that the highways pass through continue. The most immediate result of globalisation, says O'Connor, has been an increase in poverty around the world, an increase in the informal economy alongside the formal economy, an increase in unemployment (20 million out of work in the European Union, she notes), and privatisation of essential social services. Even, in Western Europe — a challenge to the very concept of social security.

Winnie Karagwa Byanyima, a fully qualified flight engineer from Uganda, representing the Constituent Assembly Women's Caucus, notes that Africa was a battleground for the whole of the Cold War, so Africans greeted its end with relief. But since then, the rise of the ethnic nationalisms have brought increasing competition for dwindling resources, coupled with men's greed for power, so the longed-for peace has not eventuated. There is, instead, she says, a widening gap between rich and poor. Another African, Esther Ocloo from Ghana, representing the Sustainable End of Hunger Foundation, observes that the new production technologies have deprived women of employment by displacing manual labour, leading to the current crisis of poverty and lack of education.

There is a concerted critique of national and international colonialism. Winona Laduke, Native American representative of the Indigenous Women's Network, tells us that, although Native Americans meet all of the criteria defining a nation-state in international law, they are still treated as merely a minority group, and that they are the most bombed nation on earth, since all of the United States' nuclear testing has been conducted on their land. Amelia Rokotuivana, representative of the Young Women's Christian Association in Fiji and the Asia and Pacific Development Centre, picks up the theme: nuclear submarines are cruising the Pacific at this moment, she observes, and while formerly they were there as yet another manifestation of the Cold War, now they are there to terrify the remainder of the Communist Bloc, particularly North Korea. The French will never let go of Tahiti, she says, and other colonising powers in the Pacific continue to deny basic human rights to indigenous peoples: the Indonesian government is still waging war against the inhabitants of West Papua and East Timor; the people of Bilao are still having to fight for a new constitution; the inhabitants of Guam are still denied land-rights; the Australian government continues to delay in returning land-rights to Aboriginal Australians; and the government of Papua New Guinea, aided by the Australian military, blockaded Bougainville. Moreover, she notes, the Pacific is the principal dumping-ground for the world's nuclear waste.

One speaker, Marcia Rivera, a Puerto Rican representing the Latin American Council of Social Sciences and a member of Development Alternatives with Women for a New Era [DAWN], disentangles the critiques of colonising governments and those of the forces for globalisation of the economy. On her analysis, the most dangerous forces abroad are the multinational corporations and the international finance institutions which have harnessed the technological revolution of the late twentieth century to their own ends. The result has been, she says, a uniformisation, brought about by structural adjustment programs, based on a free-market model; these make intervention by national states more difficult, erode the rights of labour, encourage privatisation and social polarisation, and, since 95 per cent of their financial transactions are speculative, they lead to risk-taking over production, and corruption and bribery of politicians and officials. Even the international aid agencies are often unable to counter these effects, she notes, a comment which brings a cry from the floor: 'Funds to the NGOs often don't reach the people they're supposed to help. They are thieves and robbers!'

The technological revolution of the late twentieth century might be serving to democratise information in some places: one speaker, the head of Distance Education at the University of the South Pacific, tells us about a telecommunications network linking ten countries in meetings to develop educational programs. But other speakers see the revolution in communications technologies as ranging from useless to positively harmful. The new communication technologies are irrelevant to families in which women cannot afford to buy batteries for their radios, and that means that new work-training programs made available by broadcasting are useless to women in African villages, says Esther Ocloo. The new information technologies have not brought a democratisation of knowledge, notes Amelia Rokotuivana from Fiji, but the reverse. Coupled with the new intellectual and property rights of the General Agreement on Tariffs and Trade [GATT], they are privatising and commercialising knowledge, and, in the process, eliminating the specific knowledges of Aboriginal peoples. Winnie Karagwa Byanyima says that they have brought an erosion of cultural specificity through what she calls 'the vulgarity of what Hollywood calls entertainment'. This is a concern about cultural integrity and diversity. But it is also a concern about access to information and self-determination before faceless and destructive international powers. Laura Flanders, a New York-based broadcaster involved in media-watch in the United States, notes that media companies are becoming fewer and larger, and if current mergers go ahead, two of the largest will be controlled by nuclear power companies with strong military interests. Moreover, she tells us, the present Head of TCI was recently quoted as saying that it was not the purpose of the media to serve the public; any chief executive officer of a major corporation would be sacked if he began devoting resources to satisfying the demands of the public.

These are searing — if not unexpected — critiques. What do the plenary speakers recommend that the International Women's Movement do to combat these forces?

Nobel Prize-winner for Peace, Aung San Suu Kyi, on video, says that women as mothers are natural teachers, and should use these skills to act in the processes of both governance and development. Female solidarity across the world demonstrates, she says, the power of an idea to cross national boundaries. Mag Segrest, a United States-based writer, representing the World Council of Churches, speaking powerfully against religious fundamentalism as a new force for conservatism, is concerned with power-relations, domestically and globally; like Charlotte Bunch, she argues for a new definition of the family as democratic, securing the rights of each member, and including all humanity — that is, Bunch says, including gays and lesbians, and gypsies. (Segrest's paper, in which she announces that she is also speaking as a lesbian, is greeted by a homophobic and fundamentalist tirade from the floor, clear evidence that the understanding for which the plenaries aimed was not shared universally.) Both Winnie Karagwa Byanyima and Gita Sen of the Indian Institute of Management in Bangalore urge that we build the structures of civil society so that they become a force to which both governments and international corporations have to be accountable. Amelia Rokotuivana also urges us to engage with our own governments: governments are, after all, she notes, among the worst violators of human rights. For global peace, it is crucial, she tells us, that 'the south' be enabled to trade out of its debt and lack of development. Helen O'Connor argues passionately that in order to democratise the global economy and make the transnational corporations and the international finance institutions accountable to us, our primary responsibility, as women, and as the global Women's Movement, is to continue to organise. Marcia Rivera exhorts us all to participate in debate on models for development to ensure that they are based on human needs and rights rather than on the capacities of computers. We must develop new political strategies which will open up new spaces for action, new ways in which to achieve power, she says. And, as many also repeat, we must lobby the government representatives at the Fourth World Conference on Women.

Much of this could have sounded hollow, or utopian — if there had not been such extensive evidence of women organising, and demonstrating, all around the forum. This showed immense diversity. On one day, Islamic women held a press conference criticising religious fundamentalism; on another, there was a march, 300-strong, for lesbian rights; on yet another, there was a very small, pro-life march. There was, too, a huge march protesting the French nuclear tests, taking place while we were meeting. (There was a surprising quietness about Chinese nuclear testing). There was a double-life-size female figure, demonstrating for the right to drinking water as a basic human right. There was a Youth Tent in which young women organised spontaneous discussions. And the workshops ranged from debate over the current state of the international Women's Movement, with criticism by a Pakistani speaker of language using the term 'gender' as an imposition by both the IMF and the male-dominated UN, an East German workshop titled 'How We Lost Our Revolution', to Betty Friedan reading extracts from her works to a tent so crowded that people were standing on chairs three and four rows deep outside it, to a panel of Pacific and Torres Strait Islanders objecting to being always tacked onto Asia in UN language, and including one woman who said she had had to begin her journey to Beijing by canoe. As with the implicit conflict between the critiques of fundamentalism and those of reproductive rights for women, the diversity sometimes crystallised into difference — on one day, Japanese women were dancing in their raincoats with placards saying 'Japanese Government should give full apology to Asian Comfort Women' and 'Japan should be made full member of UN'; the next day, Korean women were demonstrating with placards rejecting Japanese government apologies, demanding full compensation for the Comfort Women, and objecting to full UN membership for Japan. Another Australian participant told me about a discussion she had listened to in which an assertion about the need for women working as prostitutes to be able to ensure protection of their working conditions from violence and infection had run into direct conflict with widespread anguish about the international trade in the bodies of girl-children for prostitution.

Lobbying government representatives at the Fourth World Conference proved logistically difficult given the distance, and uncertain transport, between Huairou and Beijing. The buses that left our Beijing hotels at 7.30 am went only once a day. If you missed the bus, then you had to make your way to the Worker's Stadium in Beijing, and take a shuttle bus from there. And once the World Conference on Women began, the shuttle buses all ran first to the Conference location in Beijing before they went on to Huairou, and were very slow. For coming back to Beijing in

Figure 19: A double life-size female figure demonstrating for access to drinking water to be a basic human right, Fourth Non-Government Organisation Forum, United Nations Congress on Women, Huairou, China, 1995

Photograph courtesy of Susan Magarey

the evenings, the hotel buses would assemble and wait until they were full before they would set off; this could mean waiting as long as two hours, and missing any chance of contacting government representatives. There were taxis, readily available; the hour-long journey between Beijing and Huairou cost 100 yuan, which was only about $AUS16, a reasonable sum for the distance, particularly if it could be shared by three people; but for participants from economies whose currencies are not able to purchase much in the way of US dollars, for instance, such sums were prohibitive. Further, while child care was available at the NGO Forum, it was not provided at the Conference of government representatives.

Some, perhaps all, governments had arranged for the possibility of meetings between participants in the Forum and government representatives attending the Fourth World Conference on Women. On one bus journey from Huairou back to Beijing, I heard some African women speaking with pleased excitement about their expectation that Winnie Mandela would be visiting them that evening. The Australian National Council of Women, with funds donated by Westpac, had organised a regular gathering-point, a large room in the very posh Kun Lun Hotel in Beijing, from six to nine o'clock each evening, where — I had thought — the 800 Australians attending the Forum were to be able to engage in the lobbying so strongly urged upon us. But, we were told, the Chinese security people had decreed that the space was not to be used for political meetings, so entertainment was provided — allowing us to see the Australian Women's Circus if we'd missed them at Huairou, and Playback Theatre, which was fun — and what we did in the rest of the time was described as 'networking'. This, of course, was political. On one evening, we were introduced to the members of the government delegation to the Conference. And on one evening, former Premier of Western Australia Carmen Lawrence came to speak to us, and to hear us.

On that evening, I was meeting a friend for dinner, a Greek playwright called Chrystiana Lambrinidis, who came to the Kun Lun gathering with me. When Carmen Lawrence appeared, the whole of the large space erupted with enthusiasm: women were standing on chairs to applaud, and the applause must have lasted a good ten minutes. Afterwards, Chrystiana asked me, 'Who *is* this woman?' I told her: she was the former Premier of Western Australia, at that time being subjected to a politico-legal attack on a charge of having mis-led the Western Australian Parliament. And then she said: 'Well, no politician in Greece could command so strong an affirmation — unless it were Melina Mercouri!'

When torrential rain set in, tents at Huairou collapsed and the concrete blocks forming the paths between the tents slipped sideways in the mud, making movement particularly difficult for wheelchairs. People in wheelchairs protested outside the Media Centre. The rain washed out the possibility of Hilary Clinton's address to the Forum being delivered from the Kuumba Stage on the edge of the Sports Ground, where she could probably have been heard by several thousand women. Instead, she was moved into the Convention Centre, where the plenaries had been held, where no more than about 2000 women could be admitted. Observers who had arrived at the Convention Centre to queue for admission as early as 7.30 am told me that a White House team had been there for an hour before that, and that once the Centre was full, no-one else was allowed in. By the time I arrived, at 8.30 am, the space in front of the Convention Centre was a sea of umbrellas, and security guards were closing gates and forming phalanxes to block off walkways around the Centre. This provoked very considerable annoyance: I saw some Malaysian women trying to climb a fence, and a woman in a chador beating a security guard on the chest with the handle of her umbrella and proclaiming loudly that she had paid a lot of money to get to this conference so they had no right to keep her out. I also encountered Sylvia Kinder, an English-Australian now living in Germany, in a great rage: she did not want to see or hear Hilary Clinton — since when would we have been impressed by a woman simply because of the man she slept with? she huffed — but she did want to attend a workshop scheduled to be held in one of the smaller rooms in the Convention Centre, and the security for Clinton had made that inaccessible. 'Imagine coming all this way, only to find your workshop cancelled to make way for the wife of the president of the United States!' she fulminated. Laura Flanders made a different point: the media was tight-lipped over Reagan selling police equipment to China, she pointed out, but was, at the very moment in which she was speaking, in a frenzy over security for Hilary Rodham Clinton talking about rights at a rights conference in China.

Women who did manage to get into the Convention Centre reported afterwards that they'd had to wait hours for Clinton to appear, and had been getting very restless, when a woman leapt onto stage and began to lead them in singing. Perhaps that explains a sign that appeared on the upper floor of the Centre the next day; it read: 'No dancing on the second floor', a warning, I surmised about the fragility of the structure rather than gratuitous puritanism. The singing seemed to have been the principal event of that morning; no-one told me anything about what Hilary Rodham Clinton had said.

There were moments, amid the immense cultural variety of these crowded days, when I wondered if there were any specifically Chinese features of this major international conference. After all, I was staying in a hotel much like hotels in many parts of the world, and certainly much better equipped than several of the hotels for which I had paid much more in, just for instance, Russia in 1991. The television in my room (illustrating critiques by some of the African speakers) showed CNN's version of events at the government conference. Excellent Chinese food can be found in many parts of the world, not only in Beijing. Smog in a hot and humid climate is not exclusive to China. The highway between Beijing and Huairou was broad and well-made, and took us over a newly opened fly-over. While our buses whisked past a multitude of people on bicycles, and past lotus-plantations, they also took us past what appeared to be agricultural buildings with solar panels and sky-television disks on their roofs. And a taxi into Beijing could bring us into the midst of a street-market cheek-by-jowl with a Kentucky Fried Chicken outlet.

Many of us had been led to expect a specifically Chinese experience, in the most negative possible ways. Pre-Forum stories in the Australian press had ranged from accounts of UN indignation about the site of the Forum being moved from the Workers' Stadium in Beijing to 'a dusty village' several hours' distance away, to an extraordinary report of Chinese officials being issued with sheets in case protesting Western women should proceed to take off all their clothes in public places. There had also been stories, coupled with accounts of the summary despatch of a demonstration by Amnesty International in Tienanmen Square shortly before we all arrived, of excessive and officious security measures. A great many of us had been kept waiting until only days before we were due to board our planes for the documentation necessary to gain visas. My own arrived by courier — courier! — from Beijing.

I know everyone has a different conference, even when the conference is small, particularly if each person's expectations differ widely. I embarked for Beijing with a great deal of optimism. In many respects, it was justified. Huairou was, without doubt, some distance from Beijing, but it was also a township designed *as* a convention centre, surrounded by gardens, beside an extraordinarily beautiful lake and only twenty minutes' drive from a segment of the Great Wall, where there was a cable-car making access possible even for the rushed, or like me, lame (though the climb at either end would have put that still out of reach of anyone in a wheelchair). The security measures that occasioned so much comment and complaint in the Australian press, even while we were there, I learned later, were checkpoints just like the security checks you go through in an airport. Given the numbers present at the Forum, I found that I was thankful for them, even when queueing to pass through them meant that I was so rained on I could afterwards have wrung out my bra; after all, such an environment would have been a gift to a terrorist organisation wanting worldwide attention.

Yet, reading the Australian press reports of the Forum when I returned home — their harping upon intrusive security and apparent deafness to the issues that we had been discussing — was a bit like time-warping back into the Cold War 1950s. We had been warned of this, though, while we were still in Huairou. At a plenary on 'Media, Culture & Communication, Challenges & opportunities', Kamla Bhasin (from India) told us that friends at home had been telling her that reports on the Forum were uniformly negative, focusing on questions about security — and once again — ignoring the issues that we were discussing. And Laura Flanders, having opened her paper by addressing us as 'the largest gathering of marginalised experts in the world', went on to tell us about the only attention given to the Forum by the *New York Herald Tribune*. This paper had ignored the Forum for most of the week, she noted, but had then included an opinion piece on the Forum by a woman who is not a feminist and was not attending either of the gatherings in China. This was an art critic who had become famous for mouthing some old anti-feminist stuff that had something to do with blood-lust in rape over the past few years, she said, a woman called Camille Paglia.[565]

Nevertheless, there were disappointments while we were there. The roadside banner announcing 'Equality, Development and Peace' should also have included 'Democracy': is it naïve to ask why it had been left out? I heard about Tibetan women who had come to the forum from Australia being hassled by Chinese security people to such an extent that the Australian Ambassador had to intervene. I have been told since I returned that as many as 10 000 women were unable to gain visas to attend the Forum. The total number of Forum participants was revised in the *China Daily*'s publication for the Forum, *World Women*: by 7 September, 25 549

---

[565]   See my reference to Paglia at the end of Chapter Nineteen.

overseas participants had arrived in Huairou, a ratio between applicants and actual attendance which, this paper stated, 'is very high for an international meetings' [*sic*] (9 September 1995). On 9 September, the *China Daily* reported a spokesman for the Chinese Foreign Ministry refuting the accusation that China had refused visas to people like this:

> The United Nations and the Chinese side [*sic*] did not approve the attendance of some organizations because their purpose or activities are not related to the theme of this conference or because some of them would conduct activities that run counter to the goals of the UN Charter, relevant resolutions on the UN assemble and goals of the women's conference or even pose a threat to the security of the conference.

An Australian who had spent time in China teaching Australian Studies arrived late because her visa had been delayed; a North American academic, teacher of Women's Studies, did not manage to secure a visa at all. Neither of them came anywhere near meeting the description in the Chinese Foreign Ministry's statement.

Clambering away from sodden paper and puddles among collapsed tents into the Media Centre, funded by Apple and packed with computers and fax machines, was a experience of difference made poignant, later, in a workshop on establishing an international network of Women's Studies Associations: when we sought to exchange email addresses, one woman from Africa said, 'We don't have enough money for pencils and paper in our schools'.

Burmese Nobel Peace Prize Winner, Aung San Suu Kyi, spoke of the urgency of 'spending less on the war toys of grown men and more on tolerance, human rights, peace, and democracy'. Since the French were carrying out their nuclear tests at the very time that we were meeting, it would be difficult to say that governments were paying attention to such statements, and in any case we will have to look to the report of the resolutions passed at the World Conference for evidence that they are. But the NGO Forum made it clear that if they are not, then they are likely to face organised action by women across the globe. The international Women's *Movement* seems larger and stronger than ever before.

References

Articles and Books

Aaron, Jane, and Sylvia Walby (eds), *Out of the margins: Women's Studies in the nineties*, The Falmer Press, London, 1991.

Adkins, Lisa, and Maryanne Dever, 'Gender and labour in new times: an introduction', *Australian Feminist Studies*, vol. 29, no. 79, June 2014, pp. 1-11.

Albury, Rebecca M., '"Babies kept on ice": aspects of Australian press coverage of IVF', *Australian Feminist Studies*, vol. 2, no. 4, Autumn 1987.

Alexander, Sally, and Barbara Taylor, 'In defence of "patriarchy"', *New Statesman*, February 1980, reprinted in Raphael Samuel (ed.), *People's history and socialist theory*, Routledge & Kegan Paul, London, 1981.

Allen, Judith, and Paul Patton (eds), *Beyond Marxism? Interventions after Marx*, Intervention Publications, Sydney, 1983.

Allen, Judith, and Elizabeth Grosz, 'Editorial', *Australian Feminist Studies*, vol. 2, no. 5, Summer 1987.

Allen, Margaret, 'Inaugural Australian Women's Studies Association Conference', *Australian Feminist Studies*, vol. 4, no. 10, 1989.

Anderson, Benedict, *Imagined communities: reflections on the origin and spread of nationalism*, Verso, London, 1983.

Anderson, Helen, 'The choice before us', National Women's Conference on Feminism and Socialism, 5-6 October 1974, duplicated papers.

Archer, Robyn, *The Robyn Archer songbook*, McPhee Gribble Publishers, Melbourne, 1980.

Armitt, Lucy (ed.), *Where no man has gone before: women and science fiction*, Routledge, London, 1991.

Association Choisir, *Abortion: the Bobigny affair: a law on trial: a complete record of the pleadings at the court of Bobigny 8 November 1972*, 'Introduction' by Simone de Beauvoir, trans. Beryl Henderson, Wild & Woolley Pty Ltd, Marrickville, NSW, 1975.

Atwood, Margaret, *The handmaid's tale*, Jonathon Cape, London, 1986.

Atwood, Margaret, *Oryx and Crake*, Bloomsbury, London, 2003.

Bakhtin, M.M., *Speech genres and other late essays*, trans. Vern W. Gee, Caryl Emerson and Michael Holquist (eds), University of Texas Press, Austin, 1986.

Baldock, Cora V., and Bettina Cass (eds), *Women, social welfare and the state*, George Allen & Unwin, Sydney, London and Boston, 1983.

Barclay, Lesley, 'Menstruation: a life span view', *Australian Family Physician*, vol. 11, no. 6, June 1982.

Barrett, Michèle, *Women's oppression today: problems in Marxist feminists analysis*, Verso, London, 1980.

Barrett, Michèle, 'The Concept of "difference"', *Feminist Review*, no. 26, Summer 1987.

Bashford, Alison, 'The return of the repressed: feminism in the quad', *Australian Feminist Studies*, vol. 13, no. 27, 1988.

Bassnett, Susan, 'Remaking the old world: Ursula Le Guin and the American tradition', in Lucie Armitt (ed.), *Where no man has gone before: women and science fiction*, Routledge, London, 1991.

Bennett, Tony, 'Cultural Studies', in *Knowing ourselves and others: the humanities in Australia into the 21st century*, 3 vols, prepared by a Reference Group for the Australian Academy of the Humanities, Australian Government Publishing Service, Canberra, April 1998, Vol. 2.

Berkson, Dorothy, '"So we all become mothers": Harriet Beecher Stowe, Charlotte Perkins Gilman, and the new world of women's culture', in Libby Falk Jones and Sarah Webster Goodwin (eds), *Feminism, utopia and narrative*, University of Tennessee Press, Knoxville, 1990.

Bevege, Margaret, Margaret James and Carmel Shute (eds), *Worth her salt: women at work in Australia*, Hale & Iremonger, Sydney, 1982.

Bleir, Ruth, *Science and gender: a critique of biology and its theories on women*, Pergamon Press, New York & co., 1984.

The Boston Women's Health Book Collective, *Our bodies, ourselves: a book by and for women*, Simon & Schuster, New York, 1971.

Boumelha, Penny, 'Culture in the age of information: knowledge and research in the humanities and social sciences', in Susan Magarey (ed.), *Social justice: politics, technology and culture for a better world*, Wakefield Press, Adelaide, 1998.

Bowman Albinski, Nan, *Women's utopias in British and American fiction*, Routledge, London, 1988.

Boxer, Marilyn J., 'For and about women: the theory and practice of Women's Studies in the United States', in Keohane et al. (eds), *Feminist Theory: a critique of ideology*, Harvester Press, Brighton, 1982.

Bramley, Gwenda W., and Marion W. Ward, *The role of women in the Australian National University*, Australian National University, internal publication, Canberra, 1976.

Branson, J.E., 'The nature of Women's Studies and its potential role within the university', typescript, Monash University, 1974.

Brontë, Charlotte, *Shirley*, Penguin, Harmondsworth, 1974 (1849).

Broom, Dorothy H. (ed.), *Unfinished business: social justice for women in Australia*, George Allen & Unwin, 1984.

Brown, Wendy, 'Feminism unbound, revolution, mourning, politics', in Wendy Brown, *Edgework: critical essays on knowledge and politics*, Princeton University Press, Princeton, 2005.

Brownmiller, Susan, *Against our will: men, women and rape*, Simon & Schuster, New York, 1975.

Brownmiller, Susan, *In our time: memoir of a revolution*, Aurum Press, London, 2000.

Bryson, Lois, *Welfare and the state: who benefits?*, Macmillan, London, 1992.

Bulbeck, Chilla (ed.), *Proceedings of the Australian Women's Studies Association Seventh Conference*, Adelaide, April 1998.

Campbell, Beatrix, and Val Charlton, 'Grunwick women, why they are striking and why their sisters are supporting them', *Spare Rib*, no. 61, August 1977.

Campbell, Beatrix, and Anna Coote, *Sweet freedom: the struggle for Women's Liberation*, Pan Books, London, 1982.

Campbell, Beatrix, 'Speak up for feminism', in 'Letters', *London Review of Books*, 26 January 2012.

Capek, Mary Ellen (ed.), *A women's thesaurus: an index of language used to describe and locate information by and about women*, Harper & Row, New York, 1987.

Carter, Angela, 'Truly, it felt like Year One', in Sara Maitland (ed.), *Very heaven: looking back at the 1960s*, Virago Press Limited, London, 1988.

Cass, Bettina, 'Women's place in the class structure,' in E.L. Wheelwright and Ken Buckley (eds), *Essays in the political economy of Australian capitalism*, vol. 3, Australia and New Zealand Book Company, Sydney, 1978.

Cass, Bettina, 'The changing face of poverty in Australia: 1972-1982', in *Australian Feminist Studies*, vol. 1, no. 1, December 1985.

Cass, Bettina, 'The feminisation of poverty', in Barbara Caine, E.A. Grosz and Marie de Lepervanche (eds), *Crossing boundaries: feminisms and the critique of knowledges*, Allen & Unwin, Sydney, 1988.

Cass, Bettina, 'Gender in Australia's restructuring labour market and welfare state', in Anne Edwards and Susan Magarey (eds), *Women in a restructuring Australia: work and welfare*, Allen & Unwin in Association with the Academy of Social Sciences in Australia, Sydney, 1995.

Cass, Bettina, and Heather Radi, 'The family: old and new — bread and circuses', paper presented to the *Wrong Way — Go Back conference*, in association with the Bicentennial History of Australia project, Sydney University, February 1979.

Cass, Bettina, et al., *Why so few? Women academics in Australian universities*, Sydney University Press, Sydney 1983.

The changing experience of women, 16 Units, Open University Press, Milton Keynes, 1982, repr. 1983.

Chodorow, Nancy, *The reproduction of mothering: psychoanalysis and the sociology of gender*, University of California Press, Berkeley, 1978.

Cohen, Stanley (ed.), *Images of deviance*, Penguin, Harmondsworth, 1971, Introduction.

Couani, Anna, and Pamela Brown, 'Sydney women writers' workship', *Lip*, 1978-79, pp. 188-9.

Connell, R.W., and T.H. Irving, *Class structure in Australian history: documents, narrative and argument*, Longman Cheshire, Melbourne, 1980.

Connell, R.W., *Masculinities*, University of California Press, Berkeley, 1995.

Coombs, Anne, *Sex and anarchy: the life and death of the Sydney Push*, Viking, Melbourne, 1996.

Coyner, Sandra, 'Women's Studies as an academic discipline: why and how to do it', in Gloria Bowles and Renate Duelli Klein (eds), *Theories of Women's Studies*, Routledge & Kegan Paul, London, Boston, Melbourne and Henley, 1983.

Cox, David, 'Working married women and youth unemployment', Women's Advisory Unit, Premier's Department, South Australia, Adelaide, October 1978.

Curthoys, Ann, 'History and Women's Liberation', *Arena*, no. 22, 1970, reprinted in Ann Curthoys, *For and against feminism: a personal journey into feminist theory and history*, Allen & Unwin, Sydney, 1988.

Curthoys, Ann, 'Women's studies, the university, and the Women's Movement', typescript, June 1975.

Curthoys, Ann, 'The Women's Movement and social justice', in Dorothy H. Broom (ed.), *Unfinished business: social justice for women in Australia*, George Allen & Unwin, Sydney, 1984.

Curthoys, Ann, 'The theory of Women's Liberation', in Ann Curthoys, *For and against feminism: a personal journey into feminist theory and history*, Allen & Unwin, Sydney, 1988.

Curthoys, Ann, 'Cosmopolitan radicals', in Barbara Caine, Moira Gatens, Emma Grahame, Jan Larbalestier, Sophie Watson and Elizabeth Webby (eds), *Australian feminism: a companion*, Oxford University Press, Melbourne, 1998.

Curthoys, Ann, 'Women's Studies at the Australian National University: the early years', *Australian Feminist Studies*, vol. 13, no. 27, 1998.

Curthoys, Ann, 'Gender in the social sciences in Australia — a review essay,' prepared for the Review of the Social Sciences by the Academy of the Social Sciences in Australia, *Challenges for the social sciences and Australia*, 2 vols, Australian Government Publishing Service, Canberra, July 1998.

Curthoys, Jean, Mia Campioni, Pat Vort-Ronald, Liz Jacka, 'A discussion on the political economy of housework', First Australian Political Economy Conference, Sydney, 18-20 June 1976, duplicated note.

Daly, Mary, *Gyn/Ecology: the meta-ethics of radical feminism*, The Women's Press, London, 1979.

Daniels, Kay, 'Womens [sic] liberation national conference June 10-12, a personal report', in *Liberaction*, no. 3, 1972, pp. 4-5.

Daniels, Kay, Mary Murnane and Anne Picot (eds), *Women in Australia: an annotated guide to records*, 2 vols, Australian Government Publishing Service, Canberra, 1977.

Daniels, Kay, and Mary Murnane (comp.), *Uphill all the way: a documentary history of women in Australia*, University of Queensland Press, St. Lucia, 1980.

Darroch, Dorothy [see also Broom, Dorothy], Maria Miranda, Angelica Marx, Lucy Parish, Anne Stanton, Frances Sutherland, Carolyn Traill and Helen Williams, *The public secret: a story about menstruation*, Canberra, 1981.

Davies, Bronwyn, Shirley Fisher and Lenore Coltheart, *The violet pages: the Women's Studies research directory*, University of New England, 1985.

Davis, Mark, *Gangland*, Allen & Unwin, Sydney, 1997.

Davis, Natalie Zemon, *Society and culture in early modern France: eight essays*, Stanford University Press, Stanford, 1975.

Deleuze, Gilles, 'Philosophie et minorité', *Critique*, no. 369, February 1978.

Deveson, Anne, *Australians at risk*, Cassell Australia Ltd, Stanmore, NSW, 1978.

Discussion of the Hobart Women's Action Group Paper 'Sexism in the women's liberation movement' at the Mount Beauty Conference, January 1973, transcribed by Sue Wills, August 1997, in Sydney First Ten Years Collection, Mitchell Library, State Library of New South Wales.

Dobson, Rosemary (ed.), *Sisters poets 1*, Sisters Publishing Ltd, Carlton, 1979.

Dowse, Sara, 'Power in institutions — the public service', paper given to the Women and Politics Conference, Canberra, 1-5 September 1975.

Dowse, Sara, 'The Women's Movement fandango with the state: the Movement's role in policy since 1972,' in Cora V. Baldock and Bettina Cass (eds), *Women, social welfare and the state in Australia*, Allen & Unwin, Sydney, 1983.

Dowse, Sara, 'The bureaucrat as usurer', in Dorothy H. Broom (ed.), *Unfinished business: social justice for women in Australia*, George Allen & Unwin, Sydney, 1984.

Dowse, Sara, 'Bride price — 1958', chapter of unpublished autobiography, personal communication, email March 2014.

Duffy, Maureen, *Gor saga*, Methuen, London, 1983.

Dugdale, Mrs. H.A., *A few hours in a far-off age*, McCarron, Bird & Co., Melbourne, 1883.

Dux, Monica, and Zora Simic, *The great feminist denial*, Melbourne University Press, Carlton, 2008.

Dworkin, Andrea, *Pornography: men possessing women*, The Women's Press, London, 1981.

Eade, Susan, see Magarey, Susan.

Echols, Alice, *Daring to be bad: radical feminism in America 1967-1975*, University of Minnesota Press, Minneapolis, 1989.

'Editorial', *MeJane*, no. 1, 1 March 1971.

Edwards, Anne, and Susan Magarey (eds), *Women in a restructuring Australia: work and welfare*, Allen & Unwin, Sydney, 1995.

Edwards, Meredith, 'Taxation and the family unit: social aspects', paper delivered at seminar organised by the Taxation Institute Research and Education Trust, Sydney, May 1979.

Ehrenreich, Barbara, *The hearts of men: American dreams and the flight from commitment*, Pluto, London, 1983.

Eisenstein, Hester, 'Comment on the Women's Movement and social justice', in Dorothy H. Broom (ed.), *Unfinished business: social justice for women in Australia*, George Allen & Unwin, Sydney, 1984.

Eisenstein, Hester, *Gender shock: practising feminism on two continents*, Allen & Unwin, Sydney, 1991.

Elshtain, Jean Bethke, 'Response', in Libby Falk Jones and Sarah Webster Goodwin (eds), *Feminism, utopia and narrative*, University of Tennessee Press, Knoxville, 1990.

Encel, Sol, Norman Mackenzie and Margaret Tebutt, *Women and society: an Australian study*, Cheshire, Melbourne, 1974.

Evans, Gareth and John Reeves (eds), *Labour essays 1980*, Drummond for the Australian Labour Party (Victorian Branch), Richmond, 1980.

Ezekiel, Judith, *Feminism in the heartland*, Ohio State University Press, Columbus, 2002.

Farley Kessler, Carol, 'Distribution of utopias by United States women 1830-1980', in Carol Farley Kessler, *Daring to dream: utopian stories by United States women, 1836-1919*, Pandora Press, Boston, 1984.

'Feminist Forum', *AUMLA: Journal of the Australasian Universities Modern Language Association*, May 1986 (Panel discussion at AULLA 23rd Congress, 1985).

Fems, Red, 'The implications of technological change for women workers in the public sector', in Margaret Bevege, Margaret James and Carmel Shute (eds), *Worth her salt: women at work in Australia*, Hale & Iremonger, Sydney, 1982.

Fernon, Christine, 'Women's suffrage in Victoria', *Refractory Girl*, no. 22, 1981.

Firestone, Shulamith, *The dialectics of sex: the case for feminist revolution*, Paladin, London, 1972.

First National Women's Housing Conference, Adelaide, March 1985.

Flood, Alison, 'Elegant, popular and enduring', *Guardian Weekly*, 26 September 2014, p. 39.

Fox Keller, Evelyn, 'Feminism and science', in N.O. Keohane et al. (eds), *Feminist theory: a critique of ideology*, Harvester Press, Brighton, 1982.

Fox Keller, Evelyn, *Reflections on gender and science*, Yale University Press, New Haven and London, 1985.

Franzway, Suzanne, 'With problems of their own: femocrats and the welfare state', *Australian Feminist Studies*, vol. 1, no. 3, Summer 1986.

Franzway, Suzanne, Diane Court and R.W. Connell, *Staking a claim: feminism, bureaucracy and the state*, Allen & Unwin, Sydney, 1989.

Freeman, Jo ['Joreen'], 'Trashing: the dark side of sisterhood', *Ms.*, April 1976.

Freeman, Jo, 'The tyranny of structurelessness', reprinted in Rosalyn Baxandall and Linda Gordon (eds), *Dear sisters: dispatches from the women's liberation movement*, Basic Books, New York, 2000.

Freibert, Lucy M., 'World views in utopian novels by women', *Journal of Popular Culture*, vol. 17, Summer 1983.

Froines, Ann, 'Outsiders within — outsiders without?', *Women's Review of Books*, vol. 15, no. 5, February 1998.

Furlong, Mark, 'i-dolatry', *Arena: The Australian Magazine of Left Political, Social and Cultural Commentary*, no. 101, 8 September 2009.

Game, Ann, and Rosemary Pringle, 'Women and the Labor Government 1972-75', duplicated paper read to the First Australian Political Economy Conference.

Game, Ann, and Rosemary Pringle, 'The making of the Australian family', *Intervention: Revolutionary Marxist Journal*, no. 12, April 1979, pp. 63-83.

Game, Ann and Rosemary Pringle, 'Sexuality and the suburban dream', *Australian and New Zealand Journal of Sociology*, vol. 15, no. 2, 1979.

Game, Ann, and Rosemary Pringle, 'The making of the Australian family', in Ailsa Burns, Gill Bottomley and Penny Jools (eds), *The family in the modern world:*

Australian perspectives, George Allen & Unwin, Sydney, 1983.

Game, Ann, and Rosemary Pringle, *Gender at work*, Allen & Unwin, Sydney, 1983.

Garner, Helen, *Monkey grip*, McPhee Gribble Publishers, Melbourne, 1977.

Gatens, Moira, 'Towards a feminist philosophy of the body', in Barbara Caine, E.A. Grosz and Marie de Lepervanche (eds), *Crossing boundaries: feminism and the critique of knowledges*, Allen & Unwin, Sydney, 1988.

Gatens, Moira, 'Woman and her double(s): sex, gender and ethics', *Australian Feminist Studies*, vol. 4, no. 10, Summer 1989.

Gatens, Moira, *Feminism and philosophy: perspectives on difference and equality*, Polity, Cambridge, 1991.

Gatens, Moira, *Imaginary bodies: ethics, power, and corporeality*, Routledge, London and New York, 1996.

Gatens, Moira, 'A critique of the sex/gender distinction', in Judith Allen and Paul Patton (eds), *Beyond Marxism? Interventions after Marx*, Intervention Publications, Sydney, 1983, republished in Moira Gatens, *Imaginary bodies: ethics, power and corporeality*, Routledge, London and New York, 1996.

Glaspell Keating, Susan, 'A jury of her peers', in Lee R. Edwards and Arlyn O'Fermond (eds), *American voices, American women*, Avon, New York, 1973, www.learner.org/exhibits/literature/story/fulltext.html.

Gollan, Daphne, 'The Women's Movement and the revolutionary critique of capitalism', paper distributed at Feminism-Anarchism Conference, Canberra, 11-12 October 1975, also printed as 'The Women's Movement — revolutionary?', *International*, no. 44, October 1975.

Gollan, Daphne, 'The Memoirs of "Cleopatra Sweatfigure"', in Elizabeth Windschuttle (ed.), *Women, class and history: feminist perspectives on Australia 1788-1978*, Fontana/Collins, Melbourne, 1980.

Gollan, R.A., *Radical and working class politics: a study of eastern Australia 1850-1910*, Melbourne University Press, Melbourne, 1960.

Goodnow, Jacqueline, and Carole Pateman (eds), *Women, social science, and public policy*, Allen & Unwin, Sydney, 1985.

Gough-Brady, Catherine, '"You don't want to be an artist, do you Babe?": Social change and the women's art movement', BA Hons Thesis, The University of Adelaide, 1992.

Grahame, Emma, 'Sisterhood', in Barbara Caine, Moira Gatens, Emma Grahame, Jan Larbalestier, Sophie Watson and Elizabeth Webb (eds), *Australian feminism: a companion*, Oxford University Press, Melbourne, 1998.

Graycar, Regina, 'Feminism comes to law: better late than never', *Australian Feminist Studies*, vol. 1, no. 3, Summer 1986.

Greer, Germaine, *The female eunuch*, Flamingo, London, 1971; 1993.

Grieve, Norma, and Patricia Grimshaw (eds), *Women in Australia: feminist perspectives*, Oxford University Press, Melbourne, 1981.

Grieve, Norma and Ailsa Burns (eds), *Australian women: contemporary feminist thought*, Oxford University Press, Melbourne, 1994.

Griffin, Susan, *Rape: the power of consciousness*, Harper & Row, San Francisco, 1981.

de Groot, Joanna, and Mary Maynard (eds), *Women's Studies in the 1990s: doing things differently*, Macmillan, London, 1993.

Gross, Elizabeth, 'Contemporary theories of power', in Deakin Women's Studies Course Team (comp.), *Feminist knowledge as critique and construct*, Study Guide, parts A & B, in production 1985.

Gross, Elizabeth, 'Conclusion: what is feminist theory?', in Carole Pateman and Elizabeth Gross (eds), *Feminist challenges: social and political theory*, Allen & Unwin, Sydney, 1986.

Grosz, Elizabeth, 'Notes towards a corporeal feminism,' *Australian Feminist Studies*, vol. 2, no. 5, 1987.

Grosz, Elizabeth, *Volatile bodies: toward a corporeal feminism*, Allen & Unwin, Sydney, 1994.

Gunew, Sneja (ed.), *Feminist knowledge: critique and construct*, Routledge, London and New York, 1990.

Gunew, Sneja (ed.), *A reader in feminist knowledge*, Routledge, London and New York, 1991.

Haley, Eileen, 'The long haul', *Politics*, vol. 8, no. 2, November 1973.

Haraway, Donna, 'A manifesto for cyborgs: science, technology and socialist feminism in the 1980s', *Australian Feminist Studies*, vol. 2, no. 4, Autumn 1987.

Hargreaves, Kay, *Women at work*, Penguin, Ringwood, 1982.

Henderson, Margaret, *Marking feminist times: remembering the longest revolution in Australia*, Peter Lang, Bern, 2006.

Hetzel, Basil S., *Health and Australian society*, Penguin, Ringwood, 1974.

Higgs, Kerryn, 'Afterword', in Kerryn Higgs, *All that false instruction*, Spinifex, North Melbourne, 2001.

Hirst, Paul. H., *Knowledge and the curriculum*, Routledge & Kegan Paul, London and Boston, 1974.

Hobshawm, E.J., *Industry and empire*, Penguin, Harmondsworth, 1970 (1969).

Hobshawm, E.J., *The age of revolution: Europe 1789-1848*, Cardinal, London, 1973.

Hobshawm, E.J., 'From social history to the history of societies', first published in *Daedalus*, vol. 100, no. 1, Winter 1971, republished in M.W. Flinn and T.C. Smout (eds), *Essays in social history*, Clarendon Press, Oxford, 1974.

Hobsbawm, E.J., *The crisis and the outlook*, Socialist Society, Student Union, Birkbeck College, London, 1975.

Hunter, Thelma, 'Reform and revolution in contemporary feminism', *Politics*, vol. 8, no. 2, November 1973.

Hunter, Thelma, *Not a dutiful daughter: the personal story of a migrant academic*, Ginnindera Press, Charnwood, 1999.

Huws, Ursula, 'The New Home Workers', *New Society*, 22 March 1984.

Iremonger, Duncan (ed.), *Households work: productive activities, women and income in the household economy*, Allen & Unwin, Sydney, 1989.

Irigaray, Luce, 'This sex which is not one', in Elaine Marks and Isabelle de Courtivron (eds), *New French feminism: an anthology*, Harvester Press, Brighton, 1982.

Jennings, Kate (ed.), *Mother I'm rooted: an anthology of Australian women poets*, Outback Press, Fitzroy, 1975.

Johnson & Johnson Pty Ltd Sydney, *Enjoy being a girl especially now you're growing up*, pamphlets dating from the 1980s.

Keiko, Nakajima, 'Women organize to tackle the world of new technology', *Japan-Aisa Quarterly Review*, vol. 15. no. 2, 1983.

Kelly, Petra Karin, 'Women must link arms and have a planetary vision', address to Section 44, Women's Studies, 54th Congress of ANZAAS, Australian National University, Canberra, 15 May 1984.

Kelly-Gadol, Joan, 'The social relation of the sexes: methodological implications of women's history', in *Signs: Journal of Women in Culture and Society*, vol. 1, no. 4, Summer 1976.

Kelly, Joan, 'The doubled vision of feminist theory', in Judith L. Newton et al. (eds), *Sex and class in women's history*, Routledge & Kegan Paul, London, Boston, Melbourne, Henley, 1983.

Kinder, Sylvia, *Herstory of the Adelaide women's liberation movement 1969-1974*,

Salisbury Education Centre, Adelaide, 1980.

Kingston, Beverly, *My wife, my daughter, and poor Mary Ann*, Thomas Nelson, Melbourne, 1975.

Kingston, Beverly (ed.), *The world moves slowly: a documentary history of Australian women*, Cassell, Camperdown, 1977.

Koedt, Anne, 'The myth of the vaginal orgasm', in Leslie B. Tanner (ed.), *Voices from Women's Liberation*, Signet Books, New York, 1971.

Kornegger, Peggy, 'Anarchism: the feminist connection', *The Second Wave*, Spring 1975.

Kuhn, Annette, 'Structures of patriarchy and capital in the family', in Annette Kuhn and Ann Marie Wolpe (eds), *Feminism and materialism: women and modes of production*, Routledge & Kegan Paul, London, 1978.

Kuhn, Thomas S., *The structure of scientific revolutions*, University of Chicago Press, Chicago and London, 1970 (1962).

Kuhse, Helga, 'Ethical Issues in *In Vitro* Fertilisation and Related Technologies', Section 44, Women's Studies, 54th Congress of ANZAAS, Australian National University, Canberra, 16 May, 1984.

Lake, Marilyn, *Getting equal: the history of Australian feminism*, Allen & Unwin, Sydney, 1999.

Laqueur, Thomas, *Making sex: body and gender from the Greeks to Freud*, Harvard University Press, Cambridge, MA, 1990.

League, Sparticist, 'Towards a Communist Women's Movement', National Women's Conference on Feminism and Socialism, duplicated paper.

Lefanu, Sarah, *In the chinks of the world machine: feminism and science fiction*, The Women's Press, London, 1988.

Le Guin, Ursula K., *The left hand of darkness*, Orbit, London, 1997 (1969).

Le Guin, Ursula K., 'Winter's king', in Ursula K. Le Guin, *The wind's twelve quarters*, Granada, London, 1978 (1975).

Le Guin, Ursula, *The dispossessed*, Panther Books Ltd, St Albans, 1975.

Le Guin, Ursula K., 'The day before the revolution', in Pamela Sargent (ed.), *More women of wonder: science fiction novelettes by women about women*, Vintage Books, New York, 1976.

Le Guin, Ursula K., 'Science fiction and Mrs. Brown', in Ursula K. Le Guin (ed.), *The language of the night: essays on fantasy and science fiction*, with introductions by Susan Wood, Berkley Books, New York, 1982 (1979).

Le Guin, Ursula K., 'Is gender necessary? Redux', 1987 (1976), in Ursula Le K. Guin, *Dancing at the edge of the world: thoughts on words, women, places*, Grove Press, New York, 1989.

Lees, Stella, and June Senyard, *The 1950s — how Australia became a modern society, and everyone got a house and car*, Hyland House, Melbourne, 1987.

Leeton, John, 'Present and future aspects of infertility treatment: *in vitro* fertilisation, frozen embryos, donor eggs, surrogacy', Section 44, Women's Studies, 54th Congress of ANZAAS, Australian National University, Canberra, 16 May 1984.

Liddicoat, Kerry, 'The health implications of screen based equipment for women workers', Section 44, Women's Studies, 54th Congress of ANZAAS, Australian National University, Canberra, 17 May 1984.

Lloyd, Genevieve, *The man of reason: 'male' and 'female' in Western philosophy*, Methuen, London, 1984.

Lumby, Catherine, *Alvin Purple*, Currency Press, Strawberry Hills, NSW, 2008.

McArdle, Allen, 'Unemployment — a question without an answer?', unpublished address to the Industrial Relations Society of New South Wales at Bathurst, 22 April 1976.

Maccoby, Eleanor, and Carol Jacklin, *The psychology of sex differences*, Oxford University Press, Oxford, 1974.

McDonough, Roisin, and Rachel Harrison, 'Patriarchy and relations of production', in Annette Kuhn and Ann Marie Wolpe (eds), *Feminism and materialism: women and modes of production*, Routledge & Kegan Paul, London, 1978.

Macintyre, Stuart, 'History,' in *Knowing ourselves and others: the humanities in Australia into the 21st century*, 3 vols, prepared by a Reference Group for the Australian Academy of the Humanities, Australian Government Publishing Service, Canberra, April 1998, Vol. 2.

MacKenzie, Norman, *Women in Australia*, F.W. Cheshire, Melbourne, 1962.

McLaughlin, Andrea, '"Acting on it": feminist theatre: politics and performance', *Lip*, 1984, pp. 75-7.

McLeod, Mary (Manpower Forecasting Unit, South Australian Department of Labour), 'Repetition injury — recognition and prevention', unpublished paper, 12 July 1983.

McPhee, Hilary, *Other people's words*, Picador, Sydney, 2001.

Magarey, Susan, 'The First Feminist Wave in Australia', unpublished paper read to

Women's Liberation Conference, Guthega, January 1972.

[Magarey] Eade, Susan, 'Social history in Britain in 1976 — a survey', *Labour History*, no. 31, November 1976, pp. 38-52.

Magarey, Susan, 'Women and socialism', in Bruce O'Meagher (ed.), *The socialist objective: Labor & socialism*, Hale & Iremonger, Sydney, 1983.

Magarey, Susan, ' *Labour History's* new sub-title: social history in Australia in 1981', *Social History*, vol. 8, no. 2, May 1983, pp. 211-28.

Magarey, Susan, 'Questions about "patriarchy"', in Broom, Dorothy H. (ed.), *Unfinished business: social justice for women in Australia*, Allen & Unwin, Sydney, 1984.

Magarey, Susan, 'That hoary old chestnut, free will and determinism: culture vs. structure, or history vs. theory in Britain. A review article', *Comparative Studies in Society and History: an International Quarterly*, vol. 29, no. 3, July 1987.

Magarey, Susan, Lyndall Ryan and Susan Sheridan, 'Women's Studies in Australia', in Norma Grieve and Ailsa Burns (eds), *Australian women: contemporary feminist thought*, Oxford University Press, Melbourne, 1994.

Magarey, Susan, 'Women's Worlds: The Sixth International Interdisciplinary Congress on Women, Adelaide, 21-26 April 1996', *Australian Feminist Studies*, vol. 11, no. 24, 1996.

Magarey, Susan (ed.), *Social justice: politics, technology and culture for a better world*, Wakefield Press, Adelaide, 1998.

Magarey, Susan, 'Editorial', *Australian Feminist Studies*, vol. 20, no. 47, July 2005.

Magarey, Susan, and Susan Sheridan, 'Greenham Common — 12 December 1982', *Canberra Women's Liberation Newsletter*, n.d.

Magarey, Susan, and Susan Sheridan, 'Women's Studies in Northern Europe', *Hecate*, vol. 9, nos. 1 & 2, 1983.

Magarey, Susan and Susan Sheridan, 'Women's Studies Conferences in Australia in 1985', *Women's Studies Quarterly*, The Feminist Press, City University of New York, vol. 14, nos. 3 & 4, Fall/Winter 1986.

Magarey, Susan and Susan Sheridan, 'The Seventh Berkshire Conference on the History of Women', *Australian Feminist Studies*, vol. 2, no. 5, Summer 1987.

Malinowitz, Harriet, 'Introduction', in Kerryn Higgs, *All that false instruction*, Spinifex, North Melbourne, 2001.

marie claire, 'Women on top', a report with photographs and extensive quotations of a gathering to which Jackie Frank (publisher/editor of *marie claire*) and Di Webster (features editor-at-large of *marie claire*) attended at The Lodge with Prime Minister Julia Gillard and six of her senior female ministers, *marie claire*, December 2012, p. 48. A full transcript of this meeting is at *www.marieclaire.com.au*.

Marks, Elaine, and Isabelle de Courtivron (eds with Introductions), *New French feminisms: an anthology*, Schocken Books, New York, 1981.

Matthews, Jill Julius, 'Deconstructing the masculine universe: the case of women's work', in Margaret Allen, Jean Blackburn, Carol Johnson, Margaret King and Alison Mackinnon (eds), *All her labours*, 2 vols, Hale & Iremonger, Sydney, 1984.

Mead, Jenna (ed.), *Bodyjamming*, Vintage/Random House, Milson's Point, NSW, 1998.

Meeting to Expel Spartacist League from the General Meetings of Sydney Women's Liberation, 17 April 1977, tape transcribed by Sue Wills, June 1977, in Sydney First Ten Years Collection, Mitchell Library, State Library of New South Wales.

Mellor, Anne K., 'On feminist utopias', *Women's Studies*, vol. 9, no. 3, 1982.

Mercer, Jan (ed.), *The other half: women in Australian society*, Penguin Books, Ringwood, 1975.

Millett, Kate, *Sexual politics*, Rupert Hart-Davis, London, 1970.

Milner, Andrew, Matthew Ryan and Robert Savage, 'Introduction', in Andrew Milner, Matthew Ryan and Robert Savage (eds), *Imagining the future: utopia and dystopia*, Arena Publications Association, North Carlton, Vic., 2006.

Mitchell, Juliet, 'Women: the longest revolution', *New Left Review*, no. 40, November-December 1966.

Mitchell, Juliet, *Woman's estate*, Penguin, Harmondsworth, 1971.

Mitchell, Juliet, *Psychoanalysis and feminism*, Allen Lane, London, 1974.

Mitchell, Juliet, and Ann Oakley (eds), *What is feminism?*, Basil Blackwell, Oxford, 1986.

Moers, Ellen, *Literary women*, Doubleday, New York, 1977.

Morgan, Robin (ed.), *Sisterhood is powerful: an anthology of writings from the Women's Liberation Movement*, Vintage Books, New York, 1970.

'National Conference — Sydney 10-13 June', *Canberra Women's Liberation Newsletter*, no. 22, July 1972.

Oakley, Ann, *Sex, gender and society*, Temple Smith, London, 1972.

Oakley, Ann, *Housewife*, Penguin, Harmondsworth, 1976.

O'Donnell, Carol, and Jan Craney, *Family violence in Australia*, Longman Cheshire, Melbourne, 1982.

O'Loughlin, Mary Ann, 'Wear blue line away from body: early adolescent girls' knowledge about menstruation', *Refractory Girl*, vol. 17, March 1979.

Out from under: a journal of women and power, April 1976.

Pappas, Dee Ann, 'On being natural', first published in *Women: A Journal of Liberation*, Fall 1969; republished in Leslie B. Tanner (comp. and ed.), *Voices from Women's Liberation*, A Mentor Book, New York, 1970.

Pateman, Carole and Gross, Elizabeth (eds), *Feminist challenges: social and political theory*, Allen & Unwin, Sydney, 1986.

Perkins Gilman, Charlotte, *Herland*, 1915, republished with Introduction and Notes by Ann J. Lane, Pantheon Books, New York, 1979.

Piercy, Marge, *Women on the edge of time*, The Women's Press, London, 1979.

Pinchbeck, Ivy, *Women workers and the Industrial Revolution 1750-1850*, Frank Cass, London, 1977 (1930).

Pocock, Barbara, *The work/life collision: what work is doing to Australians and what to do about it*, Federation Press, Annandale, 2003.

Poiner, Gretchen, 'Report on Women's Studies at Macquarie University', unpublished paper, 1992.

Poland, Louise, 'The devil and the angel? Australia's feminist presses and the multinational agenda', *Hecate*, vol. 29, no. 2, 2003, pp. 123-39.

Powell, J.P., 'Towards a definition of interdisciplinary studies', *Vestes*, vol. 17, no. 2, 1974.

Power, Margaret, 'Women and economic crises: the Great Depression and the present crisis', Women and Labour Conference Paper, Macquarie University, May 1978, published in Windschuttle, Elizabeth (ed.), *Women, class and history: feminist perspectives on Australia 1788-1978*, Fontana/Collins, Melbourne, 1980.

Power, Margaret, Christine Wallace, Sue Outhwaite and Stuart Rosewarne, *Women, work, and labour market programs*, prepared for the Committee of Inquiry into Labour Market Programs, August 1984.

Prerost, Sandra, 'Technological change and women's employment in Australia', in Margaret Bevege, Margaret James and Carmel Shute (eds), *Worth her salt: women at work in Australia*, Hale & Iremonger, Sydney, 1982.

Ramsay, Janet, 'Liberation or loss? Women act on the new reproductive technologies', *Australian Feminist Studies*, vol. 1, no. 3, Summer 1986.

'Redstockings Manifesto', 1969, in Leslie B. Tanner (ed.), *Voices from women's liberation*, Mentor, New York, 1970, also in Robin Morgan (ed.), *Sisterhood is powerful: an anthology of writings from the Women's Liberation Movement*, Vintage Books, New York, 1970.

Reiger, Kerreen M., *The disenchantment of the home: modernizing the Australian family 1880-1940*, Oxford University Press, Melbourne, 1985.

Reinharz, Shulamit, *Feminist methods in social research*, Oxford University Press, New York, 1992.

Reita, Rayna R. (ed.), *Toward an anthropology of women*, Monthly Review Press, New York, 1975.

Rich, Adrienne, *The dream of a common language: poems 1974-1977*, Norton, New York, 1978.

Rich, Adrienne, 'Compulsory heterosexuality and lesbian existence', in *Signs: Journal of Women in Culture and Society*, vol. 5, no. 4, Summer 1980.

Rich, Adrienne, *A wild patience has taken me this far: poems 1978-1987*, W.W. Norton & Co., New York, 1981.

Richards, Lyn, *Having families, marriage, parenthood and social pressure in Australia*, Penguin, Ringwood, 1978.

Rigg, Julie, and Copeland, Julie (eds), *Coming out! Women's voices, women's lives: a selection from ABC radio's Coming Out Show*, in association with the Australian Broadcasting Corporation, Nelson, Melbourne, 1985.

Riley, Elizabeth, pseud. (see also Higgs, Kerryn), *All that false instruction*, Angus & Robertson, Sydney, 1975.

Rosaldo, Michelle, and Louise Lamphere (eds), *Woman, culture and society*, Stanford University Press, Stanford, 1974.

Rose, Hilary, and Stephen Rose (eds), *Ideology of/in the natural sciences*, Schenkman Publishing Co., Cambridge MA, 1980, with an introductory essay by Ruth Hubbard.

Rosen, Ruth, *The world split open: how the modern women's movement changed America*, Viking Penguin, New York, 2000.

Rosor, Lillian, 'Working Class Women', National Women's Conference on Feminism and Socialism, 5-6 October 1974, duplicated paper.

Roszak, Theodore, *The making of a counter culture: reflections on the technocratic society and its youthful opposition*, Faber, London, 1970 (1969).

Rowbotham, Sheila, *Woman's consciousness, man's world*, Penguin, Harmondsworth, 1973.

Rowbotham, Sheila, *Hidden from history: 300 years of women's oppression and the fight against it*, Pelican Books, Harmondsworth, 1975.

Rowbotham, Sheila, 'The trouble with "patriarchy"', *New Statesman*, December 1979, reprinted in Raphael Samuel (ed.), *People's history and socialist theory*, Routledge & Kegan Paul, London, 1981.

Rowland, Robyn, 'Reproductive technologies: the final solution to the woman question?', in R. Arditti, R. Duelli Klein and S. Minden (eds), *Test tube women: what future for motherhood?*, Routledge & Kegan Paul, London and Boston, 1984.

Rowland, Robyn, 'Of women born? The relationship of women to reproductive technology', draft course-book for Women's Studies, Deakin University.

Rubin, Gayle, '" The traffic in women": notes on the "political economy" of sex', in Rayna R. Reita (ed.), *Toward an anthropology of women*, Monthly Review Press, New York, 1975.

Rubinstein, Linda and Martha Kay [Ansara], paper distributed at the 'Hevvies' Theory conference, Mt Beauty, 27-29 January 1973.

Russ, Joanna, 'When it changed', in *The Zanzibar cat*, Arkham House Publishers, Inc., USA, 1983.

Ruthven, Ken, 'The future of disciplines: a report on ignorance', in *Knowing ourselves and others: the humanities in Australia into the 21st century*, 3 vols., prepared by a Reference Group for the Australian Academy of the Humanities, Australian Government Publishing Service, Canberra, April 1998.

Ryan, Edna, *Two thirds of a man: women and arbitration in New South Wales 1902-1908*, Hale & Iremonger, Sydney, 1984.

Ryan, Edna, and Anne Conlon, *Gentle invaders: Australian women and work 1788-1974*, Nelson, Melbourne, 1975.

Ryan, Julia, Women's Movement Notes, Book I.

Ryan, Julia, Women's Movement Notes, Book II.

Ryan, Julia, 'Tweedledum and Tweedledee — some comments', Ts. in Julia Ryan's Women's Movement file.

Ryan, Julia, 'Capitalism and the Family', *Refractory Girl*, no. 7, November 1975, pp. 18-19.

Ryan, Penny (ed.), *A guide to Women's Studies in Australia*, Mulgrave, Melbourne, 1973.

Ryan, Susan, *Catching the waves: life in and out of politics*, HarperCollins Publishers, Sydney, 1999.

Ryan, Susan, and Gareth Evans, *Affirmative action for women: a policy discussion paper*, Australian Government Publishing Service, Canberra, 1984.

Samuel, Raphael, 'History and theory', in Raphael Samuel (ed.), *People's history and socialist theory*, Routledge & Kegan Paul, London, 1981.

Samuel, Raphael (ed.), *History Workshop: A Collectanea 1967-1991*, History Workshop 25, Oxford, 1991.

Sargent, Lydia (ed.), *Women and revolution*, South End Press, Boston, 1981.

Sargisson, Lucy, *Contemporary feminist utopianism*, Routledge, London, 1996.

Sayers, Janet, *Biological politics: feminist and anti-feminist perspectives*, Tavistock Publications, London and New York, 1982.

Segal, Lynne, *Making trouble: life and politics*, Serpent's Tail, London, 2007.

Selby-Smith, Joy, 'Developments in microelectronic technology and their impact on women in paid employment', *Australian Quarterly Review*, Summer 1990.

Shelley, Mary, *Frankenstein; or the modern Prometheus*, first published in three volumes, 1818; republished in Peter Fairclough (ed.), *Three Gothic novels*, Penguin, Harmondsworth, 1968.

Sherfey, M.J., *The Nature and evolution of female sexuality*, Vintage Books, New York, 1973.

Sheridan, Susan, 'Ada Cambridge and the female literary tradition', in Susan Dermody et al. (eds), *Nellie Melba, Ginger Meggs and friends: essays in Australian cultural history*, Kibble Books, Melbourne, 1982.

Sheridan, Susan, '"Transcending Tauromachy": The beginnings of Women's Studies in Adelaide', *Australian Feminist Studies*, vol. 13, no. 27, 1988.

Skolnick, Arlene, *The intimate environment exploring marriage and the family*, Little, Brown and Co., Boston, 1973.

Skolnick, Arlene, 'The family revisited: themes in recent social science research', *Journal of Interdisciplinary History*, vol. 5, no. 4, Spring 1975.

Somay, Bülent, 'Towards an open-ended utopia', *Science-Fiction Studies*, vol. 11, no. 1, 1984, pp. 25-38.

Sontag, Susan, 'Notes on "Camp"', in Susan Sontag, *Against interpretation and other essays*, Dell Publishing Co., Inc., New York, 1969.

Spence, Catherine Helen, *A week in the future*, serialised in the *Centennial Magazine: An Australian Monthly*, December 1888-July 1889. Republished with Introduction and Notes by Lesley Ljungdahl, Hale & Iremonger, Sydney, 1987.

Spivack, Charlotte, *Ursula K. Le Guin*, Twayne Publishers, Boston, 1984.

Stevens, Joyce 'The autonomous women's movement and revolutionary social change', National Women's Conference on Feminism and Socialism, 5-6 October 1974, duplicated paper.

Stimpson, Catharine R., 'Women's Studies: the state of the art (1986)', paper delivered to a conference on Women's Studies as a Transdisciplinary Enterprise organised by the Research Centre for Women's Studies at Adelaide University, August 1986.

Stimpson, Catharine R., with Nina Kressner Cobb, *Women's Studies in the United States*, Ford Foundation, New York, 1986.

Stoke, Christine, 'The Daylesford embroidered banner project', *Lip*, 1984, pp. 6-13.

Stone, Janey, 'A Strategy for the Women's Liberation Movement, National Women's Conference On Feminism and Socialism, 5-6 October 1974, duplicated paper.

Strathern, Marilyn, 'Dislodging a worldview: challenge and counter-challenge in the relationship between feminism and anthropology', *Australian Feminist Studies*, vol. 1, no. 1, December 1985.

Summers, Anne, 'Where's the Women's Movement moving to?', *MeJane*, no. 10, March 1973, reprinted in Jan Mercer (ed.), *The other half: women in Australian society*, Penguin Books, Ringwood, 1975.

Summers, Anne, *Damned whores and God's police: the colonization of women in Australia*, Penguin, Ringwood, 1975.

Summers, Anne, 'The Women's Movement', *Nation Review*, 7-13 March 1975, reprinted in Henry Mayer and Helen Nelson (eds), *Australian politics: a fourth reader*, F.W. Cheshire, Melbourne, 1976.

Summers, Anne, *Ducks on the pond: an autobiography 1945-1976*, Viking, Ringwood, 1999.

Sussex, Lucy, 'Introduction', in Lucy Sussex and Judith Raphael Buckridge (eds), *She's fantastical*, Sybylla Co-operative Press and Publications Limited, Melbourne, 1995.

Taylor, Barbara, 'Our labour and our power, *Red Rag*, no. 10, Winter 1975-76.

Taylor, Jean, *Brazen Hussies: a herstory of radical activism in the women's liberation movement in Victoria 1970-1979*, Dyke Books Inc., East Melbourne, 2009.

Threadgold, Terry, 'Gender Studies and Women's Studies', in *Knowing ourselves and others: the humanities in Australia into the 21ˢᵗ century*, 3 vols., prepared by a Reference Group for the Australian Academy of the Humanities, Australian Government Publishing Service, Canberra, April 1998, vol. 2.

Thurstans, Margaret, 'Restructuring the Workplace for Keyboard Workers', Section 44, Women's Studies, 54ᵗʰ Congress of ANZAAS, Australian National University, Canberra, 17 May 1984.

Tilley, Lorraine, 'Impressions of the Worker's Control Conference', CWL *Newsletter*, no. 13, June 1973.

Toulmin, Stephen, *Human understanding: the collective use and evolution of concepts*, The Clarendon Press, Oxford, 1972, vol. 1.

Trow, Martin, 'The American academic department as a context for learning', *Studies in Higher Education*, vol. 1, no. 1.

Truscott, Margaret, *Women's access to universities: a pilot study*, Research Centre for Women's Studies, University of Adelaide, 1985.

Walby, Sylvia, *Patriarchy at work: patriarchal and capitalist relations in employment*, Polity Press, Cambridge 1986.

Walker, Beverly, and Margaret Smith, 'Women's Studies courses in Australian Universities', *Women's Studies International Quarterly*, vol. 2, no. 3, 1982.

Ward, Biff, 'The politics of feminism', duplicated paper in Ryan, Women's Movement Notes, Book II, also given at the Women and Politics conference, 1975.

Ward, Biff, 'The way forward for the revolutionary women's movement: understanding trashing and sectarianism', paper for the Marxist-Feminist Conference, Sydney, June 1977, in the Edna Ryan Papers, National Library of Australia, MS 9140, box 13, folder 73.

Watson, Sophie (ed.), *Playing the state: Australian feminist interventions*, Verso, London, 1990.

West, Donald J., *The young offender*, Penguin, Harmondsworth, 1967.

West, Roderick (chair), *Learning for life: review of higher education financing and policy: a policy discussion paper*, Australian Government Publishing Service, Canberra, May 1998.

Wheelwright, E.L., *Capitalism, socialism or barbarism? The Australian predicament. Essays in contemporary political economy*, Australia and New Zealand Book Company, Sydney, 1978.

Wheelwright, Ted, 'Transnational corporations and the new international development of labour: some implications for Australia', in Gareth Evans and John Reeves (eds), *Labour essays 1980*, Drummond for the Australian Labour Party (Victorian Branch), Richmond, 1980.

White, Donna R., *Dancing with dragons: Ursula Le Guin and the critics*, Camden House, Columbia, 1999.

White, Robert, 'The State of English Studies in the 1990s', in *Knowing ourselves and others: the humanities in Australia into the 21st century*, 3 vols., prepared by a Reference Group for the Australian Academy of the Humanities, Australian Government Publishing Service, Canberra, April 1998, Vol. 2.

Williams, Raymond, 'Utopia and science fiction', in *Problems in materialism and culture*, New Left Books, London, 1980.

Wills, Sue, 'The politics of women's liberation', PhD Thesis, University of Sydney, 1981.

Wilson, Elizabeth A., 'Feminist science studies', Elizabeth A. Wilson Guest Editor, *Australian Feminist Studies*, vol. 14, no. 29, April 1999.

Windschuttle, Elizabeth (ed.), *Women, class and history: feminist perspectives on Australia 1788-1978*, Fontana/Collins, Melbourne, 1980.

Women and Labour Publications Collective [Margaret Allen, Jean Blackburn, Carol Johnson, Margaret King and Alison Mackinnon] (ed.), *All her labours*, 2 vols, Hale & Iremonger, Sydney, 1984.

Women's Publishing Collective, *Papers on patriarchy: conference, London 76*, Women's Publishing Collective, London, 1976.

Wood, Susan, 'Discovering worlds: the fiction of Ursula K. Le Guin', in *Ursula K. Le Guin*, edited with an introduction by Harold Bloom, Chelsea House Publishers, New York, 1986.

Woolf, Virginia, *Three guineas*, Harbinger, New York, 1966 (1938).

Woolf, Virginia, *Orlando: a biography*, Triad/Panther Books, St. Albans, 1977.

Wotherspoon, Garry, *'City of the plain': history of a gay sub-culture*, Hale & Iremonger, Sydney, 1991.

Yeatman, Anna, 'The liberation of women', *Arena*, no. 21, 1970.

Yeatman, Anna, *Bureaucrats, technocrats, femocrats: essays on the contemporary Australian state*, Allen & Unwin, Sydney, 1990.

Young, Iris, 'Beyond the unhappy marriage: a critique of dual systems theory', in Lydia Sargent (ed.), *Women and revolution*, South End Press, Boston, 1981.

Interviews

Ansara, Martha, interview with Tristan Slade, 29 September 1997.

Allen, Yvonne, interview with Deborah Worsley-Pine, 4 July 1996.

Bebbington, Laurie, interview with Ruth Ford, 1 December 1997.

Chapman-Davis, Jan, interview with Ruth Ford, 29 October 1997.

Clarke, Renfrey, interview with Anastasiya Posadskaya, published in *Green Left*, 11 September 1991.

Levy, The Hon. Anne AO, interview with Deborah Worsley-Pine, 25 July 1996.

Newmarch, Annie, interview with Deborah Worsley-Pine, 22 August 1996.

Nicolson, Joyce, interview with Ruth Ford, 9 October 1997.

Ryan, Lyndall, interview with Ann Genovese, 25 September 1997.

Schaffer, Kay, interview with Kate Borrett, 18 June 1996.

Sheridan, Sue, interview with Sarah Zetlein, 29 February 1996.

Summers, Anne, interview with Ann Genovese, 30 April 1998.

Taylor, Jean, interview with Ruth Ford, 12 December 1997.

Treloar, Carol, interview with Deborah Worsley-Pine, 1 August 1996.

Williams, Sue, interview with Deborah Worsley-Pine, 19 August 1996.

Wills, Sue, interview with Tristan Slade, 26 September 1997.

Occasional Sources

ANU Reporter, 24 May 1974; 28 November 1980.

The Australian, 26 April 1996.

Blackburn, Maurice and Co., *Newsletter*, no. 8, November/December 1983.

The Bulletin, 17 September, 1977.

Canberra News, 8 March 1972.

Canberra Times, 7 April 1971; 27 November 1975; 1 May 1979.

'Canberra Women's Liberation', duplicated sheet in *Newsletter* file, Lobelia Street, O'Connor.

Canberra Women's Liberation Archives, Jessie Street National Women's Library, Sydney.

Canberra Women's Liberation [CWL] *Newsletter*: no. 2, November 1970; no. 5, February 1971, no. 8, May 1971; no. 18, March 1972; no. 19, April 1972; no. 22, July 1972; no. 26, November 1972; no. 47, February 1975; no. 48, March 1975; no. 49, April 1975; no. 51, June 1975.

Department of Science and Technology, 'National technology strategy: discussion draft,' April 1984.

The Feminist Theatre Group, directed by Anne Dunn and Eva Johnson, *Is this seat taken?*, The Space Theatre, Adelaide Festival Centre, 1989.

Hawke, Hon. R.J., 'Official opening speech', National Technology Conference, *Proceedings and Report*, Canberra, 26-28 September, 1983.

Hypatia, vol. 15, no. 2, Spring 2000, Special Issue titled 'Going Australian: reconfiguring feminism and philosophy'.

Liberaction, passim, 1972-75.

MeJane, no. 1, March 1971; no. 3, July 1971, p. 6; no. 5, November 1971, p. 4; no. 5, November 1971, n.p.

'Minutes of a meeting', 12 June 1974, 6 November 1974, 5 February 1975, 5 March 1975, 16 April 1975, CWL Minute Book 1974-5, Lobelia Street, O'Connor.

News (Adelaide), 23 March 1970, n.p.

The Ovarian Sisters, *Beat your breasts*, Candle Music Company Pty Ltd, Hobart, 1980.

The redhead's revenge, The Space Theatre, Adelaide Festival Centre, 3-13 May 1978.

'Reports of refuge meetings', 22 July 1974, 9 October 1974, reports of meetings with Department of the Capital Territory, 18 October 1974, 6 November 1974, all in Ryan, Women's Movement Notes, Book I.

Strathern, Marilyn, 'Out of context: the persuasive fictions of anthropology', Frazer Lecture delivered at the University of Liverpool, 1986.

A technology strategy for South Australia, a draft for Parliamentary Debate, 12 April 1984.

'Research Centre for Women's Studies confirmed', press release, 30 April 1985, in Special Collections, Barr Smith Library, University of Adelaide.

Refractory Girl, no. 6, June 1974.

Social History, 1 January, 1976, p. 1.

The Weekend Australian, 5-6 January 2008.

Women's Bureau Department of Employment and Youth Affairs, *Facts on women at work in Australia 1978*, Australian Government Publishing Service, Canberra, 1979.

Women's Studies Quarterly, vol. 25, nos. 1 & 2, Spring/Summer 1997: *Looking back, moving forward: 25 years of Women's Studies history*, The Feminist Press at the City University of New York.

'The Movement in Canberra — Report June 1972', duplicated paper in *Newspaper* file, Lobelia Street, O'Connor.

Williams, Sue, 'A decadent dancing delight for women who waltz', Burnside Town Hall, Adelaide, 1977.

Women's Action Group, Hobart, 'Sexism and Women's Liberation or "Why do straight sisters sometimes cry when they are called lesbians?"', paper distributed at the 'Hevvies' Theory conference.

Women's Electoral Lobby [WEL] *Broadsheet*, no. 1, February-March 1972.

Vort-Ronald, Pat, 'Women and class'; Clarke, Jocelyn, and Bebbington, Laurie, 'Lesbian oppression and liberation', National Women's Conference on Feminism and Socialism, duplicated papers.

Web Sources

Arndt, Bettina, 'Bodies without evidence', *Sydney Morning Herald*, 21 September 2002, on http://www.bettinaarndt.com.au/articles/bodies-without-evidence.htm, accessed 25 July 2012.

Borton, Marita, 'Government officials in hot water over planned new tax on tampons', *Dateline Australia*, April 2000, on http://www.socialism.com/drupal-6.8?q=node/1160, accessed 25 July 2012.

Kowalski, Sarah, 'Welcome This New Day for Womanhood: Tampons in American History', December 1999, on http://www.sccs.swarthmore.edu/users/01/sarahk/hers/school/tampon.html, accessed 25 July 2012.

http://about.nsw.gov.au/collections/doc/rely-brand-sanitary-tampon-and-applicator, accessed 25 February 2011, accessed 25 July 2012.

http://www.powerhousemuseum.com/collection/
database/?irn=12141&search=women, accessed 25 July 2012.

http://margepiercy.com/about marge/biography, accessed 23 July 2012.

Letters

Bonner, Frances, to Susan Magarey, email communication, 16 September 2003.

Grimshaw, Patricia, to Susan Magarey, 30 January 1980.

This book is available as a free fully-searchable ebook from

www.adelaide.edu.au/press

www.ingramcontent.com/pod-product-compliance
Lightning Source LLC
Chambersburg PA
CBHW051312020426
42333CB00027B/3310